Village Building
at the
End of the World

**THE COLLAPSE OF INDUSTRIAL SOCIETY,
AND THE BIRTH OF A NEW VISION**

CHRIS WILSON

2QT (Publishing) Ltd

First Edition published 2022 by
2QT Limited (Publishing)
Settle, N. Yorkshire

Publisher Disclaimer:
The events in this book are described according to the Authors
recollection; recognition and understanding of the events and
individuals mentioned and are in no way intended to mislead or
offend. As such the Publisher does not hold any responsibility for
any inaccuracies or opinions expressed by the author. Every effort
has been made to acknowledge and gain any permission from
organisations and persons mentioned in this book. Any enquiries
should be directed to the author.

Cover images: shutterstock.com

Printed by IngramSpark

A CIP catalogue record for this book is available
from the British Library

ISBN 978-1-914083-46-4

DEDICATION

To the many people all over the world who are showing, in their own lives, that real change is possible.

and ACKNOWLEDGEMENTS

Several good people have helped me to make this book more readable, including my sister Sarah, my wife Gina, and my friends and colleagues Els van Ooijen, Simon Bramwell, Emma Palmer and Jacqui Bortoft – and of course my long-suffering editor at 2QT, Karen Holmes.

I also want to acknowledge my debt to writers like Charles Eisenstein, Paul Kingsnorth, Iain McGilchrist, John Michael Greer, Paul Levy and Llewellyn Vaughan Lee, who have been inspirational in helping me understand the 'big picture'.

Contents

Introduction

WE'RE IN A gigantic mess. Our civilisation is collapsing, and we're dragging the whole Earth down with us. How do we make sense of such an awful situation?

I started researching this tangled question a few years ago, and the more I learned, the more astonished I was at how little attention the world was paying to the potential disasters that are coming our way, especially climate breakdown. It wasn't until January 2020, when we saw the terrible Australian forest fires on our TV screens, that it began to be widely recognised and debated in the mainstream media. And then, with impeccable timing, the pandemic arrived and pushed the burning forests and the melting glaciers into the background again. At least, for a while.

Covid and climate breakdown are not separate, isolated problems but *symptoms* of a life-threatening condition that runs very deep in our culture. Global warming is perhaps the most dangerous symptom of this condition, just as a high fever is often the most dangerous symptom of a viral infection. They are warning us that our ultra-sophisticated lifestyles have now gone way past their natural limit – because they depend on an industrial economy which has finally grown into a monstrous, life-destroying machine[1].

✿

This 'Death Machine' has a very long history. Its effects have often been disastrous for those people and places directly affected, but until recently these were not widespread and didn't usually involve whole ecosystems. It's only in the last two or three centuries, and particularly the last few decades, that it has grown big and powerful enough to threaten all life on this planet.

'The Machine' refers to a symbolic entity, of course, but over a long period of time this symbolic entity has been taking on a form which has now become just as substantial as the one we call 'Nature'[2]. My feeling (inspired by the work of Jacques Ellul[3] and the visionary ideas of Rudolf Steiner[4]) is that *this entity has become autonomous in its own right*, and has dragged us into this mess because we haven't been able to control it. We have tried to control everything else in the world *through* it, but I think it would be more accurate now to say that *the Machine itself is in control, using us as its willing servants.*

This seems like a radical suggestion but, when you contemplate the history of our European culture over the last thousand years or so, you can see that it's not as far-fetched as it sounds. It's one of the main reasons why our European nation-states have been responsible for such a degree of misery and violence over such a long period of time[5]. And it's the reason why we are now compelled to come to terms with a market-based culture that puts zero value on caring for each other, or for the Earth that sustains us[6].

2

When you take a good look at its historical, cultural and psycho-spiritual roots, as I have set out to do in this book, it becomes clear that this all comes from a particular way of perceiving the world. This mode of perception (and thinking) has been very successful, as it's ideally suited to the project we call 'progress'. But it has also left us with unintended consequences in every sphere of life, for which we are now paying a heavy price.

Like many other people before me, I've been on a journey trying to understand how we got into this predicament, what it really means for us, and why our responses to it so far have been so ineffective. It seems to me that we are still held back by our unbalanced dependence on the same way of thinking about the world.

We need to find a way of freeing ourselves from its dominant position so that we can re-balance our lives, otherwise we will continue trying to 'solve the problem' of climate breakdown by using the same kind of thinking, without questioning the assumptions on which it is based. This will only lead us deeper into the predicament because (as I argue in the book) the Machine will only see it as another opportunity to consolidate its grip on our lives, and this may be the worst possible outcome.

❧

This book is really a collection of essays, but it is held together by my own personal story. This is replete with false starts, sad endings and strange episodes, but I've used it as a backdrop in the hope that the book will feel less like a collection of sermons and more like what it really is: the diary of a somewhat naive explorer.

This really has been a journey for me. Four years ago, when I started writing it as a series of blog posts[7], I thought I knew how it was all going to end. I have a fondness for disaster movies and this looked to me like the biggest disaster movie of all time. I have to confess that part of me derived a perverse satisfaction from this, a smug feeling that I knew better than the 'sheeple'. I've noticed something similar in some of my contrarian friends with a leaning towards conspiracy theories. This is perhaps understandable because they are picking up on something that most people prefer not to notice, which is the way we are being manipulated – and to some extent controlled – by unseen forces that do not have our well-being at heart.

If I had read this sentence two or three years ago, I would probably have dismissed it as just another paranoid delusion. But with Steiner's vision [8] in mind, and having seen some of the outrageous greenwashing carried out by the corporates and the politicians as they shape-shift to accommodate the demands of the Machine, I now have no doubt that there is a very powerful 'unseen force' at work. However, this one isn't controlled by a shadowy group of power-possessing humans; if anything, it's the other way round.

🌿

So my journey has taken me to some surprising places and hasn't been at all like I expected it to be. I began to see that the end of our 'story of progress' may look like an unmitigated disaster, but it also *potentially* marks the beginning of a new story. It is this new story that needs our attention now as the world seems to be sliding inexorably in the wrong direction.

At the moment, there seems to be very little prospect that we can stop the slide but, like every crisis, this is also an opportunity. There's a new world waiting to be born. There are many indications of this, some of which I write about in the book. It's not hard to find them if we take the time to search. There are many ways in which we can help each other not only to resist the power of the Machine and limit the damage it can do, but to go much further than this and lay the foundations of what Eckhart Tolle calls 'a New Earth'[9].

We are being invited into a very different future – more caring, more inclusive, more intimate and heart-based, and much less dependent on the Machine. This vision is already 'out there'. It is for us to discover how it is resonating within us, as it will be in some way for most human beings on this Earth even if they aren't yet aware of it. Then, if we can nurture it, act from it, and share it with like-minded friends, we will *call it into being* and make it real. This may be hard for us, as it involves sailing in the opposite direction to the prevailing currents of the artificial world we have created around us but, if we can embark on this difficult journey, it will have incalculable value for future generations.

And if we can't, I doubt if they will be able to forgive us.

References

1 In his book *Climate: A New Story* (North Atlantic Books, 2018), Charles Eisenstein shows how the ecological devastation caused by our industrial economy is at least as important as our primary CO2 emissions in generating climate breakdown.

2 For a complete history of this process in its proper context, see Jeremy Naydler, *In the Shadow of The Machine* (Temple Lodge, 2018).

3 Jacques Ellul, the celebrated French 'anarchist Christian' and independent thinker, whose 1954 book *La Technique ou l'enjeu du siècle* was translated as *The Technological Society*. (Vintage Books, Random House, 1964).

4 Rudolf Steiner was a prolific visionary whose work extended into many spheres of life, but I'm referring here mainly to his work on Lucifer and Ahriman. See *The Influences of Lucifer and Ahriman* (Rudolf Steiner Press, London, 1954).

5 I'm referring here to the violence involved in colonialism, extractivism, the financial debt culture and resource wars.

6 A point well made by psychoanalyst Sally Weintrobe in *Psychological Roots of the Climate Crisis: Neoliberal Exceptionalism and the Culture of Uncare* (Bloomsbury Academic, 2021).

7 On the website of a short-lived training organisation in Bristol known as The Lightning Tree Collective.

8 Introduced and discussed in Chapter 4.

9 Eckhart Tolle, *A New Earth* (Penguin, 2005).

The Trouble with Lizzie

I WASN'T AWARE of the true scale of the ecological devastation our industrial societies are causing in the natural world until after my wife Jane died, fourteen years ago. Like most of us, I preferred not to think about it too much because it didn't affect me personally. The mines, the clear-cut forests, the polluted rivers, were almost always 'somewhere else'. Somebody else's problem, terrible for those directly affected, but not for me. I didn't even think about the ecocide caused all the way up the food chain by our poisoned fields. Surely we learned our lesson with DDT in the sixties, didn't we? Everything they use nowadays is supposed to be 'safe'.

Jane and I were more concerned about the human wreckage caused by a rapidly changing society. The accepted wisdom seems to be that these changes are an inevitable side effect of 'progress', but as a society we really don't seem to care very much about the unintended consequences they bring with them. Ultimately, we end up with grotesque caricatures like Donald Trump, expert manipulators of the anger and frustration felt most keenly by people who have been betrayed by the system which abandoned them as 'surplus to requirements' and left them to fend for themselves in their impoverished communities.

Jane was passionate about social justice – we first got together after a protest meeting addressed by that wonderful old warhorse Tony Benn during the 1984 UK miners' strike – so while we were together, we focused our energy on issues like poverty and mental health. She worked for a debt charity and I re-trained as a psychotherapist, which isn't perhaps the most obvious choice for someone who'd spent most of his life as a carpenter. If it hadn't been for her, I probably wouldn't have even considered it.

After she died, I spent a lot of my time going for long walks in the woods, full of grief and sadness that she couldn't be there with me, wondering what to do with myself now that she was gone. But the deep stillness of the trees also felt like a homecoming. It was as if they were inviting me to find the same stillness in the depths of my own soul. Through them, I gradually came to see how the psycho-social problems Jane and I were concerned about are actually symptoms of a much deeper malaise.

I'd been working for several years with unhappy and stressed-out people and it wasn't hard to see how their distress was related to our hyper-individualistic, alienated lifestyle. But I hadn't really acknowledged that what lay behind it was a spiritual sickness, a sickness of the soul, which has been exemplified for a long time by our relentless war on Nature.

✿

A few years later, I responded to my feelings of grief and sadness by winding down my therapy practice and joining a group of people who wanted to escape from the burgeoning insanity of twenty-first century life and at least try to live in a better state of harmony with the natural world. We sold our homes, formed a co-op and bought a fourteen-acre farm in Devon. We called ourselves 'Heart of Devon Permaculture Community', which leaves a warm feeling when you say it, as long as you keep your fingers crossed.

The accommodation was fairly basic, but the land was beautiful; it was like living in Paradise. Jane would have loved it. Her favourite tree was a pink-flowering hawthorn, so I planted one down there on the tenth anniversary of her death, and looked forward to seeing it grow and produce clouds of pink blossom every spring.

Not very far away from the farm where we lived was a land-based learning community known as Fire Valley[1], which was (and apparently still is) dedicated to inspiring leadership in the struggle to establish a more just and sustainable world. I was lucky enough to be able to spend a lot of time there developing a psycho-spiritual training course for the volunteers.

Those volunteers, and the staff who worked with them, were an inspiration. Life wasn't easy for them and, on the whole, the management didn't try to make it much easier. The accommodation was spartan and very cold in the winter months. The food was good but they were expected to work long hours with very basic tools and resources to grow it, and to help run the educational courses that Fire Valley existed to provide.

Unfortunately the management were just a tad too ambitious and embarked on a prestige eco-building project that eventually cost them a lot more than their funding was able to bear. As a result, just as we were getting the volunteers' course under way, the place went through a management convulsion; in the end they had to close it down while they tried to sort themselves out.

Going against the grain, trying to live a life that doesn't conform to the paradigm of consumption and growth, was never going to be easy. Within three years, our Heart of Devon enterprise had also fallen apart. We couldn't cope with the sheer intensity of life in such a small community, nor could we find a way to reconcile the contradictions between our ideals and the need to survive within a money economy based on a completely different set of values. Although we had all the 'right' procedures (weekly meetings to air our difficulties, consensus decision making, etc.), there were too many underlying tensions between us which people were unwilling to really look at. Finally, two of the youngest and most hard-working individuals decided they'd had enough and left. As a result, those underlying tensions came to the surface and soured relationships between us so much that we had to abandon our dream, swallow our pride and put the place back on the market.

❧

The lesson I took away from Heart of Devon was that if you want to join a community, especially a small, close-knit one like ours, it's a good idea to check that the people who are the real 'driving force' behind it are also self-aware and emotionally literate. It isn't enough to have the right procedures. Any members who have big ideas but little self-awareness, no matter how enthusiastic they are or how technically competent or what good company they are down the pub, are likely to cause problems – if not sooner, then later. I should have known this, of course, but opportunities like Heart of Devon don't often arise and I was carried away by my enthusiasm for the project.

It took three years to sell the farm, during which time I was working on a training project in Bristol similar to the one I'd started at Fire Valley. I was working with a group that called itself the Lightning Tree Collective, trying to find a way of helping people to prepare for what's coming down the line. My friend Max, with whom I had worked before at Fire Valley, knew only too well how activists often end up quarrelling with each other over tactics, or burn out because they don't know how to look after themselves psychologically. We wanted to develop a psycho-spiritual training that didn't sound too 'woo-woo', because a large proportion of activists have nothing but contempt for people they call 'navel-gazers'. But, in principle, we also wanted to honour the sacredness of our Mother Earth, as well as teaching the kind of practical self-awareness that people need to develop if they want to work harmoniously with each other in such a difficult enterprise.

In an effort to understand our global predicament a bit better, I gradually acquired (and read) a shelf full of books about everything from ecology to eschatology, which I was surprised to find means 'the theological study of death, judgement, and the final destiny of the soul of humanity'. (I had confused it with 'scatology', which is definitely not the same thing.)

The more I engaged with the predicament we're in, the worse I felt. It's not possible to look at what's happening, think about it a lot and then remain unaffected, as many of my friends have found. It can creep into your soul and destroy your *joie de vivre*, replacing it with a pervasive anxiety that begins to see TEOTWAWKI (The End of The World As We Know It) round every corner, in every shadow, everywhere.

It's not easy trying to survive on a basic state pension in an expensive city like Bristol. I soon ran out of friends with spare rooms and ended up looking after my poor confused mother-in-law, living in the spare bedroom in her comfortable 1930s semi in Radstock. She had somehow survived on her own for ten miserable years since Jane had died, and I was fated to be with her for another two until she finally gave up the ghost at the age of ninety-seven and the house was sold.

It was a strange life, thinking all the time about how to prepare for 'collapse' while living with my poor old mother-in-law. She had no clear idea of who I was, let alone what I was doing there, because she was falling further and further into a cruel and unforgiving fog of senile dementia.

*

Living with someone who's suffering from dementia can be at least as difficult and intense as working with a bunch of environmental activists. I couldn't help noticing some striking similarities between her personal disorder and the global disorder that we were so concerned about so, when I started converting my blog posts for Lightning Tree into a book, I thought she should take her rightful place in the story. After all, it was she who had enabled us to keep the collective going by the simple act of letting me live rent-free in her house.

So, let me introduce her to you. An unfortunate relic of a

bygone age, like a coelacanth stranded on Brighton Beach, she was christened a century ago by her adoring parents as Elizabeth Grace but to us she was known as 'poor old Lizzie'.

Dementia is a strange condition. Some people with dementia turn into the nicest, sweetest old dears that you can imagine. My mother was like that; she spent most of her life being irritable and depressed, then her dementia took over and she became almost beatific in her last years. But many of them change in the other direction and their behaviour becomes unrecognisably awful as the dementia takes hold. It can feel terrifying to lose your mind, so perhaps it's not surprising that some of them react like that.

Lizzie's behaviour had always been 'difficult'; she didn't undergo a personality change, her behaviour just became difficult in a more obviously bizarre and insistent way. As a rule she wasn't particularly aggressive; she just spent most of her time demanding attention, rehearsing her dramas and cultivating her obsessions. She needed to feel that she was still in control but, of course, she knew on some level that she wasn't.

It seems to me that we're all in a similar predicament to the one in which poor Lizzie found herself. On some level we can sense that our whole way of life is 'out of control', but we don't really know what that means or how to deal with it so we displace our hopes and fears onto irrelevant and exhausting dramas like Brexit. (The Brexiteers' favourite rallying cry was always 'Take Back Control'.) At the same time, we invent artificial lives to display on Facebook and Instagram so we at least feel that we can control other people's perceptions of us. Meanwhile, in the 'developed' world, we continue to act in ways that will ensure that everything that's currently going wrong can only get worse.

The similarities go deeper than this. Dementia attacks the capacity to form and hold on to memories and to knit them together into a coherent narrative. People who suffer from dementia have forgotten how to extract meaning from what happens in their lives. Something similar has happened to all of us in our fragmented, fast-moving, spiritually impoverished world. We have forgotten what we're here for, we no longer recognise our true home, and we're thrashing about in a state of deep *anomie*, trapped in a world of phantoms that promise everything but have no soul.

Lizzie needed to feel loved – or rather she needed to feel admired, which is not quite the same thing. Unfortunately people tended to be put off by her narcissistic self-absorption because she was such a drama queen. She'd never been very self-aware, and now that she had dementia she wasn't so adept at concealing it so her dramas didn't work as well as they once had. Sometimes I felt really sorry for the old bat, as long as I wasn't too closely involved with the current drama.

She told everyone that she was all alone in the world, which was quite true in a way. My wife Jane had been her only child. Lizzie moved to Radstock at the ripe old age of eighty-two because she hoped (or rather assumed) that Jane would look after her. It wasn't long after this that her daughter's cancer was diagnosed, and two years later Jane was dead. Things could have turned out better for the old relic (Lizzie, I mean, not Jane) but once again they didn't.

Jane's relationship with her mother was fraught with guilt and animosity. I remember one incident when Lizzie got into an argument with Jane about the 'Coal not Dole' poster[2] in our front window. (Despite being a mine-worker's daughter, Lizzie was a staunch supporter of Margaret Thatcher.) The argument escalated into a shouting match, which ended with Lizzie threatening to cut Jane out of her will. Jane's response was 'I don't want your *fucking* money, so you can either stop criticising me *now*, or you can get the *fuck* out of my house!'

I was quite startled by this outburst; although Jane had a deep reservoir of anger, she wouldn't normally express it as openly as that unless she was seriously provoked. But Lizzie airbrushed this incident (and others like it) out of her memory, replacing it with a warm and fuzzy fiction in which Jane had been a model of daughterly closeness and love. It made her bereft-and-alone-in-the-world drama much more plausible.

As it turned out, Jane never did get her mum's *fucking* money because she died first. I was well aware that I wouldn't be getting any of it either. My stepchildren inherited whatever was left, which is just as well because I would probably have spent it all on some hare-brained scheme to annoy the powers that be, like buying some land in the Welsh mountains and training a herd of rebellious goats to commit acts of sabotage on the HS2 line.

🍂

Jane's father left home when she was only nine. She remembered him as a warm, affectionate man who was probably driven mad by Lizzie's constant demands for attention. His departure left a big scar but Jane didn't blame him, despite her mother's furious attempts to rewrite history. She endured eight years of Lizzie's unquenchable bitterness before her mother married again.

Lizzie's second husband, George, was an Alderman in Newcastle-under-Lyme. I never found out what an Alderman actually does, but I suppose it means that he was a 'pillar of the community'. Jane didn't like her new stepfather and had as little as possible to do with him. 'He was a cold fish,' she said. 'He only cared about money and status. The ideal husband for my mother.'

Evidently George was more interested in being an Alderman than bringing up his family because his two sons – Lizzie's stepsons – were both a bit of a disaster. They were about the same age as Jane, but she never got on with them. She told me that one of them drank himself to death in the 1980s, and the other one spent time in jail for indecent exposure. This one, who went by the unlikely name of Jolyon, popped up again later and played a major role in Lizzie's last two years, as we shall see.

Lizzie never really bonded with me as I wasn't respectable enough to be a proper son-in-law, so I managed to avoid having too much contact with her ... until she decided she wanted to live nearer to Jane and bought that nice little 1930s' semi down the road from us in Radstock. From that time onward, until she became very ill, Jane had to do the weekly visit. As a ritual this was a bit pointless as nothing she did was ever good enough. From time to time I used to go with her when things were getting really fraught, just to give her some support, but her mother and I were never 'friends'.

Respectability was always very important to Lizzie, which I guess would account for her choosing a stuffed shirt like George as her second husband. She complained to Jane that I never cleaned my shoes properly or wore a suit. She used to look down at my feet when I walked in the door as if she were still hoping to see a shiny pair of leather shoes instead of my old blue trainers.

Some of her obsessions are not unusual in old age, such as the belief that everyone who cared for her secretly wanted to steal her possessions or the fear that she would run out of money. As it happens, she was surprisingly well-off because George was moderately rich and his house in Newcastle-under-Lyme was worth a lot more than the house in Radstock that Lizzie bought with the proceeds. Her fear of destitution probably went back to the late 1920s when her dad was made redundant. He was a highly skilled pattern-maker in a colliery engineering workshop who would have been quite well paid, so the impact on the family was devastating. Lizzie would have been about seven or eight at the time.

A few of her obsessions were completely bizarre, like her conviction that Jane (whose body had been well and truly reduced to ashes at the local crematorium) was somehow still alive, only they weren't allowed to meet or communicate with each other because the mysterious 'people in charge' wanted to punish her. Lizzie was convinced she'd lived a blameless life so this caused her enormous grief and outrage. One of her fantasies was that Jane was being held hostage by these mysterious people in a basement somewhere 'down the road'. When prompted, she could remember that we had scattered Jane's ashes on a hillside in North Yorkshire but it seemed easier for her to believe in both of these stories at different times, depending on how she felt, rather than choosing one of them because it was 'true'.

She also believed that she owned several other houses (originally it was one house then it grew until there were four or five of them) in Newcastle-under-Lyme. Or alternatively, the houses she owned were here in Radstock, where she'd lived for more years than she could count. She wanted me to spend my time searching, either for Jane or for 'the houses', and became angry with me when I didn't seem very enthusiastic. She was desperate to move 'back home' to one of these fantasy houses with her one-and-only dead daughter so they could both be happy again. I can easily imagine what Jane would have said about *that*.

❧

The old lady was as mad as a box of frogs, but the dementia inside the house didn't feel that much different from the collective dementia that's lurking everywhere out there in the streets beyond the front door. The world today feels fraught, unhappy, pre-dystopian. Many people think we're in the terminal phase of Western civilisation before it finally goes down under the weight of its own internal contradictions. There have been signs of it for a long time, but now it's popping up all over the place like a plague[3]. It's an embarrassing plague that we don't really want to talk about. It scares us, because it strikes at the roots of our belief in 'progress'.

It's undeniable that we've had a few hundred years of

'progress', but it seems like we haven't been willing to pay the full price. We exported the cost to countries less developed than our own, where people will do our dirty work for a lot less money. It wasn't so long ago that we enslaved millions of black and brown people and forced them to work for no money at all. Now we have exported the cost to our children by running up collective debts that have grown so huge that they can never be paid off. Above all, we have exported the cost to Mother Nature and trashed large parts of our beautiful planet in the process.

The writer Paul Kingsnorth, in a recent documentary about the battle against climate change[4], summed it up like this: *The flush toilet is a good metaphor for the civilisation we live in. You crap into a pipe, you flush it away, and you never see it. You never have to deal with your own shit... And then you end up deep in it.*

And that's where we are now. The stuff we've been flushing away has been backing up for a long while; now it's flooding the basement, we can't avoid the bad smell any longer or just pretend it's not happening[5]. As a result, we're becoming more and more anxious and those of us who can't deal with their anxiety are getting very angry. The established norms of a civilised community are breaking down and no-one knows how to stop the rot from spreading. Like all the so-called 'baby boomers', I've lived my life in a time of unparalleled prosperity; now it seems to me that the party's over and some very nasty chickens are coming home to roost.

Lizzie's situation wasn't so very different. She was desperate to believe that nothing was wrong, that everything would somehow come right in the end: Jane would come back home and the two of them would live happily ever after. But death was stalking her like a shadow and, as a result, she was gripped with a horrible sense of anxiety and furious that she could no longer control the way her life was going. There was only one way her story could end, which is the same for every sentient being that has ever enjoyed the gift of life on this planet. It's also the same for all the social forms that we humans have invented to give shape to our complicated lives, from tribes to nation-states and, ultimately, for this industrial civilisation too. Apparently we still haven't learned one of the most fundamental lessons of history:

This, too, will pass.

References

1 Some names of people or places have been changed to avoid causing offence.

2 Coal Not Dole: A slogan much used in the 1984 UK Miners' Strike.

3 I made this reference to a metaphorical plague some time before Covid-19 hit us with a real one.

4 See https://www.youtube.com/watch?v=Q_s8Vo00Xug

5 For some uniquely disturbing insights into this flood of psychological sewage, see Chris Hedges, *America: The Farewell Tour* (Simon & Schuster, 2018). Hedges, a prizewinning journalist, author and Presbyterian minister, went on a two-year fact-finding tour of the USA in search of the symptoms of its collective dystopia and despair. This book is an unforgettable account of what he found.

- 2 -

Into The Madhouse

TUESDAY 8 NOVEMBER 2016

TODAY THE CITIZENS of the USA are electing their forty-fifth president.

The Democratic candidate is clearly destined to win. She's a very experienced political animal, a master of sharp practice and devious to a degree. She's backed by the dark forces of the so-called 'deep state', so there's no chance she's even going to be *allowed* to lose. Opposing her is a political outsider, famous as the star of his own 'reality' TV show, who is widely regarded as a liar, a cheat and a psychopath. He behaves more like the leader of a cult than a serious contender for high office, but his Republican fans just can't get enough of him so the GOP had to put on a brave face and adopt him as their official candidate. None of the po-faced pundits believe this clown can win.

There are times when that dark, primitive part of ourselves that we've repressed for so long turns round and says 'fuck you, this is my time now' and comes roaring out, to everyone's horror and amazement. 'Oh my God,' we say. 'It must have been there all the time and I never knew!'

But we should know by now that such beasts can't be kept chained up out of sight for ever. They just bide their time until the wheel turns.

🍂

My mother-in-law Lizzie knows nothing of this urgent drama and cares even less. She has been cooped up in a care home for about three months now. She was persuaded to go there for respite care 'for a week or two' by someone on the pastoral care team at the local Methodist Church, but the care home spotted her dementia and couldn't let her go back to her own home until they were sure it would be safe for her. She's been there far too long, and she's getting desperate.

Meanwhile, since our Heart of Devon community collapsed, I've been hanging out most of the time with friends in Bristol. I begin to find anguished phone calls from Lizzie on my voicemail. I manage to ignore her for a while but, when eventually I do visit her, she tries desperately to persuade me to take her home. I say 'I'll see what I can do,' and talk to Sylvia, the care-home manager, to find out more about the situation.

Sylvia tells me that they can't send her home without an arrangement known as a 'care package'. Lizzie had one before but the care providers are refusing to work for her again.

'Why is that?' I ask.

'Well,' says Sylvia, 'they say she was – how shall I put it – rather rude to the carers. And apparently she used to call the duty manager on the emergency number at 4am demanding to know why she hadn't yet had her tablets. So...'

No surprises there, then.

Sylvia tells me that there have been several weeks of negotiations between various relevant bodies as to whether Lizzie can safely be sent home without round-the-clock care, which she's evidently reluctant to accept. From what I know of Lizzie, I can easily imagine that she wouldn't want any strangers – especially dark-skinned ones – invading her space and taking control of her life. Sylvia says they can't impose anything on her because, although she obviously suffers from dementia, she doesn't have a proper medical diagnosis for the simple reason that the cunning old survivor refuses to take the necessary tests. She's been diagnosed with 'mild cognitive impairment', but nevertheless her doctor insists she 'has capacity'.

'What does that mean?' I ask.

'You tell me,' says Sylvia, with a wry laugh. 'We might be able to get her home if there was someone there who could look after her,' she says, giving me a meaningful look. 'You know, see her regularly, make sure she's okay, that kind of thing. Or better still, live with her. She has enough room in the house, or so I'm told.'

'Yes, I know she has,' I say. 'I'll have to think about it.'

Actually I've already thought about it, and I find myself in an agony of indecision. I'm swiftly running out of money so I need to find a cheap place to live. The prospect of sharing my misanthropic mother-in-law's house in Radstock is daunting, but I'm fairly sure that if I help her to get back home she'll let me live there rent-free while I sort myself out, as long as Social Services are able to arrange another care package.

I can't say I like her very much, but she really does seem to be in a lot of distress. The care-home manager tells me she's pretty sure Lizzie would do much better if she could go

24

home, so I find myself feeling sorry for the old bat despite all the warnings.

I call Sylvia and say, 'Okay, let's see what we can arrange.'

I consult various friends about what it's like to live with someone who suffers from dementia and they all say, 'Don't go there.' My sister gives me a graphic description of her own mother-in-law's dementia and what it has cost them in anxiety and stress. 'Anyway, you know Lizzie well enough already,' she says. 'Even without the dementia she was always a self-centred, mean old drama queen, and she'll make your life hell.'

The sane, common-sense part of me instantly agrees, but the part that likes a challenge jumps up and says, 'Well, I've been working with distressed and dysfunctional people for nearly twenty years and she's just a crazy old woman. I should be able to handle it...'

'You have no idea what you're getting yourself into,' says my sister.

But it's too late to back out now. Because I've said I might be able to look after her, the care home is finally able to get the care package they think she needs with a different provider. This involves the usual three visits a day to make sure she's fed, watered, washed and medicated. At last I am able to abandon my mate's sofa, load my few remaining worldly goods onto my ancient Ford Focus estate and take them down to Lizzie's 1930s' semi in Radstock.

She evidently sleeps in the back bedroom so I commandeer the front one, open all the windows to let in some air, contemplate the exuberant jungle that used to be Lizzie's garden, and start thinking, 'Maybe this won't be so bad after all.'

Three days later I go back to the care home, bundle her

bony frame into my car and take her home. As she stumbles into the house, I have my first preview of what is to come. 'Oh dear,' she says, as she steps over the threshold. 'I think I've had an Accident.'

She has indeed. The evening care worker isn't due to come for another three hours, and I'm appalled at the prospect of having to clean her up, so I advise her to go upstairs and do the best she can. After all, I remind myself, the doctor says she 'has capacity'.

Lizzie disappears into the bathroom, leaving me to unload the car. Ten minutes later she reappears at the top of the stairs with her skirt bunched up around her waist and calls me. 'I don't seem to have any pants,' she announces. The truth of this statement is immediately obvious. I notice that she was once a natural redhead and I'm astonished that it still shows.

'Well, I don't know where they are,' I say nervously, ashamed of my morbid interest in the ginger undergrowth. I mean, she's ninety-five, for Heaven's sake.

At this stage, I'm still not aware that when Lizzie says 'pants', she means incontinence pants. This is one of the many things the care home has forgotten to warn me about. Soon enough, I'll be buying them from Tesco in packs of twelve.

🍃

I wake up next morning to find myself in the madhouse. First Lizzie barges into my room at 5am and switches on the light. I raise my head off the pillow and glare at her. She looks shocked. 'What are you doing here?' she asks.

I explain, but it takes a while for the news to register. Later

I turn on the radio, expecting to hear that Hillary has been voted in as the first female president of the USA. Instead the unthinkable has happened; it looks like the orange golem is likely to get there first.

With hindsight, we all know that this shouldn't have come as such a surprise. In the much-quoted words of the Irish poet W. B. Yeats:

> *The best lack all conviction, while the worst*
> *Are full of passionate intensity*
> *...And what rough beast, its hour come round at last*
> *slouches towards Bethlehem to be born?*[1]

🌿

There was a part of me that quite admired The Donald, because of his contempt for the entrenched power of the deep state, his stated desire to row back on America's forever wars and his refusal to join in with the demonisation of Russia. I hadn't yet read Naomi Klein's riveting account of what he does actually stand for[2] because she hadn't yet written it.

With my middle-class English background, I found his shameless vulgarity a bit shocking. I wondered how our esteemed ex-Prime Minister felt when she found herself being forced to be nice to the old bastard. Did she just close her eyes and think of England? Or is he as intelligent and charming in private as he is vain and stupid in public? People who work with him say no, he is exactly as he appears. Those who know him say that he routinely behaves like a psychopath, so perhaps we should infer that he can be as charming as he needs to be in order to blindside those people he intends ruthlessly to shaft.

I wondered if there was something in our Anglo-Saxon DNA that was causing us all to self-destruct, because our own government was overwhelmed by its own brand of chaos at the same time as the Barnum & Bailey show on the other side of the Atlantic. There's not a great deal of difference between Boris Johnson and Donald Trump except that The Donald is perhaps just a tiny bit madder – and he's certainly a lot richer. They both seem to be afflicted with the same hideous self-absorption, and neither of them seemed to realise that they were turning their mother country into a global basket case.

_

We baby boomers grew up expecting that social change would always proceed in the 'right' direction, so we're finding this sudden leap backwards very challenging. Like our parents and our grandparents before us, we were brainwashed into looking at history through the lens of 'progress', so perhaps that's not surprising.

Secular progress is an integral part of the mindset of our Western civilisation; in fact, I'd say it's the nearest thing to a kind of default religion for us now that our traditional Christianity has been reduced to a lifestyle choice. This religion of progress ('Progressivism', perhaps?) doesn't have a God, but it does have a strong sense that things ought to be moving onwards and upwards towards a bright new dawn.

If you ask people what they mean by 'progress', chances are that some of them will talk about social justice but most of them will talk about technology or material wealth. Both versions have historical links with Christianity, but only one of them is recognisably linked to its religious teachings. As far as I'm aware, material wealth *per se* has nothing to do with anything that Jesus said or did, apart from the time when he threw the money-changers out of the Temple.

The link with Christianity is relatively modern, especially in the corrupt form embraced by some of the American evangelical cults whose rich leaders love to flaunt their wealth. It's exemplified by the way we use the word 'good', which is in one sense a value and in another sense a thing. In this way, 'goods' (and their ownership) have come to be equated in a semi-conscious way with what is morally 'good'.

So Progressivism has a somewhat ambiguous relationship with the spiritual world. On the one hand, as Social Progressivism it behaves like any other religion in terms of its ability to mobilise a sense of moral purpose. The prime example of this is Communism, which is strictly materialistic but takes its morality very seriously. On the other hand, as Material Progressivism it has no relationship at all with 'good' as a moral value; in fact in some ways it stands for the very essence of the amoral.

*

In common with many other people, I have come to see the present political and social dysfunction as a classic symptom of the long-term systemic breakdown of our Western civilisation. There have been multiple warning signs of this, going back more than a century. *The Limits to Growth*,[3] a classic study by a team at MIT published in 1972, was the first time researchers had given it some scientific backing and put an approximate date on it, but it has been 'in the air' for a long time. Both Covid-19 and climate change are *symptoms* of this ongoing breakdown rather than causes.

During the last century, the religion of progress was amply validated by the huge increase in industrial production that fossil fuels (especially oil) made possible. We've had lots of goodies out of it, and in compensation for its many downsides we were (until recently) able to pay for a great deal of State-sponsored social welfare. But as a 'religion', or let's say an ideal, it isn't entirely new. About 200 years ago, for example, when the industrial economy was just getting under way but long before it had materially improved most people's lives, the German philosopher Hegel was writing about the inevitable march of history towards some ideal state. Hegel was one of the main inspirations for many subsequent German philosophers, including such diverse figures as Nietzsche and Karl Marx, so the theme of 'progress' has become deeply embedded in our European culture even though different writers may disagree about what actually constitutes 'progress'.

A recent manifestation of this theme came up thirty years ago when Francis Fukuyama wrote his famous End of History essay, in which he wondered whether Western liberal democracy was near enough the perfect form of society, and therefore we had reached the best of all possible worlds. Fukuyama was active in the notorious think tank known as the Project for a New American Century, so we shouldn't be at all surprised that he shared their values.

🍃

One aspect of 'progress' that stands out very clearly is its association with the patriarchy. There's a very, one has to say, *masculine* feeling attached to it. This has become an increasingly difficult bone of contention in the last forty or fifty years, and it's very revealing to explore some of its historical roots, which go back a long way.

Richard Tarnas, in his epic study of the history of Western thought, *The Passion of the Western Mind*[4], traces the history of masculine dominance back 4,000 years to the time when the warrior seafaring cultures of the Eastern Mediterranean began to invade and conquer the goddess-worshipping matrilineal peoples of Europe and the Middle East. Tarnas sees our civilisation adopting an increasingly 'masculine' view of the world over this entire period of time until, in our own time, it has culminated in an existential crisis that can only be addressed by abandoning the heroic quest and (as he put it) 're-embracing the Feminine'.

The masculine/feminine imbalance is not the only way in which our civilisation has been thrown out of kilter, but it remains one of the most significant symptoms of its malaise. Not surprisingly, this imbalance has often been regarded as another by-product of Christianity. That isn't totally justified by the historical record but it's true to say that the Church has been an enthusiastic fellow-traveller, responsible over the last 2000 years for an almost totalitarian suppression of the Feminine. This became distinctly brutal about 500 years ago with the persecution of the 'wise women' who were demonised as 'witches' and ruthlessly hunted down and killed by the Church.

That was a very significant and destructive move, because only the perspective given to us by this kind of earth wisdom (whether or not it is embodied by women) can really enable us to comprehend the extent of the damage we are inflicting on the natural world. We can get a sense of this when we read about what is happening to the indigenous people of the Amazon who are under enormous pressure from the oil, mining, agriculture and logging interests of Western-style economies. Having lived successfully for thousands of years in partnership with the forest and all the other beings with whom they share it, they see their homelands being torn up and lost forever to meet the endless demands of consumers who live in cities thousands of miles away.

🍃

Our devotion to the ideal of material progress is a product of the historical rejection by our civilisation of the eternal spiritual values that were once universally believed to underpin and unify all life on Earth, and their replacement by a mechanistic cosmology that prioritises our human ability to control and dominate Nature. It's hard for us, saturated as we are with our own cultural values, to really appreciate what it was like to inhabit the inner world of someone who lived in a civilisation like that of the ancient Egyptians but it was a very different world from the one we inhabit now.

Jeremy Naydler's 2018 study, In the Shadow of The Machine[5], is a masterly history of this process, which he traces all the way from ancient agricultural engineering to modern information technology. He shows in great detail how we came to reduce the whole of what we now call 'Nature' (meaning everything that's alive but isn't human) to a kind of alien 'thing' that exists solely for us to exploit and use in whatever way we please. This is the same 4,000-year-long process that Richard Tarnas characterises as having an undeniably 'masculine' feel.

It wasn't until the late sixteenth and early seventeenth centuries, when rationalism started to replace the dogmas of the Church, that this mechanistic cosmology became a really significant force. That was when Rene Descartes first described with great clarity the now-familiar opposition between mind and body, which in turn drew a very firm line between our human world and the world of 'unthinking' Nature. Descartes was able to justify the practice of vivisection (i.e. cutting up animals without anaesthetic while they were still alive, despite their screams and struggles) because, he pronounced, they couldn't really experience pain. Only humans could do that, because only humans could *think*.

And now these 'thinking' humans feel that it's okay to inflict painful and degraded lives on millions of their own farm animals so that someone can make more money out of them. We cram these unfortunate animals into concrete and steel cages with no room to move, inject them with hormones to make them grow faster and antibiotics to kill everything that gets in the way, slaughter them without ceremony, cut them up, package their body parts in plastic and send the packages to supermarkets thousands of miles away for disposal.

The harsh extremism of Descartes' position may be obvious to at least some of us now, but it marked the beginning of the period known (without a trace of irony) as 'the Enlightenment', so called because religious dogmas and popular superstitions were first openly challenged by empirical observation and rational thinking. Enthusiasts for Progressivism, like Stephen Pinker, tend to glorify the Enlightenment chiefly because of the way many of its thinkers emphasised the freedom of the individual. They are also keen to remind us of the undoubted material benefits it has brought over the last three centuries. But they tend to minimise the 'dark side' of progress, including the devastation that has resulted from the war on Nature.

With hindsight, we could say that the seventeenth-century English natural philosopher Francis Bacon summed up this dark side quite well when he described the new science as 'putting Nature to the torture'. You can only perform such gruesome practices as vivisection if you ignore all your natural instincts and take up residence firmly in your head, where it's possible to objectify the natural world to such an extent that you lose all contact with your natural feelings of empathy.

It's not difficult for ordinary men and women to do this. Ordinary bureaucrats in the Nazi Third Reich routinely sent Jewish people, gypsies and homosexuals to their deaths. Even concentration camp guards were 'ordinary' men and women just like you and me. Ordinary politicians and bureaucrats in my own country have been doing it in slightly less drastic ways, but just as ruthlessly, in their treatment of refugees, drug users, benefit claimants and other despised minorities. (Bankers and politicians could also be described as 'despised minorities' but the people who despise them don't have quite the same clout, so they end up with God on their side.) Ordinary farmers, who for centuries were the custodians of our intimacy with Mother Nature, are compelled by the economics of farming to do it to the natural world by using vast quantities of artificial fertilisers and toxic pesticides. In fact, our civilisation is riddled with this kind of inhumanity. It's the dark side of 'progress', and it can be very dark indeed.

♠

The problem that some Christian religionists have with women in particular, and 'the Feminine' in general, goes back a long way. It has also given rise to some grotesque distortions in our thinking. One of these is that, ever since the time of the Troubadours and even perhaps as far back as the Biblical story of the Virgin Mary, the patriarchy has needed its women – or rather, I suppose, its *anima* figures – to be 'pure', to help those bad, beastly males to civilise themselves.

The twelfth-century cult of Mary Mother of God served an important re-balancing purpose at the time, but it's now way past its sell-by date because it also created a collective female 'shadow side' that had to include everything that was loud, angry, raucous or sexually active. All these unwanted manifestations then had to be rigorously suppressed in case they threatened the authority of the patriarchy and thus the stability of our entire civilisation. What a burden for women to carry! Every woman was supposed to model herself on a fantasy picture of the Virgin. It's no wonder they have decided they've had enough.

The archetypal Feminine hasn't always been seen as submissive, nurturing, sweet and all the other rather bland qualities that our civilisation tried so hard (until recently) to confer on her. The older polytheistic religions, such as Hinduism, paid much more regard to the darker side of all this sweetness. The Hindu goddess Kali is seen as wielding enormous power – destructive as well as constructive – and isn't in any way submissive to masculine authority figures. The same was true of the ancient Egyptian Sekhmet and the Greek Artemis.

There's a quality of wildness about these mythical figures, sometimes called 'Chthonic', meaning untamed, uncivilised, archaic, belonging to the Underworld. This quality of wildness (unpredictability, disobedience, disorder) can feel very threatening to people who are trying hard to be a good Christians, so of course they don't like it. That, to my mind, is one reason for their endless denial and repression of everything associated with 'the Feminine'.

It's only about a hundred years since women in our culture started collectively to break the bonds of their oppression when the Suffragettes demanded to be treated as the democratic equals of their menfolk. At around the same time, D. H. Lawrence was writing about female sexuality in a way that shocked his contemporaries but opened the door to the realisation that to deny a woman's emotional freedom – her passion, if you like – is to rob her of an essential part of her nature and leave only the abstract shell of a person. If you succeed in domesticating a lioness, all you're left with is a very large pussy cat, shorn of its natural power, prone to bouts of embarrassing histrionics and very expensive to feed.

The essential balance between 'Maleness' and 'Femaleness' is beautifully expressed in the ancient symbol known to us as the Yin/Yang diagram.

The symbol itself, which is probably as old as the fourth century BC, is the foundational signature of Taoist spirituality. It describes how the universe is set up, how it is reflected in our own constitution and how the practice of bringing the two sides into balance is an essential part of any transformational path.

The outer circle represents the *Tao*, which means 'Oneness' or the 'Path of Inner Transformation', and contains a perfect balance between the complementary principles of Yin and Yang.

Yin (the black 'fish' with the white eye) is usually translated as 'feminine', although the original meaning is 'dark'. Yin is also thought of as soft, diffuse, cold, wet, or passive, and is associated with water, earth and the Moon.

Yang (the white 'fish' with the black eye) is usually translated as 'masculine', but the original meaning is 'light'. Yang is thought of as having the opposite qualities (hard, focused, hot, dry, active), and associated with fire, air and the Sun.

The presence of the black eye in the white fish, and vice-versa, means 'There is Yin here in the Yang, and there is

Yang here in the Yin' or, more specifically, 'Yin is the *eye* of Yang, and Yang is the *eye* of Yin'.

It's important to understand that the symbol is *not* about duality (Yin vs. Yang) but about 'Three-ness' (Yin, Yang and Tao). We tend to see everything as a duality (force/resistance, good/bad, Heaven/Earth, etc.). As the formidable cosmologist G. I. Gurdjieff put it, we are 'third-force blind'. In effect, the symbol is saying that there can only be a true balance between Yin and Yang when they are reconciled in the Tao, the path of transformation.

The complementarity between the darkness and the light is one of the central mysteries of the universe we live in. In its institutionalised form, Christianity has concentrated almost entirely on the light; it has tried to banish its devil from civilised life, with terrible results because you can't banish the devil. If you chase him out of one room, he'll take up residence in another; if you chase him out of all your rooms, he'll take up residence under the floor or in the attic; from there he'll wreak much worse havoc because you won't know where it's coming from and there's nowhere else you can banish him to. Institutional Christianity never seems to have realised that you have to make a relationship with your devils or they will never leave you alone.

All too often you'll try to get rid of your devils by projecting them onto other people. If you regard these people as inferior, there's no limit to the cruelties you may feel entitled to inflict on them. This is amply illustrated by the history of our Christian civilisation.

✍

Despite its tendency to prioritize the light, Christianity also recognises a pair of qualities that complement each other in the same sort of way as Yin and Yang. These are the two fundamental attributes of the divine, known as 'transcendence' and 'immanence'. Transcendence means that God (who is traditionally masculine, of course) is above and beyond anything we can imagine, all-powerful, almighty and all-knowing, everlasting, the creator of everything that is, etc., etc. This is clearly associated with our notion of 'the Masculine', if only because attributes like knowledge and power have been comprehensively abrogated by the patriarchy.

Immanence, on the other hand, means the way that God shows Himself in the wonder and beauty of His creation. The theatre where all this immanence manifests is known to us as Mother Nature, who is clearly a feminine entity. She is seen in a poetic sense as abundant, mysterious, wild, beautiful, nurturing and awesomely powerful. Nevertheless until quite recently, she was seen in a *rational* sense as doing what she was set up to do, following the natural law that the transcendent God (masculine) laid down for her to follow. She is awesomely powerful but *He owns her*. This is a perfect representation of the power of the patriarchy and very convenient for secular rulers whose authority was seen, until quite recently, as historically sanctioned by God.

Some Native American peoples have a very neat way of reconciling the balance between masculine and feminine where authority and power are concerned. Authority lies with the tribal chiefs (male), *but the Chiefs are chosen by the Mothers*. When I heard about this, I was reminded of a cryptic comment that my American friend Renee made to me, many years ago: *'Men have the authority,'* she said, *'but women have the power.'* I have often pondered this comment, because, although it isn't reflected in our social order, it seemed 'right' to me at the time and it still does. We have simply confused authority with power, and this has caused untold harm to the natural order.

❦

The Sufi mystic and teacher Llewellyn Vaughan Lee has written[6] about the vital need for what he calls 'the Divine Feminine' to be re-established in our minds and hearts, to restore the spiritual equilibrium of a seriously out-of-balance world:

If God is totally elevated to the heavens it is easy to lose touch with the divine in everyday life. We come to know Him only as a distant authoritarian father. Our present culture resonates with the feelings of alienation and individual impotence that reflect the remoteness of our masculine God. We easily feel uncared-for and unprotected, isolated, no longer an integral part of the great wholeness of life.

The sacred wholeness of life belongs to the feminine aspect of the divine, the Great Goddess. For Her every act is sacred; every blade of grass, every creature is part of the Great Oneness. In contrast to his awe-inspiring transcendence, She embodies the caring divine presence...

Banishing God to the heavens, we lost touch with the sacredness of the earth and its many forms of life. We are slowly becoming conscious of this imbalance and the danger caused by the rejection of the Goddess. We see how our whole planet is suffering from the abuses of masculine technology. Women have had to confront both individual and collective experiences of abuse. The masculine power principle has been recognised as responsible for tremendous feminine suffering, to the individual and to the ecosystem.' (pp.32–33)

This, to my mind, sums it up very well.

*

The way that 'male' and 'female' qualities complement each other spiritually is replicated in a most interesting way in our individual psychology, and again shows how unbalanced our current way of life has become.

The inventor of 'embodiment coaching', Philip Shepherd, suggests that we can recognise in ourselves two complementary poles of intelligence: the head, which is more associated with a 'masculine' orientation, and the body, which represents a more 'feminine' orientation. This is how he describes the difference between the two and the way we prioritise one of them over the other[7]:

The relationship we have with our body celebrates one part of our intelligence (what the head knows) and demeans another part (what the body knows). It celebrates the part that is able to abstract, disconnect, systematize, gain perspective, establish known relationship and seek control. And it demeans the part that is able to come into felt relationship, integrate, attune to the Present, know things without words and feel wholeness. If it's true, as I deeply believe, that we are all endowed with gifts of both male and female strengths within us, we might see the abstracting strengths of the head as expressions of the male side of our consciousness, and the sensitized attunement of the body's intelligence as an expression of the female side of our consciousness. Again, all of us are endowed with both male

*and female strengths, however we might identify our gender.
But if a primary feature of how we relate to our body is that
we demean the female strengths of our intelligence and exalt
the male, we should expect to find that reflected in how we
relate to the world. And indeed, in our culture 'maleness' has
been held up as the standard for a normal human being and
'femaleness' has been considered nonstandard, unreliable,
inferior, weak, not worth listening to and certainly not fit to
be in charge. It is a heinous, ludicrous cultural imbalance –
and the seed of it lies in how we have come to relate to the
body.*

To understand a bit more about this mysterious faculty
which Shepherd calls 'the body's intelligence', I would
recommend taking a look at the psychological self-care
practice known as Focusing. This was first developed in
the seventies by American philosopher Eugene Gendlin,
who was interested in how we create meaning through
language[8]. His unique discovery was that our capacity
to understand and relate to the situations that we find
ourselves in actually comes from a holistic sense of them
(or rather, of our place within them) that we hold *in our
bodies*. This 'felt sense', as he called it, is much more
intricate and penetrating than a mere statement of 'what
happened' and 'what it made us feel like'. If we pause and
listen to what our bodies are telling us through the felt
sense, we are more likely to understand what's really going
on in our lives and how we might be able to change the
ways in which we relate to the situations that really matter
to us[9]. If, on the other hand, we just listen to what the
'intelligence in our head' says, we are more likely to get a
formulaic or second-hand response based on what we've
learned out of a book, what other people have said or what

our childhood conditioning told us a long time ago.

Focusing works through what I like to call 'embodied intelligence', the same faculty that Shepherd calls 'sensitized attunement'. There is no suggestion that women are better or worse at it than men, but in my experience it does take a certain degree of emotional maturity, especially the ability to listen with compassion without giving advice or telling someone how they should be feeling. I have practised it for the last twenty years with several different Focusing partners (it's usually done in pairs) and I've found it very valuable – and, of course, it's a good deal cheaper than psychotherapy.

Another way of understanding the psychological complementarity between these two different kinds of intelligence is to look at the relationship between the right and the left hemispheres of the human brain. This has been explored recently in exquisite detail by the psychiatrist Iain McGilchrist[10]. It has been known for a long time that there are significant differences in the way that the two hemispheres of the brain do their work[11], but most of the discussion about this difference has assumed that it's about functionality (i.e. that each hemisphere carries out different functions or tasks). McGilchrist made a detailed study of all the evidence and came to the conclusion that both of them are involved in carrying out all the necessary functions but they do it in entirely different ways, corresponding with different ways of paying attention to the world.

The right hemisphere experiences the world in a

more holistic way and is capable of appreciating the organic wholeness of a living structure. It is far better at appreciating music, much more involved in feeling life and much more empathetic. The left hemisphere, on the other hand, is better at separating everything out into categories from which predictions can be made. It sees the world more as a set of abstractions, and is good at using tools and working with mechanisms. It is much more involved in 'doing' than in 'being'.

As McGilchrist is careful to point out, these differences are not gender-related (in other words, they don't describe the difference between men and women) but they do bear a strong resemblance to the observations that Philip Shepherd makes about the differences between a more 'male-oriented' (separative, head-based) and a more 'female-oriented' (holistic, body-based) type of intelligence. This might mean that the right hemisphere of the brain is much better at listening to what the body is trying to tell us. My experience with Focusing suggests that the body presents us with a whole *gestalt*, which is easily destroyed if we try to force it into the kinds of ready-made categories with which the left hemisphere usually works. The focusers that I know tend to be introverted, emotionally literate, good listeners and more interested in people than things.

The essential conclusions that McGilchrist set out in *The Master and His Emissary* are summed up (or should I say 'elegantly compressed') in his recently published booklet, *Ways of Attending*. There is a chilling section at the end of this booklet where he suggests that ...*the world in which we live has come increasingly to reflect the view of the left hemisphere alone* (i.e. in Shepherd's language, the dominance of the masculine)[12]. McGilchrist reflects in detail on what it might look like if we were to rely exclusively on the left hemisphere as our only means of interpreting reality. This starts with the bald sentence: *First of all, the whole picture would be unattainable: the world would become a heap of bits. Its only meaning would come through its capacity to be used.*

This has enormous implications, of course. For example, if it is taken together with the absence of any feeling of sacredness, then the whole of Nature becomes reduced to a superstore full of 'resources' which we are free to exploit in whatever way we want. This is a subject which I will explore more thoroughly in Chapter 8, because it's key to understanding the fundamental imbalance in our world-view. It also applies to our relationships with each other: *Exploitation rather than cooperation would, explicitly or not, be the default relationship between human individuals and between humanity and the rest of the world.*

The left hemisphere doesn't see the whole picture because its attention is much more narrowly focused. This, McGilchrist says, *would lead to an increasing specialisation and technicalising of knowledge. This, in turn, would promote the substitution of information ... for knowledge, which comes through experience. Knowledge, in its turn, would seem more 'real' than what one might call wisdom, which would seem too nebulous, something never to be grasped.*

In the immortal words of T. S. Eliot, from his pageant play *The Rock*:

Where is the wisdom we have lost in knowledge?
Where is the knowledge we have lost in information?

McGilchrist would reply: *Knowledge that has come*

through experience... would be replaced by tokens and representations – formal systems, to be evidenced by paper qualifications.

We are all well aware of some common examples of this. The tendency to denigrate practical education (e.g. apprenticeships) in favour of academic education (e.g. degrees) is one of the more obvious. This is very hard to reverse because a degree has always been associated with a much higher social status. As a result of this: ... *fewer people would find themselves doing work involving contact with anything in the real, 'lived' world, rather than with plans, strategies, paperwork, management and bureaucratic procedures.* Anyone over the age of about sixty will be familiar with this trend; our bureaucratic structures in both private and public sectors of the economy have grown enormously since the end of the Second World War.

At the same time, ...*Increasingly, the living would be modelled on the mechanical. This would have an effect on the way bureaucracies would deal with human situations ... and a certain inflexibility would result.* Again, anyone familiar with the Byzantine complexity of the social welfare and immigration systems in the UK and their often insensitive, and sometimes brutal, application in practice, will have no trouble recognising this.

Bureaucracies, he writes, would find it harder to tolerate ambiguity or to rely on implicit meaning. This, in turn, would mean *a rise in explicitness, backed up by ever-increasing legislation... As it became less possible to rely on a shared and intuitive moral sense or on implicit contracts between individuals, such rules would grow ever more burdensome.* I return to this subject in Chapter 10, which explores some of the difficulties our 'rational' bureaucracies face when they try to turn ethical values into law.

Another characteristic feature of the left-hemisphere world is its addiction to control: *The left hemisphere cannot trust and is prone to paranoia. It needs to feel in control. We would expect governments to become obsessed with issues of security above all else, and to seek total control.* This is an important subject, which I return to in many parts of this book, especially in Chapter 4.

McGilchrist pays great attention to detail[13], and it's difficult in a short summary like this to do justice to the picture he paints, so his account is well worth reading in the original. This is how he finishes: *In terms of the fable with which I began, the emissary, insightless as ever, appears to believe it can see everything, alone. But it cannot: on its own it is like a zombie, a sleepwalker ambling straight towards the abyss, whistling a happy tune.*

The fable he's referring to is one in which the master represents the intuitive, holistic knowledge of the right hemisphere, and his emissary represents the formal knowledge of the left. McGilchrist is very clear about this: he says the bicameral arrangement only works properly when the right hemisphere is in charge, and the left is his (or her) servant.

However, in our age the servant has usurped the master, and is strutting about wrecking the planet. This is because, although he's very good at what he does, he is completely incapable of appreciating his own limitations and, above all, because *he doesn't care*. Not from some kind of malice but because he's actually incapable of caring, in the same way that a rabbit is incapable of flying. So for him, an ancient forest (for example) is 'worth' nothing more than the monetary value of x cubic metres of construction timber.

If he's in charge, it's no wonder we're in this appalling mess.

✐

As an illustration of how deeply this 'split consciousness' might affect the lives that we lead, I'm reminded of the story of my friend Claire.

Claire is a bright, articulate thirty-something who now lives in a small community in Cumbria. I first met her at Heart of Devon, where she'd joined us on a WWOOF[14] scheme. One evening we were sitting round the fire telling stories, and I asked her how she came to be 'WWOOFing', as they call it.

She said she'd been brought up by middle-class parents who lived in a commuter village near London. As a young girl she was always a bit solitary, in love with Nature, and frequently helped out at a local farm where they kept goats. Her parents wanted her to do well and gave her lots of encouragement with her education, sending her to a local fee-paying day school which had ambitious standards.

She wasn't particularly academic but she worked hard and did well at school, went on to university and studied economics (which she hated), and soon landed a job in the marketing department of a prestigious company in London. She was very keen to prove herself, always trying to do better, and in the end she got very stressed out in her zeal to impress her employers. Within a couple of years she was relying on anti-depressants and often unable to sleep; after another couple of years she had a breakdown and had to take time off work.

She went home to recuperate and soon found herself

back on the farm, helping out with the animals. One day she was sitting on a log, smoking a cigarette and watching the sunset, when she became aware of a vast spaciousness – she felt that she *was* the sunset and the hillside and the bleating of the goats, and that this was somehow eternal and unchanging like a sort of infinite moment outside of time. That, she said, was when she realised that she had been living a totally false life that had nothing to do with who she really was and everything to do with the hopes and expectations of her parents, teachers, friends, bosses and everyone else who had influenced her since she was a child.

It took her another three years of struggle, argument and self-doubt before she abandoned her previous life entirely and started on this new life of travel and profound learning. She embraced Buddhism and learned to live very simply. She learned a lot of useful skills, met some really interesting people, made many good friends and was much happier than she'd ever been. She said she probably wouldn't go on living like this for ever, but she would simply carry on until she was able to move on naturally into the next phase of her life, whatever that might be.

To my mind, this is a good example of what Iain McGilchrist is talking about when he says that the emissary has usurped the master and we need to put him back in his place. Just like Claire did.

❧

So, after a thousand years of 'progress' our civilisation now finds itself in an extremely unbalanced state. We could call this 'the tragedy of progress' because we undertook this long journey in an attempt to understand the material world and explore how we could use it for the advancement of human culture. One could say that we've gone too far with this progress – but how far is too far? And how could we have anticipated that it would end up like this? Was there a point at which we should we have said 'enough is enough', or was it always fated to end in disaster?

The dark side of progress – the collateral damage, we could say – has been the ruthless exploitation of other people, and of the entire natural living world, by a 'civilised' humanity that has finally lost its way and become arrogant, materialistic and alienated from its ancient sources of spiritual and emotional nourishment. We'll be looking at this in much more detail in Chapter 8, but for now I'll finish with a suggestion from the Nigerian writer Bayo Akomolafe, who is one of the most fluent commentators on the history and consequences of the ideal of progress. In this passage, he makes the link between the way we unconsciously prioritize the left-brain version of knowledge and our obsession with the search for what we call 'happiness':[15]

...we live largely in a world governed under a kingdom of Light, and this light implies a violent and forceful dichotomization of the world. It needs everything neatly arranged and easily categorized. It cannot afford that things spill into each other. It needs binaries—an inside and outside. The things that fall on the outside are thus thought to be evil, chaotic, and corrupt...

...we should pay attention to the interesting proposal that our psychic lives are richly embroidered with darkness. And living with the inescapability of darkness, meeting the dark on its own terms, acknowledging that darkness has its own

prerogatives that are different from illumination, instead of attempting to fix it or look past it or make it a means to light, becomes our fierce focus. That is, opening closures— one of which is the closure of the dark psychic life—can help us understand how, in our modern comings and goings, happiness is so easily fetishized, so passionately pursued, and yet so defiantly in short supply.

It's worth pondering why he makes this link and what it says about our way of life. Claire, for example, believed fervently – having had it impressed on her over and over again – that the advancement of her ambition would, after all the struggles and compromises, finally make her happy. She would earn lots of money, marry another high earner, buy a house in the country, and all her problems would be solved. I wonder how many times we've all heard *that* kind of fairy story.

The more unbalanced a dynamic system becomes, the greater the internal pressure it will generate towards rebalancing. We've pushed this one to an extreme now, a logical extreme that has been made much worse by our profligate squandering of sources of energy that are finite and non-renewable. There is a price to pay and we (or more likely, our children, and their children and so on into the remote future) will have to pay it.

The Earth – Gaia – is essentially a feminine power. As 'Mother Earth' she can be very forgiving but the time for that is over because we have endlessly abused her; now she's showing us in a clear and unmistakable way that there are limits to her indulgence.

We talk about 'climate change' or 'climate breakdown' as if they were mechanical responses to us placing too much of a burden on the Earth's carrying capacity. From a rational point of view, this is obviously true. She's simply responding and adapting to the conditions we've imposed on her. But from a mythopoetic point of view, we can see it as something much more profound. Gaia will literally *burn us up* in the same way that Sekhmet, the lion-headed goddess, burned up the enemies of the Sun-god Ra. It might well take a few hundred years of wretchedness while our collapsed world recovers (or doesn't) for us to learn that it doesn't pay to abuse the Goddess.

References

1 From *The Second Coming*, by W. B. Yeats, written in 1919 and much quoted by commentators after Trump's victory.

2 Naomi Klein, *No Is not Enough* (Penguin/Random House, 2018).

3 Meadows, Meadows and Randers, *The Limits to Grown* (N.Y., Universe Books, 1972). Recently John Michael Greer published an essay on his website Ecosophia, where he shows in unmistakably clear terms that what we see playing out today corresponds almost exactly with the 'worst-case scenario' predicted by this fifty-year-old study. See https://www.ecosophia.net/a-prayer-for-nonbelievers

4 Richard Tarnas, *The Passion of the Western Mind* (Pimlico, London, 2010).

5 Jeremy Naydler, *In the Shadow of The Machine* (Temple Lodge, 2018).

6 Llewellyn Vaughan Lee, *The Return of the Feminine and the World Soul* (Golden Sufi Centre, 2009).

7 Philip Shepherd, *Radical Wholeness*, (North Atlantic Books, 2017), p.46.

8 Eugene Gendlin, *Experience and the Creation of Meaning* (Northwestern University Press, 1997).

9 For a good introduction to the technique, see (for example) Ann Weiser Cornell, *The Power of Focusing* (New Harbinger Publications, 1996).

10 Iain McGilchrist, T*he Master and his Emissary: The Divided Brain and the Making of the Western World* (New Haven, Ct.: Yale University Press, 2009).

11 For example, the work of Robert Ornstein and others in the 1970s. See R. Ornstein (ed.), *The Nature of Human Consciousness* (Freeman & Co., 1973).

12 Iain McGilchrist, *Ways of Attending: How our Divided*

Brain Constructs the World (Routledge, 2019), p.27.

13 McGilchrist has recently published a new version of the material originally developed in *The Master and His Emissary*. This is *The Matter With Things: Our Brains, Our Delusions and the Unmaking of the World*, a monumental 3,000-page account of the subject, published in two volumes, which includes all the detailed neuropsychological evidence for his basic proposition, and a considerable expansion of the conclusions he derives from it. He shows how the left hemisphere has come to dominate our world-view on two previous occasions, first with the ancient Greeks and then again with the Romans, and how on each occasion this coincided with a major civilisational collapse.

14 World Wide Opportunities on Organic Farms.

15 From *Finding the Dark: Decolonising Darkness*, by Bayo Akomolafe, at bayoakomolafe.net/project/1313

- 3 -

The Curlew's Cry

DECEMBER 2016

DONALD TRUMP NOMINATES someone called Scott Pruitt to be head of the Environmental Protection Agency[1]. There is an immediate cry of pain from everyone who cares about 'the environment' (also known as Mother Nature). This man Pruitt is a climate-change denier who opposes all attempts to protect our long-suffering mother from our frenzied assaults on her. Far from being a friend of the EPA, when he was Attorney General to the State of Oklahoma between 2010 and 2016, he sued the Agency no less than thirteen times on behalf of fossil fuel companies and other industrial polluters. He has a reputation for dodgy ethics and for using devious, barely legal manoeuvring to get what he wants. It's as if Trump had nominated Al Capone to be Attorney General of the USA.

❧

My ancient mother-in-law knows nothing of this new controversy. She is too far gone to care about 'the environment'. She never even looks out of the window at her own gloriously overgrown patch of garden.

I'm getting used to this strange life. I don't mean I'm enjoying it – just getting used to it, that's all. I cook Lizzie's food – she has appalling dietary preferences, but I just hold my nose and do it – and then she tells everyone what a good cook I am, which makes me wonder whether the old girl has a latent sense of irony that she's kept hidden all these years. The only items in the fridge that we share are milk and butter. She won't eat any fresh fruit or veg, or anything even slightly tasty apart from ketchup. She won't even eat tinned soup because most tinned soups have onions in them and, as everyone knows, onions are the devil's veg.

There's a mysterious solicitor who has financial power of attorney, and he pays for everything except my food (using her money, of course). I think he was suspicious about my motives for being here – he's been doing this kind of work for a while, so he's seen it all before – but now he's relaxed a bit. He's happy that she's living at home again, so he leaves me alone to get on with it.

Lizzie is constantly asking me when 'the girl' will be coming to dish out her tablets. She knocks on my bedroom door at 5 am, opens it, walks right in and asks me.

'She comes at 9.30,' I say. 'Please go back to bed and don't disturb me any more.'

Back she comes at 6.30 and asks me the same question.

'I've already told you,' I growl. 'She's coming at 9.30!'

'Don't you swear at me like that,' she says indignantly. 'After all I've done for you!'

After several of these performances, I buy a small brass bolt and instal it on the inside of my door so that she can't just open it and walk in. Then I write a large notice that says

*THE CARER WILL COME WITH YOUR TABLETS AT 9.30,
and stick it up prominently on the outside.*

*At 5am the next morning, Lizzie knocks on my door,
rattles it when it won't open and shouts, 'When is the girl
coming with my tablets?'*

*I get out of bed, open the door, point at the sign and ask
her if she's read what it says.*

'Yes, but she hasn't come yet.'

*'Of course she hasn't come yet,' I say. 'It's only 5am. She
won't be here for another four-and-a-half hours. Now why
don't you just go back to bed and have a nice little sleep.'*

*Lizzie sticks to her guns. 'But she should have come at
9.30,' she complains.*

*'Oh, for God's sake,' I say, and shut the door. This is one
of my first lessons in the logic of dementia. I know she's mad
and she can't help it, but all the same...*

*'The girl' (or rather the girls, as there are several of them)
come and dish out her pills three times a day. Lizzie has
a profoundly ambiguous relationship with her pills. She
worries constantly about when she's going to get them, but
when they are offered she frequently refuses to take them
because she suspects that the carers are trying to poison her.
She always refuses her Mirtazapine at night, for example,
because it's big and brown in colour, and looks kind of mean.
As a result, she's up most of the night and then all she can do
is worry about when she's going to get the next lot.*

*She leaves endless messages on the care company's office
voicemail in the wee small hours. I've heard her doing it a
couple of times when I've been awake and she does manage
to make herself sound absolutely desperate. She doesn't use
the emergency number, which would summon the manager
out of bed at 3am, but that's only because she doesn't know*

that it exists. It's listed at the bottom of the loose-leaf page in the transparent pocket on the front cover of their log book, but I've folded it over so that she can't see it. Probably illegal, but I think they'd understand.

Lizzie's predilection for drama makes me think of a girl of five who has a genuine talent for acting but is only encouraged to develop it in a way that pleases Daddy and Mummy. She just goes on playing the same small range of parts all the time, hoping that someone will notice her.

She particularly likes to see herself as a tragic heroine, and she's in her element when she's feeling bereft and abandoned. I've seen her look just as tragic when the biscuit jar is empty as she looks on Jane's birthday (that is, when she remembers it). She can become instantly and overwhelmingly tragic when she's on the phone to a friend. One minute she's happily watching Deal or No Deal on TV, then a friend calls her and she sighs convincingly as she describes how empty her life is and how lonely she feels. 'I'm all on my own,' she wails, ignoring the fact that I'm in the same room. 'It would be so nice if you could come down to Radstock and see me!'

Unfortunately, her friends are reluctant to get involved, which enables her to confirm her story about herself – that she's alone and bereft in a world where no-one cares.

She used to go to the weekly social gatherings at the Methodist Church but she stopped going a while ago, long before she was in the care home, probably because they too were reluctant to get involved with her dramas. I suspect she used to inhabit her Lady Elizabeth character, which she developed when she was married to Alderman George. (In those days, she was treated with a certain deference.) I ask her if she wants to start going again but she tells me the church socials are 'a bit common'. She'll go occasionally if they're having a 'special do', but she doesn't seem to enjoy it very much.

Jane once told me that her incurable urge to always be the centre of attention comes from the fact that she was Daddy's little princess, so I guess it's been a lifelong habit. Her parents had five boys but her dad always wanted a girl so they didn't give up until Lizzie popped out. She learned how to be the star of the show in a family full of boys, that's for sure, because she behaves completely differently when there are men around. You can sense that she's still trying to flutter and flirt and simper, but she can't do it so convincingly now that she's ninety-five.

Being Daddy's little princess must be great for a little girl, but surely they must get bored with it by the time they're sixteen, or at least when Daddy starts criticizing their boyfriends? If you keep on expecting the same kind of attention when you're no longer a little girl, it must put an awful burden on your life. I don't know how many admirers Lizzie once had – quite a few, by her account, and maybe that's true because she was once quite good-looking – but she appears to have very few left. I guess most of those that are still living are tucked away in their bungalows somewhere in the Potteries. They send Christmas cards, and one or two of them call her on the telephone every so often, but so far as I know none of them have yet bothered to travel all the way down here to see her.

So I'm afraid she doesn't have many friends. There's Sue, the next-door neighbour, who has been 'keeping an eye on her' for a while now and comes in once a week to do a bit of cleaning. Sue is a mine of information about everything that goes on in the house and loves gossiping about Lizzie's curious obsessions. I often consult her when there's something I need to know, like which brand of incontinence pants Lizzie likes to use and where I can get hold of them. Then there's Amy, who probably met Lizzie at some kind of church event. They don't have much in common and Lizzie is frequently rude to her, but Amy is determined to save Lizzie's soul and visits regularly, ostensibly to run small errands but actually to talk about Jesus. Lizzie kind of goes along with it for the sake of a bit of companionship, but she's not convinced.

🍃

I escape from this mausoleum as often as I can. Usually it's to do a bit of shopping or to meet with my Lightning Tree colleagues in Bristol, but I try as often as I can to disappear westwards into the Mendips where there are some cracking places to explore.

The biggest attraction is the famous Cheddar Gorge but there are many others that aren't so well-known, so they're less crowded with visitors. There's Burrington Coombe, for example, a delightful valley with a big pub at the bottom where Jane and I often used to go and have lunch after an exhilarating walk in the woods. I go there at least once a week, to escape from the madhouse.

During these forays into wild Nature, I often find myself thinking about the way we are trashing the planet. Usually it makes me angry, but sometimes underneath the anger I sense a profound and inexpressible sadness.

🍃

Trees are the most astonishing structures. I've always loved them but it was only recently that I became aware of just how truly *amazing* they are. When you look at a tree, you see an extraordinary balance between life and death, above and below, movement and stillness. The growing part of the tree is held up in the air by the part that's stopped growing, like an exuberant dance into the light which has been frozen in time.

More recently, I've sometimes become aware of the subtle energy field that every tree makes around itself and the way these energy fields together make up the whole energy field of the wood. It's this kind of experience that convinces me that the Earth is more like a single living being than a random collection of separate living things sharing the surface of an inanimate piece of rock.

Of course, if we all saw it this way we would find it much more difficult to continue trashing this beautiful planet in the reckless way that we are doing now.

As many poets of the natural world have noticed, trees have a certain natural presence. You can stand in front of an ancient oak and get the distinct feeling that you are in the presence of a being that is at least as wise, in its own way, as you are in yours.

I have several favourites, which I visit as often as possible. One is a huge, gnarly old horse chestnut, which reminds me of my grandpa Bert. He was a down-to-earth ex-Marine with a sense of humour, who always supported me when I got into an argument with my dad. If this tree were music, it would express a kind of trenchant despair, like one of those Russian Romantics – Tchaikovsky or Mussorgsky, perhaps. Another of my favourites is an ancient yew, which for some reason reminds me of my old mate Conrad who died thirty years ago. It's as solemn as a churchyard, and has the most interesting, complicated shape, like a seventeenth-century alchemical diagram (Conrad was fond of that kind of stuff). Yet another is a tall silver birch, which is actually in the local park (or what passes for a park). It looks ethereal, as if it isn't quite 'of the Earth'. It's lacy and delicate, like my friend Trudy who comes across like harp music or those breathy Andean pipes.

When you contemplate one of these trees, you are tapping into a whole world of meaning.

You may have read about the battle that was going on in Sheffield, where the council was paying a company of hired vandals a mountain of money to destroy thousands of trees because it was cheaper than lopping them every few years. I can understand why the people of Sheffield were so angry about it. Their trees mean something to them, and there's no way this 'something' can be measured in terms of money.

Something similar has been happening all over Europe because of 5G. It's claimed that the trees will get in the way of the cell-phone transmissions. If that's true, it's obviously crazy. I find it hard to understand why anyone would want to chop down a tree because it enabled some sort of marginal improvement in our ability to disappear down a mobile phone.

That's where 'environmentalism' starts. Something is being chopped down or bulldozed, and there is a very personal sense of loss and grief which easily translates into anger and determination. It's never just a matter of utility or monetary value, even though this is the only language the bureaucrats are allowed to speak. It can be easily derided as romantic nostalgia, but the unconscious purpose of that kind of sarcasm is to offload the secret shame that the agent of the bureaucracy is actually feeling. He probably knows in his soul that it's just wrong to cut down all those trees, but his salary depends on not admitting it so he has to project his bad feeling onto the protesters. Then *they* can be the 'bad people', and he can continue to draw his salary without feeling too uncomfortable.

❧

When I was working down at Fire Valley, my friend Max, who's a real 'environmentalist' (although he hates that description) and one of the founders of Extinction Rebellion, told me about a practice known as 'sit spot'. This means that you find a place that's as wild as possible, i.e. not usually visited by humans, and you go there as unobtrusively as possible and sit communing with Nature.

The idea wasn't altogether new to me but I'd never done it before. One day in December, when the paths were muddy and the trees were bare, I started exploring my favourite wood up at the top of Burrington Combe to see if I could find such a place. As my rickety-rackety legs are old and tired, it had to be a place where I could sit down easily and without too much discomfort, as you're supposed to sit quietly for at least half an hour to give the local fauna a chance to get used to you.

Eventually I found a wonderful place, right on the edge of a deep chasm. I think there had once been a path through it, but the path is so overgrown now that it probably hasn't been used by anyone else for many years. There's an old holm oak growing right out across the chasm with a sideways branch into which my bum fits perfectly, almost as if this branch has grown with me in mind. (Who knows? In a universe of strange serendipities, maybe it has.) I could sit facing either way, outwards with my legs dangling over a sixty-foot drop or inwards with my feet planted on the edge of the cliff.

I came to know this place in all weathers, winter and summer, and it became as much a part of my life as my own bedroom. Or perhaps even more so, because my bedroom was part of my mother-in-law's domain, whereas this belonged to no-one except perhaps notionally Her Majesty the Queen, and she wasn't about to disturb me sitting on my branch.

There are several other holm oaks thereabouts, and a couple of Scots pines. Holm oaks and Scots pines are evergreen, and there are a few rhododendrons about as well, so the place is quite leafy even in the depths of winter. In spring and summer it's a riot of colours and shapes, and especially beautiful in the late evening when the sun bathes the undersides of the leaves that face towards the East with a warm light.

I sit up there, suspended over the chasm, surrounded by a rampant Nature beyond anyone's control, and forget about cell-phones and cars and cities. Gradually a feeling for wildness creeps over me, an urge to celebrate the places we haven't yet ruined in our rush to tame Mother Nature and turn her into a food factory or a theme park.

🍃

Here's what the Sufi teacher Elias Amidon wrote recently about wildness[2]:

Mother Nature – how accurate that we call her a "mother",

the mother of all this life around us. To call Mother Nature mother means she's "woman", though not a woman, but womanish in her way which is wild, untamed, fecund and free-spirited. She follows no path; she moves everywhere. She stirs the ocean into unruly waves, she tangles the grasses like unkempt hair. She's wild. Womanish wild.

And yet in her wildness – how does she do it? – she's perfectly skilled and careful, fashioning each feather in the sparrow's wing, just so, the dapple on the forest floor, the veins in a leaf. From her womb everything is born, elegantly made but unscripted, perfectly formed but set free – wild. The sparrow flies in quick arcs and dips, unmanaged by anything, the shadows on the forest floor play by themselves, the veins of one leaf are never the same as another's.

We humans have done our best to tame Mother Nature, make her predictable like ourselves, fence her. We've built roofs above us to keep her wild rain from our faces. Good, we need that, we need some safety. But have we gone too far? Have we forgotten something?

...We who are so concerned with saving the world – and ourselves – perhaps we can learn something crucial to our task from our wild mother, from how her wildness is both perfect artistry and perfect freedom. So let us ask again: how, indeed, does she do it?

Not by planning certainly, though she remembers everything that has happened and creates from that wholeness. Her wildness, extravagant in the extreme, is somehow frugal too – a million sperm for one egg, every raindrop of the trillions brought back to the clouds, every falling leaf put to use. Her law above all is life! – she proceeds always towards life. Even death, which seems to us so final and tragic, is to her alive.

And if we turn our attention to the most insignificant, small-scale sounds and movements of her wildness – do they tell us anything? Things like the sound of water flowing over rocks, the turning of a hawk's head, every rustle in the forest, all give evidence of... what? Responsiveness? Perhaps that's it, her responsiveness is her mother-way, her nature, her Tao, exactly appropriate and always spontaneous.

Spontaneity! Every instant she is present and becoming something new – it's as if the moment is hers and is the source of her intelligence. What does that say to us? Could we touch that spontaneous intelligence too? Now? Perhaps it's closer than we think.

And what else? So much! We could sit at her feet and learn forever. Her fierceness teaches us caution, her indifference, humility, her nurturing, love. But let us note here just two more ways of her wildness, both of them obvious and both nearly lost to us.

First, so clear to see, she is beautiful. It is not an accident. Her beauty, in part, is how well she makes everything fit – sky to earth, river to land, tree to forest, mother to child. See how the dawn's first sunlight touches the sides of the trees! How the small blue eggs fit in the nest! How blessed we would be if we could make our doings, our cities and commerce, fit so well to her!

And then there's this – can we say it without sounding grand? – her wildness, as ordinary as rain splashing on a leaf, reveals the holiness we have longed to know and to be intimate with. Her wildness is holy wildness. Her presence is sacred presence. Her ways are sacred ways. In their wild evanescence they disclose the wholeness, livingness, responsiveness, spontaneity and beauty that can teach us what we so dearly need to learn.

I've had this strong feeling for *wildness* before, when my wife Jane and I lived off-grid up in Swaledale in the eighties. My friend Conrad lived up there in an old cottage which he'd partly renovated high above the village of Gunnerside. He knew of a derelict house near his cottage that was owned by a university lecturer who hardly ever visited, and Conrad thought he could be persuaded to rent it to us. We'd had enough of London, so we didn't need any persuading. I met the guy and offered to do some basic renovations for him if he'd let us live there, and he could use it for his holidays from time to time in the summer. To my surprise, he readily agreed to my proposition.

It was hard work, but as a lifestyle it was idyllic. In those days, I had no idea that our entire Western way of life was in trouble – or rather, this being the time of Thatcher and Reagan, I thought that our 'troubles' were about the dangers of nuclear war rather than the more insidious, less newsworthy, war that we've been waging against Nature. I'd read *The Limits to Growth*, which came out in 1972, but the ideas in it remained just that – ideas; although I took them seriously, I felt there wasn't much we could do about it, so there was no point in getting upset. The hills would still be here and the River Swale would still meander through the valley as it had done for the last hundred million years.

With hindsight, I find it hard to believe that we were so short-sighted. But we weren't yet aware of the looming catastrophe of climate breakdown and, for us, living off-grid was just a wild adventure, a wonderful escape from the serious business of 'earning lots of money and having a nice house'.

To this day the bubbling cry of the curlew makes me stop in my tracks, because it brings back the whole feeling of that time in North Yorkshire. Just like that wonderful Cyndi Lauper track *Time After Time*, which almost always brings tears to my eyes, because it carries with it such a vivid memory of the time in 1984 when Jane and I were first together.

❧

What actually is the feeling that's conjured up by the curlew's cry? For me, it's a feeling of desolate intimacy, of being at home in the ancient rolling hills of North Yorkshire, its patchwork of fields with their limestone walls meandering up the hillsides to meet the deep browns and purples of the heather on the moorland above. Having repaired a few stone walls, my hands can still feel the weight and the hardness of those stones even now. My body can recall lying in the bracken, watching the clouds moving slowly across a huge sky, smelling the damp earth and feeling the rough and ferny fronds on my face.

I remember the awesome grandeur of the dales rolling away into the far distance, with the long winding valley of the River Swale below ('Old Mother Swale', they used to sing to her when I first went up there nearly sixty years ago). I recall the deep scars left by the old mine workings where they tunnelled into the hillsides in search of lead for the church roofs of England. The feeling of history – not just the few hundred years during which we humans have occupied these hills, but the geological history that laid them down in Carboniferous times, and then spent the next 300 million years weathering them into their characteristic roundness.

This is the curlew's country. She's a magician: she invites you to disappear into her song, fills the empty air with her music, brings everything on the hillside into one timeless presence – that's the kind of magic that you don't get in cities. It's a Nature programme that you never forget when it's over, a memory that never leaves you.

I learned a lot from the birds. I remember watching the lapwings, with their peculiar dipping flight and their piercing cries: *Peee-wit*! *Peee-wit*! In their world, it is always *now*. I have been trying for a long time to live in the world of *now* through the practice of meditation – with limited success – but these birds are master practitioners, effortlessly attuned to one-ness, never estranged from the world around them like we are.

Speaking of the world of *now*, one evening when I was walking back up the hill from Gunnerside village I was spellbound by the song that a thrush (now much rarer in these islands than it was when I was a boy) was singing way up in a huge beech tree. She was literally singing out the day. The whole valley was immersed in her song, as if time had suspended itself for a while just so that every being could stop and listen. It was like living in a different kind of time, a forever time, not just the intersection of past and future but a kind of 'eternal present', an intense 'now-ness' that knew no limits[3].

Nature offers us glimpses of this kind of perfection. This is what we are trashing with our techno-narcissistic civilisation. It's beyond tragedy.

✿

As I was a Southern softie the Yorkshire folk took a bit of getting used to, but after I'd lived there for a while I grew to love them too. They're much more reserved than your usual townies, hard as nails from years of coping with Dales winters, with a dry sense of humour, but they're very ready to help out when there's trouble. There's real hardship up there as well; those who still farm there will never be millionaires. They do it because deep down they love the land, but they're a resilient community that doesn't demand sympathy and knows how to cope with adversity. (That is, when they're not fighting each other over something that happened six generations ago.)

When we were living there, the local farmer (whose name was Jamie Raggett) used to come to our cottage and chat with us whenever he was up there walking his top fields. He was a canny old man, but he was exquisitely polite, warm and friendly to us 'townies', partly because he was very curious as to why two sophisticated (as he thought) urbanites would want to live up there, summer and winter, rather than in a square brick box with central heating and a piped water supply like everyone else. We told him that we'd had enough of that kind of life but I'm not sure he believed us. He knew I kept a load of £50 notes rolled up in a jam jar; this was what we lived on for the first year, just £3,000 in cash that I'd saved up from a year's worth of carpentry. Maybe he thought we were ex-villains on the run from some bank job in New Malden that went wrong, waiting up there in our hideout for the police to lose interest.

Jamie really belonged to the land. He was a smallish, slight man, but his stride was long, and to see him striding along you'd think he had somehow arisen spontaneously out of the earth. He was no country bumpkin; he was an expert sheep breeder (the Swaledale ewe is well-known for her hardiness) and he was often away visiting the county shows around England and Scotland, meeting people, doing deals and trading sheep.

The university lecturer who owned the cottage we lived in had bought the place in a derelict state from Jamie for £300. When he wanted it back from us, we put up a fight because he'd never taken much interest before we actually made it habitable – he just collected the tiny rent and that was that – but eventually he got a court order and we had to go. He loved it so much that he put it up for sale three years later and made a cool £80,000.

Living at a basic level close to Nature all year round requires a completely different mindset. You learn skills that city dwellers consider old-fashioned, quaint or just plain redundant 'in this day and age', like co-operating with your neighbours even if you don't like them, getting your winter fuel in while it's still deliverable, knowing how to tap a spring for fresh water, living comfortably in a damp environment, disposing of your own waste products and keeping a fire going all night. Basic survival skills, really.

More importantly, you learn that it's not only possible to live much closer to Nature but that it's very enjoyable as well as deeply fulfilling. If the owner hadn't been so keen to turf us out, I've no doubt that Jane and I would have been there forever, or at least for fifteen years until she became very ill. Once you've tasted that kind of life, it's quite hard to get back to 'civilisation' again, with its frantic pace, its electronic distractions and its tendency to numb you out emotionally so that you can cope with the stress. It was hard work, but I wouldn't have missed it for anything.

References

1 Despite his past record, his nomination was confirmed on February 17, 2017. He was forced to resign in July 2018 after a series of ethical scandals that even his supporters could no longer ignore. He was, by a very long way, the worst EPA Administrator since the Agency was set up in 1970.

2 Reproduced with the kind permission of *Pir* Elias Amidon, director of The Sufi Way. 'Notes from the Open Path', April 2019, from www.sufiway.org

3 Some time after I wrote this description of the thrush singing out the day, I came across this comment on the song of the wood thrush in *Braiding Sweetgrass*, Robin Wall Kimmerer's wonderful book about science and indigenous wisdom: *The Creator gave Wood Thrush the gift of a beautiful song, with the duty to sing the forest good-night.*
Robin Wall Kimmerer, *Braiding Sweetgrass: Indigenous Wisdom, Scientific Knowledge, and the Teachings of Plants* (Milkweed Editions, 2013).

- 4 -

The Ubiquitous Machine

A REPORT JUST released by Oxfam[1] shows that just eight men own the same wealth as the poorest *3.6 billion people on Earth. Our broken economies*, says the report, *are funnelling wealth to a rich elite at the expense of the poorest in society, the majority of whom are women.* The report shows how big business and the super-rich use their money and connections to ensure that government policy works for them.

How have the business elites created this outrageous kleptocracy? Mainly by political bribery, because our 'democratic' governments (and their dependent bureaucracies) rely on the big corporations – especially the fossil fuel companies, the arms manufacturers, Big Pharma and the mining and agribusiness corporations – to keep the economy going and provide them with the lifestyle to which they've become accustomed. Why is there so little awareness of this corrupt arrangement? Because the rich elite also own almost the entire news and entertainment media. And because we, 'the people', are more interested in Kim Kardashian's ass than in the nuts and bolts of democracy.

But more than this, because our dependence on the ever-expanding industrial economy has driven us into a dead end from which there is no escape without completely crashing the system.

The weather turns wintry, so Lizzie doesn't go outside the house any more. I coax her into the front garden a few times then one day, when the weather is a bit milder, she plucks up courage and asks me to take her to the corner shop at the end of the road. As we walk, she leans heavily on my arm, uttering little gasps of pain. With some trepidation, I realise that I am in danger of being dramatised as 'the man in her life', with all the emotional baggage that might imply. Not quite a fate worse than death, but close.

By the time she's had enough of her little walk, we are still only halfway there. I leave her sitting on somebody's garden wall while I fetch the car, pick her up and take her the full fifty yards back home again. After this, she doesn't ask to go outside any more. She instructs me to turn the heating up until the house is like a sauna, then she wanders round from room to room, complaining about things that have gone missing. Books, ornaments, the dining-room table ('No, that's not my table. My table was bigger, and it was made of darker wood. Someone has walked off with it.') Sometimes I make a pretence of searching the house, just to show willing.

We have our first Christmas together. In an effort to inject some semblance of festivity, I invite Amy and her funny little husband, Ron, to join us for dinner on Christmas Eve. Lizzie puts on her most tragic face and announces that she can't enjoy Christmas without her beloved daughter by her side. This is ironic, because the few Christmases that Jane, Lizzie and I spent together in Radstock while Jane was still alive were a bit like that achingly funny Tony Hancock sketch, but without the humour. She picks at her food and makes a show of bravely trying to hold back the tears while Amy, Ron and I make jolly conversation about the weather, their holiday on the Costa del Somewhere and the endearing habits of their adorable Shih Tzu, which they were good enough to leave at home on this occasion because Lizzie doesn't like dogs. (On this occasion, Lizzie and I are in full agreement. Actually, I quite like proper dogs but definitely not bloody Shih Tzus.)

A week after this lugubrious episode, early in the morning on New Year's Day, disaster strikes. I've just gone to the bathroom and I'm enjoying my first pee of the day when I hear a heavy crash downstairs and a loud wail from Lizzie. 'Aaaaowww! Chris! Chris!'

'I'm coming!' I shout, wishing I could still pee like you do when you're young. I'm seventy-five and my pee comes out hesitantly, as if I can never be sure how much more there is. Have I finished yet? Oh no, there's a bit more... Now have I finished? Still not sure. Better keep going a bit... So there I am, trying to make a drip-free exit, while my mother-in-law downstairs is still screaming. 'Aaaaowww! Chris! Chris!'

'Oh for fuck's sake, Lizzie,' I breathe through clenched teeth. 'I'm coming,' I shout, and make my way carefully downstairs on my rickety-rackety legs, to find her lying in an awkward position in the corner of the front room.

'Don't try to move,' I command, kneeling by her prostrate body. 'Where does it hurt?'

It looks to me like she's broken her hip. The pain is real, then; she's not just being dramatic. I find a small cushion and gently push it under her head. 'It looks like you've broken something,' I say. 'I'll call the ambulance.'

The ambulance takes forty minutes, during which time she cries, moans, and clutches my hand. My left leg goes numb from sitting on the floor next to her but she won't let me go. She calls obsessively for Jane. 'Don't worry,' I say. 'We'll let her know as soon as we can, but right now we have to wait for the ambulance'.

When the paramedics ring the doorbell, I wrench myself free of her grip, stand up and immediately fall over because my left leg has gone to sleep. I work my way painfully to the front door and let them in.

They are very efficient and also very patient. There's a lot of screaming when they try to get the stretcher under her body but in the end they succeed, and she's carted off to hospital in Bath, many miles away. By now it's 9.30 and I'm very hungry, so I do myself a large fried breakfast and contemplate the new state of affairs.

I've read somewhere that old people who break a hip often don't last very long, so I wonder whether I should make a few preparations. What sort of a funeral would she want? How can I find out who to invite? Should we have it here in Radstock, or 'back home' in Newcastle under Lyme? Would anyone else in her family want to be involved, or should I expect to be doing it on my own? I don't know much about her family, Jane isn't alive to tell me about it, and my stepchildren aren't on hand to help very much. One of them still lives in North Yorkshire and the other one lives and works in Africa.

Never mind. While Lizzie's in hospital, I can invite a few of my old friends round to stay and get pleasantly plastered talking about old times. I reach for my ancient Nokia and leave a few messages. Suddenly I'm feeling 'normal' again.

🍃

I know very few people who still have ancient phones like mine, *sans* camera, *sans* Internet access, *sans* anything 'smart'. Are we Luddites by nature, or are we just incompetent and unable to master the technology? I guess we must share a kind of bloody-minded refusal to 'keep up'. Normal people with iPhones and Samsung Galaxies tend to find this a bit difficult to understand. What's wrong with us that we don't see the benefits of owning such a useful piece of kit? But I'm not trying to make a statement by having an old phone; I just don't really need a new one, so why spend all that money?

I did get myself a smart-ish phone once. At first it was fun to play with, but before long it began to really annoy me. All that tapping and swiping... I finally gave it to a friend and went back to my old Nokia, which is just 'smart' enough to do what I want it to do, and both of us were much happier.

But I do feel uneasy about the way we've become so dependent on electronic gadgetry, not only because it's unnecessarily complicated but also because it has a human cost. I first really noticed this when supermarkets began replacing some of their checkouts with automatic self-service payment machines. I'm very bad at following instructions, especially gnomic utterances like 'unexpected item in bagging area'. *WTF? It's a BAG, you moron! What do you expect to find in a bagging area? My mother-in-law?* After being made to look like an idiot a few times, while I waited for the nice lady to come and give me some help, I gave up trying to use the damn things. In any case, I'd much rather have a conversation with the person on the checkout because they obviously enjoy a bit of human contact to make up for the tedium of sitting in the same position all day, scanning barcodes and dreaming about Christmas.

Of course, this kind of hi-tech substitution racket has been going for a long while. It makes everything much more efficient but also much duller and more soulless. For example, back in the day, I used to do most of my own vehicle maintenance. It gave me great satisfaction to tune up the engine, working with the carburettor, the distributor and the spark plugs until I got just the right mix and the right timing to make it hum. Then in the eighties, the motor manufacturers abandoned all of that primitive stuff and began fitting their engines with computer-driven fuel injection systems that needed specialised machines to adjust anything. That was about when I stopped loving my car (actually the last one I loved was a 1973 Land Rover, which was a dream to maintain because everything could be stripped down and repaired). Now my car is just another over-engineered machine that somebody else looks after at great expense. If I were still able to ride a bike, I'd go back to doing that. At least bikes can still be maintained without costing an arm and a leg.

I find it really difficult to learn how to use digital devices. They work through logical decision pathways which don't respond to our right-brain, holistic sense of a situation. The way we're encouraged to deal with this difficulty (which is the same for all of us) is to fiddle with them until we get the result we're looking for, but I'm not very adept at this kind of fiddling and I'm obviously not the only one to be afflicted by this dreadful disability. Thank heavens there must be quite a few of us poor, inadequate technophobes, or the human beings still working on the checkouts would all have lost their jobs.

Now we even have 'smart fridges' that organise our entire family lives for us. Here's the blurb on an ad for one of them: *The way you cook, shop and socialise is about to be revolutionised thanks to the S___ F___ H___ Refrigerator. With the WiFi enabled touchscreen and app, you're getting so much more than a fridge freezer. You can use the F___ H___ to create shopping lists and follow delicious recipes step-by-step. With an interactive family account, you can create personalised profiles for everyone, so you can stay on top of your family's to-do list. And thanks to the clever entertainment hub, you can display your family photos with pride and even stream your favourite tunes while you unpack the groceries!*

You're not supposed to notice that what this actually does is to place a highly artificial interface between 'you' and your family. Judging by the photo, 'you' in this scenario means Mum, who's standing next to the damn thing with a big smile on her face. What kind of a mum would want or need such a device to prop up her relationship with her family? In what way is it a good idea? And do we really want to add yet another way of informing Mr Google about our everyday lives so that he can bombard us with what he calls 'appropriate' advertising?

Personally, I would rather cut off my own arm with a blunt penknife than sit there patiently learning how to program such a nightmarish device. You might think you're in charge, but actually the device is in charge because everything has to be done in a very artificial way to conform with its operating system.

It's just an expensive toy, of course – but these toys have an insidious effect. The more complex the machine, or rather the more complex the 'user interface', the more we have to close down our capacity for sensitive attunement to the world and behave like a machine ourselves. Not just *think* like a machine, but force our whole being into a kind of 'machine mode'.

There's an extraordinary amount of hype about Artificial Intelligence (AI) out there, which to my mind illustrates just how bedazzled we are by our obsession with technology. The futurists keep telling us that AI is going to transform our lives and solve all our problems, computers will soon be more intelligent than humans, we will soon be able to communicate directly with 'the Cloud', and other fantasies of that kind. Of course, if one takes a very narrow view of what the word 'intelligence' means then all this is quite conceivably true. However I'd prefer to use the word 'clever' to describe what computers can do. For me, there's a very significant difference between 'clever' and 'intelligent'.

My cat is much more intelligent than my computer, but she can't compute to save her life. Nor can I, for that matter. On the other hand, my computer is much cleverer than I am. It manipulates enormous quantities of binary data (0s and 1s) very speedily, remembers exactly what it has done, and can reliably do it again any number of times. It can even 'learn' how to manipulate data in order to make a particular kind of decision if it's programmed to do so. But it has zero inner life, it has no appreciation of values and it can't have a relationship to save its life. It's as dumb as a brick in all the ways my cat is as sharp as a teasel brush; no amount of clever programming will change that, even if it calls itself Alexa and speaks with a soft female voice.

Computers operate on the data that's fed into them using algorithms supplied by the programmer. Algorithms enable computers like mine to make very simple, value-free decisions: Does this person qualify for this benefit? How much should this person pay for his car insurance? Is this person statistically likely to offend again if we let him out of jail? and so on. It can even learn from a data set and produce its own algorithms.

Techniques like this are widely used by bureaucracies, to save time and money (even though the algorithms they use often have the social prejudices of their programmers built into them). They are also used by social media platforms, to manipulate their dopamine-hungry users into certain desired behaviours[2]. The programmers, or the users, can make spectacular mistakes, too. A recent book by Hannah Fry, *Hello World*[3], details a few of these screw-ups and, despite Ms Fry's light and humorous touch, parts of it make sobering reading.

Human (or indeed feline) cognition doesn't work through logical decision pathways. It deals with a whole gestalt all at once, to which it reacts immediately on a bodily level. Only after a measurable interval does it start to convert this reaction into attributes that it can name (or at least the human variety does; the feline variety is a bit short on names). At this point, we can perform logical procedures, if we want to. But our value judgements depend almost entirely on perceptions which – in cats as well as humans – are grounded in very complex body states[4]. They rely on intimations, subtle nuances, habits and feelings, not 'data' in a digital sense. They have an irreducible complexity that can't be expressed in a linear string of 0s and 1s. Small parts of this complexity – those which are amenable to some kind of logic – can be *simulated* to some extent, but these simulations are not at all the same as 'the real thing' and we shouldn't allow ourselves to be fooled into believing that they are.

The body states in which our perceptions are grounded are the result of a billion years of evolution. They have evolved as part of an unimaginably complex system, known as 'life', that can in no way be reduced to anything simpler. All we can do with our famous AI is to simulate a few tiny sub-sets of this complexity. These sub-sets may be very significant to us, and very powerful in the specific way they operate, *but only because they serve the purposes of the Machine in some capacity.* There's no independent intelligence in them, and certainly no *humanity*.

❧

As you can see, I'm not greatly impressed by the hi-tech world we're creating around us. It's often sold to us (at least, by implication) as if it were 'raising mankind to new heights', but as the great peacemaker Martin Luther King once said[5], *Nothing in our glittering technology can raise man to new heights, because material growth has been made an end in itself, and, in the absence of moral purpose, man himself becomes smaller as the works of man become bigger.*

In particular, there's something that makes me very apprehensive about the huge amount of attention we're giving to the development of smartphone technology, such as the potential horror show known as 5G. I know it's 'reasonable' to regard a smartphone as no more than a convenient device but it's being increasingly used as the portal to a whole world of 'applications' which are becoming essential for our lives as citizens of the twenty-first century. On another level, it looks to me like the latest and most effective way of persuading us, like poor old Dr Faustus, to sell what remains of our souls to some evil power that wants to use our hi-tech addiction to rob us of our humanity.

The words 'evil power' remind me of the lectures that Rudolf Steiner, the influential Austrian mystic and occult scientist, gave just after the First World War about the dark god, *Ahriman*[6]. Ahriman was the name given to the Devil in the ancient Zoroastrian religion. Steiner saw our Christian devil, Lucifer, as a completely distinct and different being. Ahriman is Lucifer's dark twin, the bearer of spiritual darkness rather than light.

His cosmic mission, according to Steiner, was to bring humanity into a closer relationship with the material world as a necessary stage in the developmental history of our species. If this is his mission he seems to have succeeded very well, but his success has given him a very powerful 'dark side'. As Steiner said, if we get too identified with our own cleverness, Ahriman will take us over and cut us off completely from the spiritual world. He effectively becomes the great god of materialist reductionism, which is ironic because reductionists are absolutely sure that there can't possibly exist any such things as gods.

The comforting dreams of the techno-futurists, the self-appointed priesthood of the Machine, remind me very much of what Steiner wrote about this dark god. For all their boyish enthusiasm, these guys sound quite rational and many of them even see themselves as a new kind of spiritual warrior. But trailing behind them in the deep shadows is an unconscious archetypal will-to-power that feels strangely inhuman, as if it comes from 'somewhere else', and this sends shivers down my spine.

Why have I suddenly taken flight into the mythopoetic world? Because our addiction to technology, especially to devices like smartphones, has arguably had a profoundly negative effect on our collective *spiritual* life, just as Steiner predicted it would. I'm not talking about the decline of religion, although that's also relevant here, but about our ever-diminishing sensitivity towards the inner world of relationships and purposes, which is grounded in Nature and animates and gives meaning to our existence.

The inner aspect of the world of relationships (by which I mean the *felt* aspect, whether it's a relationship with oneself or other human beings, or any of the other diverse inhabitants of the natural and supernatural worlds) is an embodiment of Spirit. There's no way this can be substituted or channelled by any technological device. Information can be channelled in this way to give us something called 'connectivity', but this 'connectivity' is absolutely not the same thing as a relationship.

Nowadays most of us would regard Steiner's vision as ridiculously fanciful. WTF? We've spent the last five hundred years getting rid of superstitions like that! We don't need that kind of nonsense any more; this is the twenty-first century not the sixteenth! In any case, surely it's obvious that the smartphone is a device that brings us together, connects us with one another, gives us a sense of belonging in this shattered world. It's a device that, more than anything else, helps us to live a more fulfilled life!

That's exactly what a figure like Steiner's Ahriman would want us to believe. But is it true? I don't think so. Given our hunger for some feeling of belonging in this hyper-individualistic culture, it can help to restore the *semblance* of a relationship with our fellow human beings. However, if we are hoping, albeit unconsciously, to solve the problem of our human need for community by using technology, I'd say that we are barking up the wrong tree.

Our long love affair with industrial capitalism has shattered our traditional community life, but technological substitutes don't even begin to fulfil the need for ordinary human intimacy, any more than beautifully-produced TV programmes about the Yorkshire Dales are a substitute for actually being up there, feeling the wind on your face and the peaty earth under your feet. Intimacy with the natural world is not called into being by staring at pretty pictures on a screen. And talking about smartphones, if you're a kid who's being subjected to cyber-bullying (for example), it can turn your life into a limitless and ever-present nightmare. So the smartphone is just a neutral device, then?

Of course. Much like an assault rifle in the USA.

Just to be absolutely clear, I'm *not* suggesting that the smartphone itself is somehow 'evil' – of course it isn't. It can be a very useful device if you want some information or you need to keep in touch with someone. But it's also the principal gateway to an artificial world represented

85

at present by platforms like Facebook and Instagram – a world of simulated reality where we're busily creating an *ersatz*, debased substitute for the real one with its constant difficulties and its ever-present danger of leaving us lonely and disappointed. The smartphone is already the principal vehicle for our obsession with looking cool, being liked, creating an appearance of being 'successful'. Of course, I'm not saying that *everyone* uses it like this, *all* the time, but that's undoubtedly one of the principal activities for which it is used and, as we all now have to have a smartphone, the temptation to enter into that artificial world is difficult to resist. For vulnerable teenagers struggling with questions of identity and belonging, it's almost impossible.

It's also evidently the case that platforms like Facebook, which use the smartphone to maximum effect, are a two-edged sword when it comes to bringing people together. They have an overwhelming tendency to create tribes, which are then encouraged to assert their own identities, maximise their differences and exacerbate tensions to the point where they break out into open war. This wasn't the intention of those who developed such platforms, but it has certainly been one of the unintended consequences of the algorithms they use and it's now very difficult to strip it out of the system.

This is the kind of discord that Ahriman would be intent on sowing, according to the scenario that Steiner predicted a hundred years ago. He didn't say exactly how he thought Ahriman was going to do it, but he did say that the influence of this Being would encourage us to do some unimaginably clever things in the material world. That in itself is not necessarily a bad thing, but Steiner also predicted that if we weren't vigilant we might become so identified with our own cleverness that we could easily be pulled down into a spiritual darkness so profound that we would never be able to emerge from it again.

I hardly need to add that it isn't necessary for Ahriman to exist in some disembodied but definite form, just as it isn't necessary for God to exist in that way. 'God' could just as well mean a universal, loving intelligence that stands behind the wholeness we recognise in our spiritual experience. Similarly, Ahriman stands as a symbol for a very powerful *attractor*, one that brings a high degree of artificially constructed order into the chaos of our human lives. Our preference for left-brain thinking means we are always looking for an artificially constructed order, so it has become very attractive to that way of thinking.

Steiner did also say that there would be an actual human incarnation of this symbolic entity at some future time but, even if that were not so, Ahriman as a pure symbol would still have meaning and potency. He brings together many of the diverse qualities associated with the development of the Machine, such as its compulsiveness, its relentless march in one particular direction, its spiritual emptiness and its lack of genuine humanity.

The Economic Super-organism, a recent book by Carey King[7], also refers to the industrial growth economy (the engine that powers the Machine) as a symbolic entity, but without recourse to any dark god or unseen force. King argues that it behaves more like a self-directing organism than a system of arrangements that we control. What does an organism want? It wants to survive and thrive, which means it wants plenty of food and a predator-free environment. To my mind, there's no better way of describing how the Machine looks after itself.

In his thoughtful and well-researched study of the history of 'logic machines'[8], Jeremy Naydler acknowledges that our fondness for logical thought (because it means we have to separate everything out) has contributed immensely to our modern sense of individual 'freedom', that is, freedom from entanglement in religious beliefs that held us back from our full potential and kept us ensnared in a world of relative ignorance and superstition. This was amply justified at the time but, as Naydler points out, what we gained from it is not real freedom. It's a limited, artificial kind of freedom, and it comes at a very high price. He sums up the situation like this (pp. 286–288):

If we regard the highest reach of the mind as extending no further than the ability to analyse and calculate, then we do not so much approach the source of our freedom as identify with an essentially empty and meaningless activity, for analysis and calculation alone do not give us access to meaning. Unless nourished and guided by another kind of thinking that introduces value and meaning to the content of thought, the human being is not fully present: the analysis and calculation take place in a vacuum. And so we become La Mattrie's "L'homme machine", and fall under the spell of an extraneous archetype. It is the archetype of the Inhuman – inhuman because the 'machine-man' has lost the capacity to think contemplatively, has lost contact with the real source of thought and has indeed lost contact with what is essentially human. A deeper, wiser, contemplative intelligence must be present alongside logical thought-processes and must act as their guide, for it alone recalls us to ourselves, and to our freedom.

This is exactly what Martin Luther King was getting at in the comment I quoted earlier. Naydler continues:

It is above all the inner quality of freedom that should guide us as we go towards a future in which it seems we shall be increasingly hemmed in on all sides by an ever more pervasive computer 'intelligence' which, while purporting to serve us, ties us in to an ever greater conformity. For the quality of freedom belongs to every truly human act, and its value will be inestimable in a world under the dominion of the machine. Consider the following activities whose very meaning stems from the fact that they are rooted in human freedom: acts of compassion that spring from the selfless impulse to do good to another; creative visualisation, through which we freely enter into imaginative contact with the archetypal realm; imaginative empathy through which we are able to participate in the inner life of another person or creature; and that profoundest of all human activities, prayer, in which the mind, grounded in the heart, turns towards its transcendent source.

Naydler's warning reminds me of Iain McGilchrist's observation that the 'left-brain' (logical, separative, problem-solving) style of thinking should be subordinate to the right-brain (holistic, relationship-based, contemplative) style, otherwise our humanity starts to be compromised by something machine-like whose only 'values' are utility and efficiency. It doesn't take much insight to see how perilously far we have allowed this to develop in the way our modern societies are organised and governed.

On a more political note while we are talking about 'freedom', it's worth reminding ourselves that the smartphone has become a powerful agent of the surveillance state. This is not the same kind of 'unfreedom' that Naydler was writing about (above), but nevertheless it's very real. The detailed knowledge harvested by Facebook (and its Chinese copy, WeChat) about its clients, is being used by political parties to influence voting behaviour, and (in the Chinese case) by the state to control its citizens.

On a smartphone, Facebook is an integrated addiction machine that relies on our anxious anticipation of the dopamine rush we get every time we use it – and it's supremely portable, so we use it *a lot*.

In a recent article, Jacob Weisberg writes[9]: '*In the West online surveillance is theoretically voluntary, the price we pay for enjoying the pleasure machine – a privatized 1984 by way of* Brave New World.' He goes on to describe the way WeChat is used in China, which is much more sinister. Tencent, the owners of WeChat, is connected into the Chinese government's social credit system that gives points for being a 'good citizen' and takes them away for 'bad behaviour', which includes such terrible crimes as 'spreading rumours online'. Weisberg writes: *[This] is already being used to punish people with low scores. [Such punishments include] preventing them from travelling, restricting them from certain jobs, and barring their children from attending private schools.*

According to journalist Chris Hedges[10], the BBC China correspondent Stephen McDonnell was locked out of WeChat after posting photos of the candlelight vigil in Hong Kong, which took place on the thirtieth anniversary of the brutal crushing of the Tiananmen Square protest in Beijing in June 1989. Hedges wrote: *In order to get back on WeChat, he had to agree that he was responsible for spreading 'malicious rumours' and provide what is called a 'Faceprint'.*

Hedges quotes McDonnell as saying: *'I was instructed to hold my phone up – to "face front camera straight on" – looking directly at an image of a human head. Then told to "read numbers aloud in Mandarin Chinese". My voice was captured by the app at the same time it scanned my face.'* How useful for a government that wants to control its citizens.

Technology provides many benefits but they come at a price, and there are always unintended consequences. The Internet is a good example of this: we now have almost instant access to an incredible amount of useful information; we can connect with other people who have similar interests; we can keep up with the latest info on any field of human endeavour without having to get our backsides out of the chair, and this has changed our world mostly for the better. But it has also brought unprecedented dangers, including the sexual grooming of vulnerable children, the increasing social anxieties of teenagers, the theft of people's identities, the proliferation of conspiracy theories and 'fake news', the growing menace of hate groups all over the world, and the unhindered broadcasting of their messages.

Almost any innovation you can name – the internal combustion engine, allopathic medicine, plastic packaging, and industrial farming, to mention just a few – has presented us with a proliferation of unintended consequences. This has been speeding up over the years, until it's now almost impossible for us to keep up with them. It's as if we became fascinated by the artificial world we were creating and now this fascination has become a deadly cancer that might eventually kill us. Not only because we are trashing the planet but because we are effectively creating a debased substitute for the world of Spirit, which is the source of our humanity and our true home. This is the main reason why I think of our clever technology as if it were some kind of death machine.

❧

Phrases like 'the Machine' have been used by many writers to denote not only actual devices but the entire mindset that enables us to substitute a repetitious mechanical transaction for a genuine human engagement of a more unscripted kind. This goes back a long way. If you conjured up an image of the Roman military machine, for example, there wouldn't be very many mechanical devices in it; instead, you would see hundreds of identically clad and armed human beings in tightly disciplined war formations advancing on their enemies with the kind of ruthless precision that we associate with armoured divisions during the Second World War.

One of the most trenchant critics of the Machine was the French writer Jacques Ellul, whose 1954 book *La Technique ou l'enjeu du siècle* (translated and published in 1964 as *The Technological Society*) remains a classic of its kind. Ellul's thinking was recently summed up, and brought up to date in an article by Andrew Nikiforuk[11].

Ellul referred to the Machine as *La Technique*. This included bureaucratic procedures as well as actual machines: *the totality of methods rationally arrived at, and having absolute efficiency ... in every field of human activity.* He wasn't saying that *la technique* is inherently evil, but that we should have been much more careful about the extent to which we have allowed it to take over our lives because it has a tendency to extend its domination without limit. In doing so, it destroys our humanity by colonising our minds, compromising our spiritual heritage and reinforcing our weakness for power and control.

Nikiforuk sums up Ellul's key characteristics of technology like this. *[T]he world of Technique imposes a rational and mechanical order on all things. It embraces artificiality and seeks to replace all natural systems with engineered ones. In a technological society a dam performs better than a running river, a car takes the place of the pedestrians – and may even kill them – and a fish farm offers more 'efficiencies' than a natural wild salmon migration... [It] automatically reduces actions to the 'one best way'. Technical progress is also self-augmenting: it is irreversible and builds with a geometric progression... Technology is indivisible and universal because everywhere it goes it shows the same deterministic face with the same consequences. And it is autonomous. By autonomous, Ellul meant that technology had become a determining force that elicits and conditions social, political and economic change. [He] was the first to note that technologies build upon each other and therefore centralize power and control. New techniques for teaching, selling things or organising political parties also required propaganda. Here again Ellul saw the future.*

'*Machines, whether mechanical or digital, aren't interested in truth, beauty or justice. Their goal is to make the world a more efficient place for more machines. Their proliferation combined with our growing dependence on their services inevitably [leads to] an erosion of human freedom and unintended consequences in every sphere of life.'*

Obviously this shouldn't be taken to mean that the machines themselves have some kind of conscious or unconscious intention. But if we imagine a machine and its human creator (and user) *as a system*, it's obvious that the man/machine system embodies a definite intention to make the world a more efficient place for more machines. The inner world of the machine-maker is already full of machines because the machine he's building only makes sense in the context of all the other machines.

What is it that attracts the machine-maker (or the bureaucrat, or the programmer or the futurist) so strongly to this work? What's behind the sheer fascination of it? It's worth noting that the word 'fascination' comes from the Latin verb *fascinare*, which means 'to bewitch or enchant'. Maybe you know what this fascination feels like – I certainly do. I've often been so caught up in some kind of design work or administrative arranging that I find it almost impossible to clear it out of my head even when I'm tired out from the effort of thinking about it. It's almost as if *it* won't let go of *me*, rather than the other way round.

If we want to get a sense of the sheer overwhelming power of Steiner's 'devil of darkness', maybe this kind of *fascination* is where we should start looking.

❧

The Machine has perhaps had its most dramatic effects on the world of work. In an earlier phase of the Industrial Age, it was easier to see the damage it was doing to our human relationships in the workplace because the 'old ways' were so much fresher in people's memories. William Morris (1834–1896), poet, socialist, craftsman, entrepreneur and founder of the Arts & Crafts movement in England, was an example of someone who could see this very clearly. He could understand how important it is for people to feel that their work is an opportunity to express their full *humanity*, not just a way of making enough money to continue their existence. Karl Marx's notion of *alienation* is another example of the same observation, although his view of what should be done about it was rather different from William Morris's.

Recently I came across a more up-to-date example of some of the distortions – familiar to many people on zero-hours contracts – that the Machine has been introducing into our already impoverished work relationships. I know a young man from Eastern Europe, let's call him Dan, who works as a delivery driver for Amazon. He has at least one (sometimes two) days off in every seven, but he doesn't know which days those will be until 6am in the morning, when they text him with his instructions. He is told to go to one of their distribution centres at a certain time, then he has to wait for about forty-five minutes while they load his van with the day's deliveries. There will be at least one hundred stops every day, with up to 230 items to deliver. At the same time, they load his app with the day's pre-optimised route, where every address is accurately positioned by GPS, and his paid employment begins (in theory) when he leaves the yard and starts his deliveries. He has to confirm delivery at every address, standing in a position not more than two metres from the front door so that it can be confirmed by GPS on Amazon's sub-contractor's computer. If someone is out and there's no 'safe place' information, he has to return to that address before the end of his day and make a second attempt. If that doesn't work, he's supposed to make a third attempt, as long as it's before 9.30pm He leaves the house at 7am and rarely gets back before 7pm, sometimes working until 9.30 because of unforeseen circumstances (diversions, breakdowns, missed deliveries, etc.) The schedule takes no account of meal breaks, or what the Americans call 'comfort breaks', so he's become good at eating a sandwich while driving and he's adept at spotting places where he can take a quick pee (or maybe he actually uses empty Coca-Cola bottles but is too shy to admit it).

Dan earns £120 a day, out of which he pays approximately £30 a day for the hire of his official van. As he's 'self-employed' (which is, of course, an outrageous fiction), he is supposed to pay his taxes in April at the end of the tax year, which will remove about another £10 a day. His wages work out at about £80 per eleven-hour day, which is about the level of the UK minimum wage in 2018. It isn't what you could call 'slave labour', but it's not far off it. You could say that it's just about enough to make it worthwhile for him to subject himself to this daily grind, bearing in mind that he comes from a country where the money he earns will go an awful lot further than it will over here.

Meanwhile his boss, Jeff Bezos, is worth approximately *$150 billion*[12]. Apparently he earns as much in ten seconds as Dan does in a year. He got there by developing working practices for his employees that maximise efficiency (he calls that 'doing it better'), which in effect means that Amazon squeezes every available drop of juice out of every one of them. This isn't a new idea, of course – it was pioneered by Henry Ford in his auto factories a century ago – but Bezos has certainly raised it to a new level of sophistication.

He's an interesting guy, full of contradictions. He comes across (at least, to some) as warm and friendly, which he probably is to those who know him intimately, but the way he *thinks* is very much as an agent of the Machine. He says he's very concerned about work/life balance, and advises all his employees not to become workaholics because it's bad for them. I ask Dan what he thinks about his boss's advice, given that he's compelled to work anything from eleven to fourteen hours a day to earn a living. '*Vorbeste prin cur,*' says Dan. His wife translates for me: 'He's talking out of his ass.'

I'm interested in what Bezos does with all that money. I read that he's invested a lot of it in something called Blue Origin, which has a long-term vision of exploring space. He thinks this is a good idea because we will soon need to get off this Earth and populate the rest of the universe (a typical futurist fantasy). When the number of humans reaches a trillion or two, he reasons, there could be several thousand Mozarts and Einsteins instead of just the pitiful one of each that we've produced so far[13]. This is pure left-brain 'reasoning', produced by a mind saturated with numbers, one that can think of quality only in terms of quantity. Bezos himself has become a symbol of the power, influence and sheer banality of a certain type of thinking.

We keep this man in the manner to which he has become accustomed because we are addicted to buying stuff at the cheapest possible price from a source that causes us the least possible exertion. This he understands very well. Amazon: look it up online, choose what you want, pay for it with your card and expect it to be delivered the following day.

This is how the Machine works. Way back in the sixties, when I was a young man, we were always being promised by its devotees that we were about to enter an 'age of leisure', when these wonderful machines would take over the dirty work and allow us all to spend our time enjoying the kind of luxurious life that only monarchs and their courtiers could have dreamed of. Instead these wonderful machines have enabled our employers to exploit us much more thoroughly, using every second of our time on the job. We still work the same hours but we are now compelled to do it much more 'efficiently', which means cutting out as much as possible of the kinds of human interaction that made such jobs bearable in the past. This has made our lives meaner, less fulfilling and much more stressful.

Jacques Ellul's vision of our subservience to the Machine has been perfectly vindicated. In 'developed' economies, the deadly combination of technology and global industrial capitalism has resulted in mass de-skilling and the replacement of real jobs with the so-called 'gig economy'. Large swathes of de-industrialised America arc now occupied by a population that's either angry and defeated or half-dead with opioid addiction. A similar fate has befallen many of our old industrial communities in the UK, especially in the mining areas of South Wales and northern England. In the developing world, peasant farming economies have been replaced by mega-cities where huge numbers of poor people who don't have access to a decent education scratch a living amongst the accumulated debris.

Seems like only guys like Jeff Bezos actually made it into the golden era. For the rest of us, the best we can aspire to is consumer choice. I'm not impressed.

'The rise of the Machine' has become a popular theme in our culture with the *Terminator* movies and their numerous imitators but, looking at it from a different perspective, what has actually happened in the last two or three hundred years is that we ourselves have become more and more machine-like. As Erich Fromm wrote:

Alienation as we find it in modern society is almost total ... Man has created a world of man-made things as it never existed before. He has constructed a complicated social machine to administer the technical machine he built. The more powerful and gigantic the forces are which he unleashes, the more powerless he feels himself as a human being. He is owned by his creations, and has lost ownership of himself.

It's been a long process. We started on this path at the dawn of history by propping up our societies with increasingly complex bureaucratic institutions, then in the seventeenth and eighteenth centuries we started to imagine that the entire material world is like a huge machine. This enabled us to investigate in greater and greater detail how it all works, at least on a mechanical level, which in turn enabled us to reshape it more and more in our own image. The more we did this, the more identified we became with our own creations.

At the same time, we began to exploit sources of energy that were somewhere between fifty and 200 times more powerful than anything we had used before, then we used them to build a whole new type of industrial society. We were forced to adapt our entire way of life to fit in with the new industrial machine, a process that was (and still is) fraught with misery and suffering for millions of people. And now that we're thoroughly used to that, we are busily adapting ourselves to live in service to our own personal machines, especially those we use to communicate with each other.

For the last 400 years, we have imagined this as a journey that leads 'upwards' towards greater control, predictability and comfort, but we didn't really see how it's inevitably balanced by an equal and opposite journey 'downwards'. What we've been losing all the time is our capacity for sensitive attunement to each other and to the entire living world of which we are a part, including the more-than-human beings that share it with us. The more head-centred we become, the more we tend to lose our bodily, heartfelt spiritual connection with Mother Nature – and as a result, the less we care about the damage we are doing to her.

For many of us in the richer parts of the world, this doesn't even feel like a problem. Many seem quite happy with their artificial lives and are not particularly bothered about ecocide, mass extinctions or climate change. In some ways this is the most dangerous aspect of the entire situation. If they have never acquired a feeling for the natural world, how are millions of 'normal people' ever going to value it enough to protest against its obliteration?

And yet it's still possible that there are enough people who do feel 'the cry of the Earth' to make a difference. There have always been such people since the time of William Blake and the Romantic poets in the eighteenth and nineteenth centuries. William Morris's Arts & Crafts Movement, mentioned above, played an important part in this, and it received a large boost in the 1960s with the

New Age and Human Potential movements.

Having lived through them, in my view the sixties represented a time of spiritual renewal, not just a 'lifestyle' thing – although that's what it soon became, once the black magicians of Madison Avenue got hold of it. It's all too easy to replace the Buddha in your mind and heart with the moulded concrete figurine on its plinth by the side of your water feature.

*

This aspect of the human condition – our tendency to forget our humanity and act like machines – has interested me from the time when I first became aware of it as a teenager. I was sent to a boarding school where (for various reasons) I became a bit of a rebel, but I was the kind of rebel who also wants to be the boss. (Thankfully, I've almost lost that inclination now.)

The only arena in which I was able to take advantage of the pervasive authority structure was the Combined Cadet Force (CCF). Schools had cadet forces in those days; the Second World War had ended only a few years earlier, and we were still eligible for National Service until the late 1950s. I was so enthusiastic about the small and exclusive Navy section of the CCF that I was the senior naval cadet by the age of sixteen and planning a career in what was then known as the Senior Service. My dad, who was a colonel in the Marines, was probably proud of me although he wasn't always very good at showing it.

Every year the school put on a big parade where the entire CCF marched round the senior cricket pitch while some Army bigwig took the salute. As senior cadet in the

Navy section, my place was up at the front, right behind the chief cadet officer. I looked forward to this with great satisfaction, mainly as a way of saying 'fuck you' to the housemaster who would be watching the parade together with everybody else. He had decided, probably quite rightly, that I was much too independent minded for him to risk making me a prefect.

However I was also an avid rugby player, which was another statement of nonconformity, this being a football school. During the previous term I had torn the lateral meniscus cartilages in both knees, which meant I had to have them removed. (This is what they did during the fifties: if it malfunctions, remove it.) As a result, when the parade came around I was still disabled after the operation so I couldn't take part.

I leaned on my crutches – those old-fashioned underarm things, made of wood – watching from the side lines, consumed with envy and frustration. How smart they look, I told myself. How wonderful to be in command of such a disciplined and magnificent army. How unfair it was that I had lost the chance to shine...

Then, when my chagrin was at its height, my perception of the whole thing suddenly flipped. I don't know why – it certainly wasn't because I'd thought long and deeply about it – but something had got into me, that's all. Moments before, I'd been seeing rows and rows of smart cadets; now I just saw rows and rows of robots. *Killing machines.* Nothing magnificent or inspiring, just ordinary young men being turned into mass-produced killing machines.

At that moment I knew I could never have anything to do with that kind of machine. I stumbled back in great distress to the grey stone Victorian Gothic house where my section of the school lived, and expressed my feelings about it in a long and tearful poem. The following day, I resigned from the Navy cadets.

'But I've just awarded you the Rooke Naval Prize!' said the RNVR dummy who ran the naval section of the CCF.

'Yes, well, I suppose you'll have to award it to someone else then,' said I, not knowing what else to say.

That was the first time I saw with awful clarity how we make the mistake of confusing *Eros* with *Thanatos*[14]. Not many years before, the Nazis had made the same mistake, idealising the so-called 'Aryan Race' and exterminating with chilling efficiency something like six million human beings barely distinguishable from themselves. It's a mistake our civilisation keeps making in one form or another, and for me this is what the CCF had come to represent.

Refusing to take any part in the CCF from then on, I came under enormous pressure from the school, which collectively thought I'd gone mad. They couldn't physically force me to march around with all the others, so they reclassified me as a sort of conscientious objector and banished me to the faraway music schools during CCF afternoons so that I couldn't infect anyone else with my madness. This was like being in heaven; I had three hours of bliss, all on my own, listening to 12-inch 78rpm Bakelite records of J. S. Bach, Mozart, Haydn, Mendelssohn and Scarlatti (among others). Thanks, Malvern College.

When I went home for the summer holiday I had some spectacular rows with my dad, who thought I was a very bad apple indeed. Our relationship didn't recover until I went sailing with him ten years later. He was a bit desperate because he'd hired a boat for two weeks with my uncle Ken, who'd had to drop out at the last minute because he'd injured his foot. Dad knew I enjoyed sailing and maybe he thought it was an opportunity to get to know me a bit better ... but that's another tale.

❧

The rise of the Machine has been intimately bound up with the long history of misery and mass killings for which our European civilisation has been responsible during the last 500 years, from the evils of slavery to the genocidal invasions of the Americas and now the monumentally stupid 'War on Terror'.

Slavery and later colonialism were the two main routes through which Britain, the principal colonial power, accumulated the capital necessary to establish and strengthen our mercantile economy in the fifteenth and sixteenth centuries. This capitalist expansion led directly to the early industrial economy. From then onwards there were many ways in which the Machine, acting through our social institutions, enabled colonialism to provide it with enough raw materials to feed its expansion until, by the end of the nineteenth century, the British Empire covered half the world.

My own boarding school was part of this process, which the psychotherapist Nick Duffell has described very well in his book about the English public school system, *The Making of Them*[15]. As Duffell points out, one of the most basic tasks of the Machine is to supply the kind of expertly brainwashed human being who can embody the disciplined, coercive power required to run an army. Another is to supply the manpower for the kind of oppressive bureaucracy that is needed to keep a subject population under control, and for colonial nations to organise their subjects into producing whatever the imperial power decides it wants to steal from them. The British, for example, under the cloak of 'civilising the natives' (also known as the 'White Man's Burden') were very good at this in Africa and India, and it was the public school system that supplied the emotionally primitive, socially conformist, physically daring people necessary to take charge of those who did the actual dirty work.

The Spanish in South America were perhaps more brutal and less of a civilising force, but they were very successful at shattering indigenous communities and stealing their gold. The polyglot Europeans who colonised North America were just as relentless in their destruction of indigenous ways of life, whether through war, disease or expropriation. But, like everyone else, they justified their genocide by claiming (with unconscious irony) to be more civilised than the 'savages' they were systematically exterminating.

To use such an epithet about a Native American like Crazy Horse, for example, the visionary Sioux leader murdered by the US Army at the age of thirty-seven, is a bit like describing Jesus Christ as a 'Jewish terrorist with a cult following amongst a few uneducated Palestinian peasants'. To the US Army, Crazy Horse was just another filthy Indian, despite earning their grudging respect as a brave and effective leader of his own Lakota people. I'm not saying that Native Americans didn't fight each other, just that they didn't set out deliberately to *exterminate* each other either physically or culturally by categorising their opponents as 'savage' and themselves as 'civilised'. They never lost their essential humanity.

The Machine is not, and never will be, capable of recognising what the word 'humanity' means. When you see the White House press secretary justifying the policy of separating immigrant children from their parents and putting them in wire cages, it feels as if you are listening to a machine rather than a person. Or, let's say, a person who has consciously consented to having her humanity surgically removed so that she can say the words she's paid to say without choking on them.

One of the characteristics of our humanity is that we are blessed with a natural conscience accessible through our feeling intelligence (the 'Intelligence of the Heart', as D. H. Lawrence called it), which doesn't need to learn an elaborate set of rules about the difference between right and wrong. I'm sure there are people working at the UK Home Office, required in their jobs to enact the inhuman 'hostile environment' policies of the British government, who will recognise what I mean. For them, it's a choice between their career and their conscience; sadly, the career (or rather the salary that goes with it) usually wins.

There arc also pcople who appear to have abandoned all pretence at possessing such a thing as a conscience. I remember a televised debate in 2003 where Richard Perle (then chairman of the US Defense Policy Board and widely known by his admirers as the 'Prince of Darkness') was justifying the invasion of Iraq. Unlike some of the cynics who inhabit the US government, he really believed in what the USA and its allies were doing. I felt chilled to the bone by his dry, soulless but deeply menacing way of describing what their aims were, and why they had to do it. The man was clearly psychotic and very badly damaged, but he was being treated as if he were just as 'human' as my mother (may she rest in peace).

I mention my mother because her father, who died before I was born, was a conscientious objector during the First World War. My admiration for him was one of the reasons I wanted to be a carpenter, despite my expensive education. He was a very good carpenter who had built his own house way back in the 1920s. The anti-war stand that he took required a great deal of courage, because the 'conchies', as they were called, were universally reviled in the madness of the British war fever. My mother found herself compelled to defend him against a crowd of school bullies when she was only eight years old.

My grandfather's humanity was intact and the Machine couldn't break him, but I wonder whether it eventually broke my mother because she ended up marrying a man who represented everything about the patriarchy that she most feared and despised. Of course I'm glad she did it, otherwise I wouldn't be here, but from a very early age I was dimly aware of something inauthentic about my dad. He wasn't what people would nowadays call a 'bad person', it was just that he had somehow *lost himself* in the effort to adapt to what society required of him.

When he was wearing his full dress uniform as a colonel, his whole demeanour changed in a subtle but quite frightening way. It was as if he had *become* the uniform and lost himself in the process. (This, of course, is the main function of uniforms.) It took me a long time to forgive him for the damage I thought he had caused because I couldn't yet see that it was actually done by the Machine, using my poor old dad as its agent.

I mentioned Crazy Horse earlier because he was a member of a noble race which, for all its 'savagery', managed to escape being corrupted by the Machine in any of its forms. The Lakota were able to live their lives with their humanity intact; indeed, many of them still do so to this day, despite the depth of their historical trauma.

.You have only to read Robin Wall Kimmerer's wonderful book, *Braiding Sweetgrass*, to get a feel for the depth and humanity of indigenous Native American wisdom[16]. This book has an extra poignancy because Kimmerer is an accomplished scientific ecologist who can make informed comparisons between the ancestral wisdom of her Potawatomi people and the very different but complementary approach of Western science.

This is what Crazy Horse is quoted as saying to Chief Sitting Bull just four days before he was murdered, in 1877[17]:

'The Red Nation shall rise again and it shall be a blessing for a sick world; a world filled with broken promises, selfishness and separations; a world longing for light again.

'I see a time of Seven Generations when all the colors of mankind will gather under the Sacred Tree of Life and the whole Earth will become one circle again.

'In that day, there will be those among the Lakota who will carry knowledge and understanding of unity among all living things and the young white ones will come to those of my people and ask for this wisdom.

'I salute the light within your eyes where the whole universe dwells. For when you are at that center within you and I am that place within me, we shall be one.'

I had to read those last two lines again slowly before I fully appreciated what he was saying. '*The light within your eyes where the whole universe dwells.*' This is a form of consciousness that we 'civilised' people have almost completely lost; it is only now being found again as a result of much pain and suffering. No doubt the ignorant white barbarians who killed Crazy Horse would have thought of it as just another savage superstition.

If this is 'savagery', then I would much rather die as a 'savage' than as a willing slave of the ubiquitous (but oh, so *civilised*) Machine.

References

1 https://www.oxfam.org/en/press-releases/just-8-men-own-same-wealth-half-world

2 The subtle way in which Facebook manipulates its users is well illustrated in the docudrama, *The Social Dilemma*.

3 Hannah Fry, *Hello World: How to be Human in the Age of The Machine* (Black Swan, 2019).

4 A good account of this is given by Antonio Damasio in *Descartes' Error: Emotion, Reason and the Human Brain* (Putnam, 1994).

5 From a talk he gave in 1967 when America was gripped by the 'space race'. Quoted by Maria Popova in her *Brain Pickings* online newsletter, 10 Oct 2021.

6 Recorded in *The Influences of Lucifer and Ahriman* (Steiner Book Centre, 1954).

7 Carey King, *The Economic Superorganism: Beyond the Competing Narratives on Energy, Growth, and Policy* (Springer, 2020).

8 Jeremy Naydler, *In The Shadow of The Machine* (Temple Lodge, 2018.)

9 Jacob Weisberg, 'The Autocracy App', in the *New York Review of Books*, 25 Oct 2018.

10 As reported in *Truthdig*, 11 June 2019.

11 In *Resilience* magazine, 16 November 2018.

12 That was the figure in 2017. After the first year of Covid-19, he was 'worth' more like $200bn.

13 Jeff Bezos interviewed by Mathias Dopfner in *UK Business Insider*, April 28, 2018. Since then, the activities of Blue Origin have become much more well-known.

14 *Eros*, which Freud called the 'love instinct', and *Thanatos*, which he called the 'death instinct'.

15 Nick Duffell, *The Making of Them* (Lone Arrow Press, 2000).

16 Robin Wall Kimmerer, *Braiding Sweetgrass: Indigenous Wisdom, Scientific Knowledge, and the Teachings of Plants* (Milkweed Editions, 2013).

17 See https://wwwwolfspirit63.blogspot.com/2012/05/final-words-from-chief-crazy-horse.html

- 5 -
Me and My Things

23 FEBRUARY 2017

TODAY MARKS THE final end of the protest camp set up by the courageous band of spiritual warriors known as the Water Protectors at the sacred site known as Standing Rock. They have been defending their ancestral lands from the depredations of the Machine.

The Dakota Access Pipeline was built to allow oil from the Bakken field to be pumped to refineries in southern Illinois. It was designed to pass under the Missouri River at Standing Rock, which is a sacred site for the Sioux nation. The Missouri River is the source of all their water. The project had been stalled by President Obama in response to environmental and cultural objections from the Standing Rock Sioux people, supported by many other Native Americans and other interested bodies. One of the first actions that Donald Trump took when he became president was to reverse the Obama decision and authorise work to go ahead.

A protest camp was set up that attracted many thousands of people who were concerned about the way the U.S. government was ignoring the people who lived on this land, which was supposed to be theirs in perpetuity under treaties between the Sioux nations and the Federal government signed in 1851 and 1868. The protesters were treated with reckless brutality by state troopers, the National Guard, the local police and private security firms, who used attack dogs on unarmed people, drenched them with water cannon in sub-zero temperatures, and arbitrarily arrested, detained and strip-searched them, among other unnecessary and vicious assaults on their human rights.

In September 2016, one of the Sioux leaders, LaDonna Brave Bull, said in a statement:

'The U.S. government is wiping out our most important cultural and spiritual areas. And as it erases our footprint from the world, it erases us as a people. These sites must be protected, or our world will end, it is that simple. Our young people have a right to know who they are. They have a right to language, to culture, to tradition. The way they learn these things is through connection to our lands and our history.

'If we allow an oil company to dig through and destroy our histories, our ancestors, our hearts and souls as a people, is that not genocide?'

Unfortunately this cry from the heart would have meant nothing to the government security apparatus for whom this kind of attachment to the land had long ago become incomprehensible in the context of the world in which they live.

As the weather became harsher in the North Dakota winter, the protest camp was reduced to a few hundred Water Protectors. David Archambault, the Standing Rock chairman, recommended that they disband and clean up the area. Most of them did eventually go, leaving just a few on the campsite who were finally evicted today, 23 February 2017.

The protest camp failed to stop the pipeline being built, but the memory of it is an inspiration for all people who want to make a stand for our humanity in the face of the war that is being waged on it by the Machine.

❦

Like most people who are just living their lives, Lizzie has no interest in pipelines or protest camps.

It turns out that she hasn't broken her hip after all; she's broken her femur in two places, and will need a steel bolt to hold it together. I can't imagine a ninety-five-year-old surviving that kind of drastic medical intervention, but somehow she does.

I don't visit her as often as I should because it's hard to bear her incessant complaints about the hospital. Everything is wrong, including the food; she can't eat the main dish if it includes onions, but then she complains that they give her too many sandwiches. She's afraid that the nurses are queueing up to steal the precious contents of her handbag which, last time I looked, included one old watch that didn't work, two ancient, tatty notebooks full of phone numbers, and about £5 in cash. She complains that no-one comes to see her, which isn't true; Amy visits the hospital regularly and so do I, but we don't count.

Six weeks later, the hospital decides she's well enough to go back home. I insist she has to have twenty-four-hour care, and (thank God) the mysterious solicitor with power of attorney agrees that she can afford it. I find out later, to my astonishment, that she's worth nearly half a million pounds in bank deposits and shares.

The hospital finds a suitable care company, EuroCare, which sends me a profile of their proposed carer. She's a sweet-looking, twenty-four-year-old Czech girl called Leona. According to her CV, she trained to be a hairdresser before she got the job with EuroCare and loves looking after her family pets. I think of her struggling to cope with a manipulative drama queen in a language she doesn't know very well. Would it be fair to put such a nice girl through such agonies? So I email them back saying, 'Let's be serious about this, please. We need someone a lot older with at least some experience of working with dementia.'

They come back with Sophia, who's a forty-nine old, no-nonsense Romanian with twelve years' experience looking after dementia patients in France and Germany. I get the feeling she'd rather cook and eat the family pet than look after it, but I don't get to say yay or nay to this one. They send her anyway because it's too late to make any more changes.

Lizzie is sent home in an ambulance. The paramedics don't spend very long here because they have other calls to make. Suddenly this house, which has been empty and quiet for the last six weeks, is full of Lizzie's complaints again.

'Someone has stolen my phone books!'

'No they haven't, Lizzie. Look, here they are in your bag.'

'No, the other phone books! Not those ones!'

'Which other phone books, Lizzie?'

'The one with the birds on the front.'

'That's this one, Lizzie. They aren't birds, they're butterflies.'

'No, the other one! The one with the blue dots.'

'There isn't one with blue dots, you're imagining it.'

'Don't you tell me what I'm imagining, young man! You don't know anything about me.'

I know that you're a pain in the ass, I hiss under my breath.

🍃

At first Sophia is very polite and well-behaved because she doesn't know me very well. Later she tells me that she has to be careful with 'the relatives' in case they are over-protective of the client and don't trust the carer. Or the other way round – that they don't give a toss about the client, and they hope she'll die so they can get their hands on the money.

Gradually she relaxes as she sees that I'm not completely taken in by Lizzie's amateur dramatics and I don't have any financial stake in her dying. We talk about Sophia's life in Romania, about my adventures living off-grid with Jane, about what's happening in the world. I get to like this roly-poly Romanian whose values seem very similar to mine.

We sit outside on the patio, smoking roll-ups and chatting. She says she's fed up with the way her country is selling its soul to the money machine. The people, she says, are abandoning their traditional communities in a desperate desire to be more like their Western European neighbours. During the 'Ceausescu time', she explains, there was no easy money and the people felt oppressed by the Communist system, so they retained a strong sense of community in order to survive. But after the revolution in 1989, the gangsters moved in and took advantage of the chaos. Now, she says, the country is gripped by the same consumerist frenzy as everywhere else, and it's run by corrupt politicians whose main aim is to line their own pockets.

I ask her what she thinks about England. She's quite complimentary about English people, apart from the staff at EuroCare who (she says) are 'idiots'. But our food is 'awful'. I suggest she might like to cook something Romanian.

'You really want the Romanian food?' she asks, incredulously.

'Why not?' I say.

So she starts by cooking chicken with garlic sauce and polenta. The garlic sauce features about a dozen cloves of raw, crushed, salted garlic in a spoonful of oil, mixed with a little yogurt. It sets my mouth on fire but I refuse to be daunted, eat all of it and ask for more.

She is astonished. 'I was told the English people don't like too much the garlic,' she says.

'I'm not your typical English person,' I splutter indignantly, and reach for the wine.

Sophia jokes with me that she comes from Transylvania; she's been told that English people are obsessed with the story of Count Dracula. She has no fangs, at least no visible ones, but she's not anyone's fluffy little pet lamb either. She's more like a brown bear, which is better avoided when it starts growling. If you cross her, you have to be very sure of your ground.

For several days, Lizzie does her best to ignore her new Transylvanian carer. She feels it's undignified to host such a person in her own house and she doesn't need a carer, even though she can't do anything by herself and can hardly even walk from the bedroom to the loo and back. But Sophia can be very gentle with the people she looks after despite being a brown bear, and my suspicious, misanthropic old mother-in-law eventually warms to her.

🌿

Ever since she broke her leg, Lizzie has been terrified of going down the stairs. I manage to persuade the solicitor with power of attorney to spend some of her money on a stairlift and he reluctantly agrees. Three weeks later it's in, and Lizzie begins to make regular afternoon trips downstairs again. Each time she comes down, she makes a big drama of clutching her handbag, which she never lets out of her sight in case someone steals her precious phone books or her hairbrush or the tattered leather purse with her nail scissors in it.

She resumes her habit of wandering round the house with her Zimmer frame, complaining that various ornaments, books, tables, chairs, etc. have gone missing. Sue tells us that this isn't new. It's one of her established ways of relating to the world.

Sometimes she makes a big drama out of something she thinks she's lost, especially if it's connected with her daughter. She says she used to have a picture of Jane as a small girl playing on the beach at Swanage in the 1950s, which she's convinced someone has stolen. If she's allowed to dwell on it for longer than five minutes, she can work herself up into a great stew of anxiety, refusing to eat her supper until someone undertakes an exhaustive search of the house in an effort to find it. Maybe there was once such a picture but I've never seen it, and Sue reckons she's imagining it.

Sophia advises me not to get caught up in this kind of story. Better to give Lizzie a cheerful reassurance that I'll look for it later, like after I've had my dinner or just 'as soon as I get the time', and rely on Lizzie's inability to remember anything for longer than five minutes. Never mind about the garlic chicken, I say to myself. Sophia's a smart woman.

Lizzie's habit of wandering around the house obsessing about her things is just another version of the strange but persistent delusion many of us share that in order to live the 'good life', it's necessary to accumulate a mountain of *stuff*. This is yet another way in which our civilisation has allowed itself to get grotesquely out of balance.

Few of us ask ourselves whether it's a good idea or not. Of course Lizzie can no longer ask herself such a question, but neither, it seems, can many other people whose brains (unlike poor Lizzie's) are still apparently intact. At least, not yet.

It should be obvious that you can't go on enjoying infinite growth on a finite planet for ever, especially when this kind of growth depends on extracting more and more raw materials from the limited stock available and then dumping more and more toxic waste into an environment that's already full of it. Nevertheless, our consumer society doggedly persists in this belief and probably won't abandon it until Gaia gets so angry with us that we're finally compelled to stop.

There seems to be an implicit hope that *if* this really is a problem, technology will solve it for us, for example, by replacing fossil fuels with 'renewables'. It's true that technology has done a lot to reduce various kinds of pollution, recycle waste, make production more efficient and so on, but the fact is that everything we make (including wind turbines and electric cars) requires raw materials, which have to be extracted from somewhere (the earth's crust, the sea, the forest, 1000-year-old aquifers, plants, animals). And because of the Law of Entropy, which is impossible to get around by any conceivable process anywhere in the known universe, *every industrial manufacturing process produces at least as much waste as useful product.*

The combination of these two facts means that the only way we can solve this problem is by manufacturing an awful lot less *stuff*, which means economic contraction instead of growth. This would mean that millions of jobs would be lost, people would suffer even more than they are suffering already, and there would be no way of restoring the kind of prosperity we've grown used to during the last fifty or sixty years of 'growth'. That is anathema to the currently fashionable, but demonstrably insane, theories according to which we organise our economic life.

There are plenty of studies that show just how insane these theories are, but they aren't written by mainstream economists, and they aren't read by politicians who rely on these economists for the advice they need to formulate economic policy. For example, *The Economic Superorganism*[1], which I mentioned in Chapter 4, was written by an energy-systems engineer. He takes into account some of the basic limitations that mainstream economics commonly ignores, like the impossibility of infinite growth on a finite planet, the central role of energy, and the real cost of so-called 'externalities' like pollution and waste. As I said, King's vivid description of the economy as a 'superorganism' sounds almost identical to the entity I am calling 'the Machine'.

So we end up caught in a horrible dilemma. Any serious attempt to change to a less environmentally damaging (i.e. non-consumerist) economy would be an economic disaster. But if we keep going as we are now and let things take their course, Planet Earth will be irreparably damaged *and the collapse will happen anyway*.

❧

It's worth taking a look at the Law of Entropy in more detail. Its proper title is the Second Law of Thermodynamics, and nowadays it's stated in such an abstract manner that only a mathematical physicist can understand it, but don't let that put you off.

The classical way of looking at it was in terms of order and disorder. It stated that order can only be created in one part of a closed system at the expense of an equivalent (or greater) degree of *disorder* somewhere else in the system. The word 'order' here is used to mean complexity, or degree of organisation, which increases when work is done to convert raw materials into a finished product. Thus a car has a much higher degree of 'order' than the raw materials that go into its manufacture (steel, plastic, copper, aluminium, rubber, etc.), and these raw materials have a higher degree of 'order' than the ores and feedstocks (hematite, chalcopyrite, bauxite, crude oil, etc.) from which they are refined. 'Disorder' means the slag-heaps, abandoned mines, poisoned rivers and all the other myriad waste products of the same processes.

All of these processes – extraction, refining, manufacture and transport – depend at one stage or another on burning fuel to create heat, sometimes in prodigious amounts. This is true of almost every physical process of creating order out of disorder, at least in the material world. These processes break down into two main categories: *refining*, which means using heat to separate out what you want from what you don't want in a naturally occurring mixture, and *heat engines*, which convert temperature differences into motion (as in a generator which produces electricity, for example). In both cases, a lot of energy has to be supplied from one part of the system in order to raise the *degree of order* in another part.

Ours is a fiery civilisation, to be sure. Both physically and metaphorically, it is intent on burning everything up and converting it as fast as possible into smoke and ashes.

For example, consider the manufacture of steel out of iron ore (e.g. hematite). First you have to mine the ore, which takes a lot of energy and heavy equipment and leaves very large holes in the ground. Then you ship it (using heavy trucks, rail wagons and often seaborne bulk carriers) to an iron foundry, which is a large, fixed installation full of even heavier equipment, where you extract the metal in a smelter. This takes a lot more energy and leaves vast heaps of ash (known as 'slag' or 'clinker') behind. Then you convert the iron into steel by blowing oxygen through the molten iron in a blast furnace (which is another fixed installation, etc.) and adding various other metals (nickel, chromium, vanadium, tungsten etc., which must also be mined, refined and shipped) using large amounts of electrical energy. Most of the heat generated in these processes is degraded and lost, and the products of combustion all disappear up the chimney where they disturb the delicate balance of atmospheric gases and make a big contribution to climate breakdown.

There are many ways in which disorder can be exported; one of them is to relocate the whole process to another country where the labour costs are cheaper. In the end it's dumped on what we call 'the environment' (i.e. as far as we're concerned, 'somewhere else'), which becomes more and more damaged and distressed but has no voice with which to complain unless we notice what's happening and provide one.

The overall effect is to provide us with goodies (structural steel for buildings, sheet steel for vehicle manufacture) while loading the Earth with relatively long-lived waste products (slag heaps, abandoned factories, greenhouse gases, the rusting carcasses of old vehicles, etc.) There is no way of escaping this, even if we use the highest of hi-tech manufacturing plants full of robotics and integrated process controls and whatever other clever ideas we can dream up.

The order that we create is converted quite quickly back into disorder. Most consumer products are made to last only a limited time and they're not very often designed with recycling in mind. According to *The Story of Stuff*[2], only about 1% of the material that flows through the manufacturing process actually appears at the other end as a product that lasts longer than six months. Even then, the culture of planned obsolescence means that most products have an unnecessarily limited life, and many of them (most smartphones, for example) are sealed units that can't be repaired if they are damaged or go wrong. This makes the 'manufacturing economy' look more like a process for extracting as much useful material as possible from the Earth, turning 99% of it into waste in the shortest possible time and then dumping all of that waste back onto the earth or into the atmosphere as long-lived pollutants.

So the amount of disorder is always increasing, and again there's no realistic way round this. Think of all the old factory estates in our decaying manufacturing cities, the toxic waste dumps and the poisoned land around them, much of which will never be revived or rescued because it will cost too much to do it after the system stops functioning smoothly. In cities like Detroit, some of these ruined areas are being transformed into urban farms, which is great, but it's a long, slow process that will take many years to make a real difference.

The creation of this kind of disorder tends to be forgotten when we talk about switching to renewable systems, but in some ways these are even worse. The raw materials we use for renewable energy structures like wind farms (steel, concrete, copper, etc.) will have to be produced by the same large-scale mining and industrial production processes that we now use for conventional energy. In addition, the move towards electrical vehicles (EVs) will cause a huge rise in the demand for minerals like cobalt, lithium and some of the rare earths[3], and for new infrastructure and additional electrical generating capacity to service the new vehicle fleet.

Charles Eisenstein wrote[4] about this in his January 2020 essay, *Extinction and the Revolution of Love*:

To scale up 'green energy' technologies such as solar panels, batteries, wind turbines, and electric vehicles would require a vast expansion of mining. Does the reader understand what a major mining operation looks like? It isn't an innocuous hole in the ground. Here's a description of the Peñasquito silver mine in Mexico:

'Covering nearly forty square miles [100 square kilometres], the operation is staggering in its scale: a sprawling open-pit complex ripped into the mountains, flanked by two waste dumps each a mile long, and a tailings dam full of toxic sludge held back by a wall that's 7 miles

around and as high as a 50-storey skyscraper. This mine will produce 11,000 tons of silver in 10 years before its reserves, the biggest in the world, are gone.'

To transition the global economy to renewables, we need to commission up to 130 more mines on the scale of Peñasquito. Just for silver.

Similar mines are necessary to meet renewable energy's increased demand for copper, neodymium, lithium, cobalt, and other minerals. Each takes a bite out of forests and other ecosystems, poisons water tables, and generates vast amounts of toxic waste. Each generates untold social misery to accompany the ecological misery, and a geopolitics just like that of petroleum extraction. One need look no further for an example than the whitewashed coup in Bolivia, which possesses enormous reserves of lithium that the ousted president, Evo Morales, had planned to nationalize.

So much for the idea of 'clean' energy.

*

We have discovered many more insidious ways to create disorder and spread it all over the planet. For example, we make a vast array of complex chemicals which either don't exist at all in Nature, or exist only in very small quantities within an environment that's capable of absorbing and/ or neutralising them without disturbing the ecosystem. Many of these substances are not easily biodegradable. Most plastics, for example, just disintegrate into smaller and smaller particles, which are ingested by various creatures (especially fish and birds) and either fill them with indigestible junk or poison their bodies and kill them slowly.

Radioactive waste is one of the most dangerous examples of this. It's been with us for the best part of eighty years now, but we still don't have a definitive solution to the problem of how to dispose of it safely.

Natural ecosystems consist of innumerable very finely balanced cyclic processes, in which the waste products of one process become the inputs for many others. This works on every scale, from the microbial level to the level of whole-Earth systems like the maintenance of the gaseous balance in the atmosphere. The industrial economy plays little or no part in this harmoniously balanced system; all it does is introduce a load of unnatural pollutants with little thought about how the system will accommodate them.

We already know about the damage caused by some of the more common pollutants, like the CFCs formerly used as refrigerants until they were banned in the 1980s. There are thousands more about which little or nothing is known. The ongoing battle over the toxic weed-killer Glyphosate shows how difficult it is to get these dangerous chemicals banned even when the damage they do is well documented, because getting them banned depends on a legal process that makes fat fees for lawyers and can easily be gamed by big corporations like Monsanto.

The regulatory systems we have put in place to guard against this kind of pollution have been made to work in a few of the more obviously grotesque cases like DDT and some of the other chemicals we've been spreading on the land to kill everything that moves. But for the more diffuse, less understood substances, these systems are worse than useless because they allow us to pretend that it's safe to go on chucking stuff into the environment – as long as we don't exceed some arbitrary level based on abstraction, compromise and political bargaining.

In his 2018 book[5] *Climate: A New Story*, Charles Eisenstein shows how the ecological devastation caused by our industrial economy is at least as important as our primary CO_2 emissions in generating climate breakdown. His argument is based on a great deal of research; it isn't just a polemic. He makes the important point that the whole political process of climate change 'mitigation' has been based on quantities that can easily be measured, like the CO_2 emissions caused by burning fossil fuels. This has led to such meaningless bargaining points as the 'concept of net zero', which was described by the authors of an April 2021 article in *The Conversation* as 'a dangerous trap'[6]. This article is well worth a read as it shows just how easy it has been for governments to game their own system and effectively get away with doing nothing at all.

🍃

Meanwhile, we're hopelessly addicted to buying *stuff*. We don't even try to conceal this addiction any longer, referring to 'retail therapy' as if it were just another harmless pastime we've invented to enjoy life more fully. Great! Let's spend all day Saturday wandering around the mall, looking at *stuff*.

The caustic writer George Monbiot wrote a brilliant essay about this madness for *The Guardian* newspaper in 2012[7].

We are screwing the planet to make solar-powered bath thermometers and desktop crazy golfers. People in eastern Congo are massacred to facilitate smartphone upgrades of ever diminishing marginal utility. Forests are felled to make

*"personalised heart-shaped wooden cheese board sets".
Rivers are poisoned to manufacture talking fish. This is
pathological consumption: a world-consuming epidemic of
collective madness, rendered so normal by advertising and
the media that we scarcely notice what has happened to us.*

Pathological consumption is the basic engine of an
economy that is intent on making our planet uninhabitable
at the fastest possible rate so as to keep the money flowing
through the system for just a few more years. (Or rather,
not flowing through it because these days an increasing
proportion of it goes straight into the pockets of the few
people who already have more of it than they know how to
use.) Of course it's insane, but it's like the maiden voyage
of the *Titanic* – neither the crew nor the passengers want
to believe there's anything wrong, even after they've heard
the ominous rumble and felt the impact, until the vessel
actually starts to sink. And then they discover that there
aren't enough lifeboats.

🌿

If the engine of the consumer economy is the extractive
industrial system, its driver is the advertising industry,
which takes advantage of our human weaknesses in the
same way that extractive industry takes advantage of the
undefended generosity of Mother Nature and the inability
of the local people to defend their land against the power
of the corporations.

Advertising acts like a giant anxiety amplifier. On some
level, the ad people 'know' what we really need but they
use this knowledge in a corrupt way to craft a clever
message, fine-tuned to convince us that we won't achieve

happiness or fulfilment unless we buy this or that thing, use this or that service, go on this or that holiday, and so on. Even if we take no notice of this stream of garbage, we are unconsciously influenced by the need to project a certain image in the way we dress, or eat, or behave in social situations. We do this just as much when we defy convention by dressing in combat gear and behaving badly.

What I'm saying here is not new; we all know it, and we may even feel slightly uncomfortable about it, but we tolerate it because everyone else does too, and we don't really want to miss out or look different. Besides, it's necessary to own quite a lot of *stuff* in order to participate in the market economy at all (ask someone who's living on the streets, and has nothing) and the economy is structured to emphasise differences in social status, which makes it very hard for us to live differently.

Like all social animals, we have a natural sense of social hierarchy – belonging, being accepted, etc. But unlike most of our four-footed friends, many of us have come to identify our status in the group as a function of how much really cool *stuff* we have accumulated for ourselves. It's hard to deny the fact that our consumerism is a collective attempt to satisfy a deep existential hunger. It's a substitute for the relationships that really matter, like our deeper connections with ourselves, with each other and with the natural world, which we're still part of no matter how much we try to transcend it.

We tend to underestimate the power of our collective unconscious dreaming because we're programmed to believe that we're all separate, self-sufficient individuals navigating our way through life by making rational choices. This 'rational choice' idea is the foundation of classical economics, but it's basically just wishful thinking and it doesn't take much insight to see through it. Most of these supposedly 'rational' choices depend on our unconscious adherence to the norms of the social group with which we tend to identify (by which I mean 'the people whose approval we value the most'). This has always been the case; the only difference nowadays is that the proliferation of social groupings has made us a lot more confused about which of them we'd rather belong to. We are members of a psycho-social matrix with a million-year history that is extremely difficult to break out of.

I've tried to buck this system for most of my life, wanting to believe I was somehow 'different' because I didn't behave like the ideal consumer. I've lived off-grid in a derelict house, got rid of most of my stuff three or four times over, and lived in a couple of converted box vans – but I still haven't escaped from the unconscious underlying structures of consumerism. The feeling of entitlement, the need for comfort, the embarrassment of being poor, these affect us emotionally just as much as our hunger for food or our thirst for water do physically. When the means to satisfy them are taken away from us, our suffering will be so much the greater.

We don't want to imagine that our consumer economy might end in disaster because we are so deeply identified with a way of life centred around our ownership of stuff. Most of us manage to hide this dependency better than my mother-in-law, who can't conceal the fact that she's terrified of losing her familiar things. As Sophia says, it's as if she's never had much of an inner life, and she finds it hard to trust people enough to make a good connection with them, so she has no alternative but to live through her dramas and find a sense of self-worth through her things. Is this really any different to the way many of us supposedly 'normal' people live, even without the dementia?

Another way Lizzie's obsession shows up is the constant, nagging feeling that she's 'bereft and alone'. Our lifelong social conditioning puts a heavy pressure on all of us to identify with our possessions as a sop for the same emotional hunger. It's a necessary part of the consumer economy that depends on us buying more stuff to make us feel better about ourselves.

Lizzie's anxiety is painful to see. It saps her energy, makes her life hell and leads her deeper into the mire of madness. I guess it's not that much different for many of us supposedly 'sane' people, except that we worry about it more discreetly. We instal locks and alarm systems; poor old Lizzie just wanders about feeling lost and alone, tormented by her anxieties and trapped forever in her tiny, obsessive little universe where nothing is safe and everyone is secretly plotting to deprive her of what little she has left.

References

1   Carey King, *The Economic Superorganism: Beyond the Competing Narratives on Energy, Growth, and Policy* (Springer, 2020).

2   An amazingly informative twenty-five-minute documentary about the process of extracting stuff from the Earth and turning it into products for the consumer economy, produced by the Tides Foundation and narrated by Annie Leonard. Highly recommended. https://www.youtube.com/watch?v=9GorqroigqM

3   The so-called rare earths are a series of seventeen metallic elements with very similar chemical properties that aren't as rare as the name suggests. However, they occur in very low concentrations and are very difficult to separate out, so extracting one ton of metal may generate more than 1000 tons of toxic waste. One of them (neodymium) is an essential component of the permanent magnets used in most (but not all) current EV engines, together with two more (terbium and dysprosium) which are added to improve battery performance at high temperatures.

4   See https://charleseisenstein.org/essays/extinction-and-the-revolution-of-love/

5   Charles Eisenstein, *Climate: A New Story* (North Atlantic Books, 2018).

6   'Climate Scientists: Concept of net zero is a dangerous trap', by James Dyke, Robert Watson and Wolfgang Knorr (*The Conversation*, April 22, 2021). Available at https://theconversation.com/climate-scientists-concept-of-net-zero-is-a-dangerous-trap-157368

7   *The Guardian*, 11th December 2012.

- 6 -

In Control

MARCH 2017

MENTAL HEALTH AND Our Changing Climate, a report published this month[1] which was sponsored by the American Psychological Association and ecoAmerica, reveals that there are serious concerns about the impact of climate breakdown on the mental health of some children. In their introduction to the report, the sponsors write:

Americans are beginning to grow familiar with climate change and its health impacts: worsening asthma and allergies; heat-related stress; foodborne, waterborne, and vector-borne diseases; illness and injury related to storms; and floods and droughts. However, the connections with mental health are not often part of the discussion. It is time to expand information and action on climate and health, including mental health.

The health, economic, political, and environmental implications of climate change affect all of us. The tolls on our mental health are far reaching. They induce stress, depression, and anxiety; strain social and community relationships; and have been linked to increases in aggression, violence, and crime. Children and communities with few resources to deal with the impacts of climate change are those most impacted.

To compound the issue, the psychological responses to climate change, such as conflict avoidance, fatalism, fear, helplessness, and resignation are growing. These responses are keeping us, and our nation, from properly addressing the core causes of and solutions for our changing climate, and from building and supporting psychological resiliency.

In a section entitled 'Children's Emotional Responses to Climate Change' (p36), Elizabeth Haase, MD, reported that direct experience with climate disasters and worrying about the future unknown effects of climate change can cause children to exhibit symptoms of PTSD, such as phobic behaviour, panic, nightmares, and anxiety.

Since this report was written, much more evidence has emerged about the effects of the climate crisis on the mental health of young people[2]. It seems to affect them in much the same way as the threat of invasion or civil war. This is hardly surprising in view of the scale of the threat. It was even suggested in one Australian newspaper that teaching them about it amounts to a form of child abuse. Unlike forcing them to sit quietly and behave themselves for six hours a day, which is called 'giving them a good education'.

❧

Lizzie exhibits some of the same symptoms, not because of climate change (about which she knows nothing and cares less) but because of her tendency to obsess about her own difficulties, most of which (unlike climate change) are imaginary. She desperately needs to feel that she's still 'in control'. Unfortunately she isn't able to appreciate how lucky she is – she thinks everything comes to her by some kind of divine right – so the fact that she's being very well looked after hasn't made her any happier. It's a shame because people are naturally sympathetic with her condition and all of us would prefer to see her having a comfortable and contented old age.

Currently she has an obsession about 'going home'. She's at home already, of course, but because she's used to living on her own and there are now three of us living here, she is convinced she's in a care home or a hospital. She's not very clear about who we are; sometimes we're 'the staff', sometimes I'm 'the man who lives here'. She refers to Sophia as 'the nurse' or 'that girl', refusing to recognise that her live-in carer has a name.

Usually when she says 'I want to go home' it turns out that she's referring to one of her mythical 'other houses'. I look at her helplessly and say I'm terribly sorry but I know nothing about them. She demands to see her solicitor so she can harangue him about them instead. He has come to see her a couple of times, but he also says he's terribly sorry but he can't find any evidence of 'other houses'. Lizzie gets very angry and frustrated when we both give the same reply, but it doesn't stop her from talking about 'going home'.

One morning Lizzie has a bad dream. She's convinced she's been 'taken down to the basement' and compelled to sleep 'in a room full of sick people'. This is probably a mangled reprise of an experience she had when she was in hospital.

She demands to know why she's still here, and when she'll be going home.

We keep telling her as gently as possible that she's just had a bad dream and we've been at home all the time, but every time we say it she becomes more bewildered and enraged by our stubborn refusal to believe her. She calls her few remaining friends one after the other. We can hear her breathlessly trying to explain to them how we won't listen to her and she's been made to sleep in the basement with a lot of sick people and she wants to go home. Most of them have learnt not to pick up when she calls, or to say something vague and reassuring, but on this occasion one of them is out and his daughter answers the phone.

Because she doesn't know Lizzie, she tries a bit of polite sarcasm. 'Well,' she says, 'if you're being kept somewhere against your will, why don't you call the police?'

Lizzie asks what number she should use to call the police.

'Oh, 999 I should think,' says the idiot, whose sense of humour knows no bounds.

Lizzie shuffles out from her bedroom and leans over the banisters. 'Is there anybody down there?' she calls.

'What is it, Lizzie?' cries Sophia from the kitchen.

'If you don't take me home, I'm going to call the police!' she announces.

'OK,' says Sophia wearily. 'Call police, then.'

So Lizzie does what she's told and dials 999. No doubt she expects a squad car to turn up with four burly policemen who will burst into the house and rescue her. Unfortunately it doesn't turn out quite like that. The call handler listens to my mother-in-law's ramblings for a while and then cuts her short. 'Is there anyone in the house there with you?'

'Oh, yes,' says Lizzie. 'The girl's here. Do you want to

136

speak to her?'

'Yes, please.'

Lizzie shuffles onto the landing again. 'Hello!' she calls. 'Is the nurse down there? The police lady wants to speak to you.'

'The police lady? Ce dracu!' says Sophia, charging up the stairs with a noise like thunder. Lizzie gives her the phone. 'Hello?... Yes, I am the carer.' She starts to walk downstairs again with the phone in her hand. 'Yes, I am here all the time...'

'They've taken my phone!' Lizzie shouts in a surprisingly loud voice. 'Help me! They've taken my phone!'

Sophia holds the phone up in the air. 'You can hear her that she shout?'

'Yes, of course,' says the call handler drily. 'Just let me take some details.'

'Help me! Someone, please come! Help me! They've taken my phone!'

Sophia disappears into the dining room. While she's answering the call handler's questions, Lizzie shuffles back into her bedroom, opens the window and leans out. 'Help!' she shouts. 'They've taken my phone! Somebody help me please!' Her voice rings out across the quiet suburban gardens.

In my imagination, fourteen curious neighbours wonder whether or not they should call the police. I stumble upstairs on my arthritic legs to try and persuade her to stop.

'Now she shout the neighbours,' says Sophia from downstairs.

'I'd better speak to her,' says the call handler.

'Lizzie! The police lady want to speak with you. Please stop to shout the neighbours!'

Sophia climbs upstairs again and gives me the phone. I hand it to Lizzie, who explains once again in a trembling voice that 'they' have brought her to this place and they won't let her go home, so she has to stay here. They made her sleep in the basement with a lot of sick people and they won't call the doctor, but she's very ill and she needs to go home.

'Where is your home, Mrs Pickton?' asks the call handler.

Lizzie struggles for a moment but nothing comes. She looks helplessly at me. 'The lady wants to know where my home is.'

'36 Darnwood Road,' I prompt.

'36 Darnwood Road,' she repeats doubtfully down the phone, as if it's the first time she's ever heard it.

And where are you now, my dear?' asks the police lady.

Lizzie turns to me in desperation. 'Where are we now?'

'36 Darnwood Road,' I say cheerfully.

'We're at Thirty-Six, Darn-wood-road,' she pronounces, as if she's never heard it before.

'Then I'd say you are already at home and you don't need to worry. All right?'

Lizzie looks at me. 'The lady says I'm already at home.' She gives me the phone.

'Thanks,' I say to the call handler. 'You dealt with that very well.'

'No problem,' says the call handler. 'We get a lot of calls like this. It's a sign of the times, I suppose.'

❧

On some level, Lizzie knows she's lost her mind but her response has been total denial and a heroic effort to stay in control. She's a very strong-willed woman. You wouldn't think so if you watched her performing 'bereft and alone', but it is so. She has been using this drama, albeit in a more covert, sophisticated form, for a long time and it has been very successful in getting people to run around doing things for her.

Unfortunately it's so obvious and so urgent nowadays that people tire of it much sooner. It doesn't help that she ends up calling them 'useless', but that does show just how strong her sense of entitlement is – rather like a two or three year old, in fact.

Her need to feel that she's in control and her sense of entitlement remind me of the obsession that has gripped many of my countrymen during the last few years: the Brexiteers' dream of 'taking back control'. It makes me wonder who exactly is going to take back control of what. It's hard to see how anyone, or indeed any government, is going to take back control of anything, especially if we move closer to America as a result of all the horse-trading.

If that happens, we're probably heading towards a deregulated free-for-all, which will benefit a few financiers and a whole class of unscrupulous entrepreneurs (and no doubt a fair few politicians) at everybody else's expense. In which case, we can kiss goodbye to what remains of our beloved NHS, our environmental standards and our social welfare system, amongst other things.

❧

We now know that the Brexiteers' dream of 'taking back control' has come at a high price in terms of economic disruption, but it's arguable that this may not make much of a difference in the long run because the entire global economy has been out of control for a while now. It is unlikely to survive in its present form for very much longer.

There are many destabilising factors but three of them seem to stand out. The first is that the world of finance has become unmoored from reality and is now highly unstable, like a Jenga tower just before it falls over[3]. The second is that an economy that depends on limitless growth needs a limitless supply of resources, especially energy, but we live on a finite planet and we are already testing the limits of what's available. And finally there is the ecological crisis that threatens the very basis of our survival on this planet, as exemplified by the rapidly advancing horrors of climate change.

*

In 2008 we almost had a financial disaster. It was forestalled by the bailouts instituted by the central banks, but the underlying causes were never really addressed, and at some point within the next few months or years it will almost certainly happen again. The central banks probably won't be able to stop it this time, because since 2008 they have taken on so much non-performing debt, and reduced interest rates to such low levels, that they have severely reduced their own capacity to mount that kind of rescue a second time. It's really no longer a question of *whether*, it's more a question of *when* and *how* the next financial crash will be triggered.

This is not a controversial point of view in the financial world. Insiders are well aware that the global financial system has been deep inside 'bubble' territory for most of the last three or four decades. This judgement hasn't penetrated very far into the ordinary world just yet, because the façade of prosperity depends on everyone in the financial business playing the same game, whether or not they actually believe their own propaganda. The central banks are supposed to be 'in control', but all they have been able to do – at great cost – is to keep the deception going by buying up huge quantities of worthless assets to stop the financial system imploding and dragging us into a really bad recession.

This is known in the trade as 'kicking the can down the road'. The hope is that somehow, at some point, the real economy will recover enough for all the debts to be paid off, but the further we go down this road, the less realistic it becomes – and the cost of the Covid crisis has made it even worse. It's a bit like a desperate gambler trying to stave off bankruptcy by juggling his credit cards: it works for a while, and then suddenly it doesn't.

We've had a stock market boom, but this is because the market has been rigged by financial trickery like very low interest rates, corporate stock buybacks and so-called 'quantitative easing' (e.g. the central banks hoovering up all kinds of worthless stock to avoid another catastrophic fall in the stock market). The ordinary professionals who manage our finances have become so used to this bubble situation that it now feels quite normal; they would prefer to keep their jobs as long as it lasts, so they continue to pretend (in public) that nothing is wrong. It looks like they will have to go on feeding the hungry monster until it suddenly falls apart as it did in October 1929, and then all of us – through our jobs, our savings accounts and our pension funds – will pay the price.

Some radical economists with a sense of history are

calling this 'the mother of all bubbles'. One obvious sign of it is asset price inflation (i.e. a lot of easy money chasing a limited number of physical and financial assets such as land, housing, natural resources and 'intellectual property'), because this kind of investment gives returns that are quicker and better than investing in the productive economy. This is a powerful engine of inequality because those who own these increasingly scarce assets are able to rent them out at higher and higher prices, which enables them to buy up more assets, etc.

The bubble economy has been characterised by gross distortions in the stock and bond markets, rampant property price inflation (and the unaffordable rents that go with it), exponentially increasing levels of debt, and the consequent inability of countries to continue to support their social welfare programs (hence 'austerity').

The 'mother of all bubbles' started inflating in the eighties after the deregulation of the banking industry and its rapid conversion into a multi-trillion-dollar casino. The most lethal weapon in this war on common sense is the market in so-called 'derivatives', which are fancy ways of betting on the future value of an underlying asset. These financial instruments may, on paper, be worth ten or a hundred times the actual value of the asset itself. They add nothing useful to the real economy, but are designed to ensure that the bets pay off in a way that is guaranteed to increase the paper wealth of the individuals and institutions that place them.

Warren Buffet, one of the most successful gamblers in this giant global casino, once called derivatives 'weapons of financial mass destruction'[4], because, in effect, they spread the risk of a local failure throughout the economy instead of keeping it concentrated in one place. This works well as long as the failures they protect against are relatively small and isolated. When there's a big enough failure, they are more likely to all implode at once because they all support each other (like the famous 'house of cards'). That's why governments have made such strenuous efforts to shore up the zombie economy, by buying up billions of dollars' worth of non-performing financial instruments (e.g. sub-prime mortgages bundled up into anonymous 'securities'), which are priced at their notional value even though they would turn out to be worthless if they were offered for sale on the open market. It's also why they will do anything to avoid a formal declaration that a country (Greece, for example) is in default on its sovereign debt. If such a default were to be officially acknowledged, the derivative explosion could spread like a nuclear chain reaction right across the globe and burn the whole edifice to the ground within weeks.

*

Financially speaking, the nearest historical situation to the one we're in now was the 'bubble economy' that led to the crash of 1929. Compared to the current situation, the amounts of money involved were quite small; nevertheless it led to the Great Depression of the 1930s.

It might be argued that we came out of that one, so why can't we come out of this one as well? Part of the answer is that in 1929 there were a lot more high-grade resources still waiting to be exploited that don't exist any longer. Whether it's crude oil, copper, coal, uranium or any of the other source materials we depend on to support *genuine* economic growth, most of the high-grade sources have been thoroughly exploited and we are left with lower-grade sources that are more difficult and expensive to extract.

Things will never again be the same as they were in the 1930s. That era has gone, never to return, and with it almost all of the light, sweet crude oil that came gushing out of the ground to fuel the seventy-year economic expansion we enjoyed during the last century before it began to stall during the first two decades of this one.

This is also the reason why using financial trickery to stimulate economic growth hasn't worked. Growth isn't actually being constrained by financial limits; it is being slowly strangled by other factors, most of which are entirely beyond the control of the central banks. One that I've just mentioned is the increasing scarcity and cost of the natural resources that need to be extracted to keep the economy going, especially oil[5]. Another is the growing disparity between the cost of a twenty-first century lifestyle and the wage levels of most ordinary families[6]. A third is the mounting cost of maintaining the enormously complex physical and bureaucratic infrastructure that keeps the global economy going[7]. None of these are of much interest to neoliberal economists who seem to inhabit a rarefied world of hyper-individualism and abstruse equations that enable them to practise a serene detachment from the trials and tribulations of the real world.

Unfortunately there's no technical way of solving these problems within the current paradigm, even if we switch to the much-touted green economy. As John Michael Greer pointed out, it's not a 'problem' that we face, or even a whole set of problems; it's a *predicament*, which means a problematic situation that can't be significantly changed

144

but must be *adapted to*. And the necessary adaptation means a complete change of lifestyle, not 'more-of-the-same-but-with-a-renewable-energy-source'[8].

🍃

What's the predicament? The short answer is that the laws of physics are more fundamental than the 'laws' of classical economics[9]. This brings us back to the main reason why the global economy is in trouble, which is energy, or more specifically oil.

E. F. Schumacher wrote about this forty-five years ago in his ground-breaking book *Small is Beautiful*[10] published in 1973. Conventional economics hardly ever refers to the fact that everything in what it calls 'the economy' is derived from raw materials that Nature provides for free. The principle of *substitutability* states that if a particular 'good' (i.e. something that the economy needs in order to function well) becomes scarce for any reason, then the price of that 'good' will increase to the point where it will become profitable to develop a substitute. This ignores the fact that some of the 'goods' that come from the primary economy of Nature – unlike the secondary 'goods' that are produced by industry – are not realistically substitutable.

The prime example is oil, which still powers 99% of the world's transport and is the feedstock for most plastic products, among other things. Quite a lot of effort has gone into finding a substitute for oil as a transport fuel, but electric cars are still much too expensive for the increasingly cash-strapped middle and working classes. Although their sales are increasing, it's not certain they can grow fast enough to replace conventional vehicles before the supply of oil becomes truly problematic.

It's already problematic in the sense that we're relying more and more on sources that are difficult to access, such as deep-sea oil, tar sands and shale oil that has to be liberated by hydraulic fracturing (fracking). These sources are expensive, energy intensive and environmentally devastating, but they are being exploited because the global demand for energy has been steadily increasing for more than a century now[11], and it shows no sign of levelling off, despite all the attention that's being given to the dangers of climate change. The Machine is truly insatiable and nothing we've done so far has been able even to slow it down, let alone to stop it. Maybe this is an area where the political and financial power of the corporates is so entrenched that only a large and determined mass movement like XR can make a difference.

Schumacher realised that energy isn't just another commodity like corn or copper. Rather, it is the unique resource category that enables us to make use of all the others. The principle of substitutability, just like the story of perpetual growth, only works if there's enough cheap energy available to make it work. Otherwise, it falls flat on its face.

*

The financial situation and the 'energy crunch' are both part of the collapse scenario that's facing us as we head into the 2020s. These predictions of collapse are appearing more and more frequently as conditions get worse, but they're not just speculative hype. They are supported by empirical studies, historical precedent and practical insight.

Some of the studies go back a long way. For example, the likely outcomes of unrestricted industrial growth on a finite planet were examined in *The Limits to Growth*, which was published nearly fifty years ago in 1972. The authors looked at the systemic interactions between five generalised variables (population, food production, natural resources, industrial output and pollution). They made some assessments of what might happen if there were significant interventions to reduce the damage on a global scale, such as imposing limits on population growth, industrial expansion or resource extraction. In almost all cases, except where the interventions were extremely tough, the outcome still looked like a collapse, although it might take a bit longer to materialise. In their worst-case scenario, where no significant limits were imposed at all, the global collapse looked likely to occur over a period of three or four decades during the first half of the twenty-first century.

The Limits to Growth was dismissed contemptuously when it came out, but in 2005 the surviving members of the team published a thirty-year update[12], which showed that their 1972 worst-case predictions were actually quite close to the current real-world data. This is perhaps not surprising, since very few significant limits were actually imposed during the intervening three decades (and this is still the case now, fifteen years later). The limits to global growth that are being felt now stem almost entirely from the laws of physics – as predicted in *The Limits to Growth* – rather than from any efforts that we have made to reduce our extravagant ecological footprint and avoid overshoot.

So here we are at the end of the second decade of the twenty-first century, and it looks as if what we are seeing now is the opening phase of the global collapse that was predicted by the MIT team fifty years ago[13].

☙

This brings us to the third reason why the global economy is in deep trouble: the arena where growth crashes head on into climate breakdown. The Intergovernmental Panel on Climate Change (IPCC) recommended in their October 2018 report that carbon emissions should be reduced to 'net zero' by 2050. Leaving out the unlikely development of Carbon Capture & Storage (CCS) technology[14], this would mean that within thirty years we would have to replace pretty much all the fossil fuels that we currently use with renewables.

In 2018 the proportions of different sources in the global energy mix were as follows:

Oil	34%	Hydro	7%
Coal	27%	Other renewables	4%
Natural Gas	24%	Nuclear	4%
Total (fossil)	85%	Total (other)	15%

How big a task would it be to replace all fossil fuels with sources that don't emit CO_2 by 2050? Chris Martenson looked at this recently on his Peak Prosperity blog[15], using calculations made by Roger Pielke, a science writer for *Forbes* magazine. To make it simple, he converted all fossil fuel use into Millions of Tons Oil Equivalent (MTOE). In 2018 the world used about 12,000 MTOE. There were approximately 11,000 days until the middle of 2050, so if we want to keep on using as much energy as we do today, we would have had to replace just over one MTOE with renewable sources every day for the next 11,000 days. To illustrate what a huge task this is, it would be equivalent to building either 16,500 new nuclear plants (that's three of them every two days)[16], or about 16.5 million wind turbines (that's 1500 every day). Presumably we would have to replace all conventional transport with electrically-powered transport as well, but Martenson was only aiming to indicate the *scale* of the problem.

Some relief could be obtained by offsetting (e.g. planting new forests to replace the ones we've cut down), but we would have to plant an enormous number of forests to make a real difference. As Martenson says, there is no way that these changes are even remotely feasible in the required timescale.

To put the nuclear choice in perspective, the new twin-reactor nuclear power station at Hinkley Point took ten years in the planning stages, will cost more than £20 billion (probably a lot more by the time it's finished), and will take at least seven years to build. And even if we managed to build 16,500 new reactors, there would only be enough uranium left to power them all for about two days.

The alternative, of course, is to cut down drastically on our energy use, but so far we seem to have been very reluctant to do this – at least on the scale required. There's a lot of pressure on governments to 'do something', and they certainly could (and should) stop subsidising the fossil fuel industry and put our tax money into subsidising renewables instead. But it's hard to see what else they can do realistically in the short term other than legislating to curb some of the activities that we are very attached to, including some that are essential to keep our sophisticated economy going. This means activities like flying, driving, heating our homes, buying lots of unnecessary stuff, and even eating beef. Can you imagine any democratic government getting enough votes from their citizens to do that? I think the answer is probably 'not any time soon'.

This doesn't augur well for the green economy that many people are proposing as a way of reconciling growth with sustainability. To support such a radical change, as Chris Martenson's example showed, we would have to divert a massive amount of investment into the production and maintenance of the machinery and infrastructure that would be necessary for green energy extraction (wind generators, nuclear reactors, solar PV panels, or whatever technical solutions are proposed), at a time when the same resources are needed to maintain and renew the existing systems, both physical and bureaucratic, that service the economy and keep it going. We would have to achieve this using production and transport facilities that are 99% based on burning fossil fuels at a time when these fuels are becoming more and more expensive to produce – a practice that can only make climate breakdown more rapid, not slower. And we would need to mine and refine very large quantities of minerals like cobalt, lithium and the rare earths, as explained in Chapter 5.

That raises the even more fundamental argument, which I also wrote about in Chapter 5, about the use of natural resources in an extractive economy that's powered by the production and sale of consumer goods. There have been three thoroughly researched studies on this, each of which has shown that, even based on the most optimistic assumptions, it is not possible to sustain such an economy without increasing resource use well beyond the agreed maximum that can be supported by our finite planet[17].

We find ourselves in the same predicament as Aesop's monkey, whose hand was trapped in the gourd because he couldn't bring himself to let go of the fruit inside it. We can't let go of our attachment to this ultra-sophisticated way of life despite the fact that we're destroying our planetary home in the process.

🍃

We could summarise our predicament like this:

- The industrial economy functions by extracting raw materials from the Earth (metal ores, fossil fuels, wood, ground water, building materials) and converting them into finished products (cars, houses, furniture, gadgets, etc.).
- These activities are financed by capital, which is generated by *fiat* (i.e. the private banks conjure it into existence by writing numbers into a computer memory) and must be repaid with interest[18].
- To generate the money required to service the interest payments, the economy must continually expand. This expansion must be exponential, meaning that it has to expand at a faster and faster rate as time goes on.
- This fast-growing economy depends on a fixed infrastructure (roads, bridges, airports, power stations, the electrical grid, etc.) that must be built, continually expanded, maintained and renewed. It also generates unwanted outputs (pollution and waste) that continually increase and must be

cleaned up or mitigated in some way. A proportion of capital must be diverted for these purposes. Most of it has to be raised by taxation, because the industries which use the infrastructure and cause the pollution are not going to pay for it unless compelled to by law. If the politicians were to demand it, these industries would simply move their operations to another jurisdiction.

- As the economy expands, the resources available (i.e. the raw materials) get used up. Naturally, the easily accessible resources (e.g. the 'super-giant' oilfields) are the first to be used up. The ones that remain (e.g. shale oil, deep-sea oil, tar sands) are progressively more and more difficult and expensive to exploit, while the associated waste and pollution increase dramatically as the quality of the source gets worse.

- A fundamental change in the principal energy source (e.g. from fossil fuels to renewables) entails building a completely different infrastructure to produce and service it. This can't be done overnight, and will require a massive diversion of capital to support it at a time when financial resources are already stretched because the principal energy resource behind the entire industrial economy (i.e. oil) is becoming more and more expensive to extract and refine.

- If all of this is converted into a mathematical model, the resulting graph is like an asymmetrical bell-curve that rises gradually to a peak but then descends much more precipitately, as if it had 'fallen off a cliff'.

The classic examination of this system was *The Limits to Growth*, the 1972 study I mentioned earlier. This made predictions based on several different scenarios. In their worst-case scenario, which could be called 'business as usual' (i.e. no significant limits imposed on the continued expansion of the existing resource-use system), the global collapse was predicted to occur sometime in the first half of the twenty-first century. I also mentioned the thirty-year update, which showed that the broad highway down which the world has so far been travelling matches very well with their 1972 worst-case prediction.

John Michael Greer has proposed a quasi-mathematical theory that draws most of this together, which he calls the Theory of Catabolic Collapse[19]. This model concentrates on four variables, Resources (R), Production (P), Maintenance (M) and Waste (W). It shows how the interaction of these four variables can lead to a state of expansion (as in the 'advanced' economies during the five decades from 1950 to 2000), which then stalls (as it has begun to do in the last two decades), and is followed by a state of relatively rapid contraction (which is what he believes faces us in the near future).

A steady-state economy (neither expanding nor contracting) is more typically associated with indigenous societies living relatively close to the land, such as pre-Columbian America and pre-colonial Africa and Australia. Alternatively, a society can oscillate regularly between expansion and contraction, as has been the case in China for pretty much the last three millennia.

Greer shows that the current slowdown can be understood as a resource depletion crisis (i.e. moving from abundant resources to increasingly hard to get, and therefore more costly, resources) together with a maintenance crisis (large parts of the necessary infrastructure all needing to be repaired at the same time, or replaced by new infrastructure with greater handling capacity, which makes heavy demands on capital already stretched by the move towards developing more expensive resources). If we add in the effect of usury (i.e. lending at interest), we get a situation of accelerated negative feedback that also increases at an exponential rate, so that once it gets under way it quickly overwhelms the system and leads to a rapid contraction in the economy (i.e. a progressive collapse).

Greer makes sense of our situation by looking at historical examples of the rise and fall of civilisations derived mainly from the work of historian Arnold Toynbee (1889–1975). Toynbee saw civilisations as organic wholes that grow, flourish, become senile and die just like plants (or rather, just like ecosystems)[20]. This is a good example of holistic thinking, but it doesn't feature much in the debate because it's regarded as too 'subjective' and therefore unreliable as a source of intelligent comment.

Once Toynbee's historical work is added into the mix, the idea of catabolic collapse becomes more nuanced in that collapse begins to look more like tumbling down a rocky slope than falling off a cliff. Collapse, Greer suggests, is a long-drawn-out step-wise process where civilisations lose their complexity in stages, stabilising for periods of time at lower levels of complexity until they bottom out at some stage and begin the long process of recovery. The prime example of this was the collapse of the western Roman Empire, which took place over a period of more than three centuries. However, since our economy now extends over the entire globe, is so highly interdependent, and we are facing the additional hazard of climate breakdown, in all probability it might not take us so long.

🍂

The American anthropologist and historian Joseph Tainter wrote a definitive study of historical civilisational collapse, which was published in 1988[21]. He used a comparative approach and came to the conclusion that the underlying process in all the collapse scenarios he had studied was the declining marginal returns of increasing complexity. All civilisations become more and more complex as they progress, but each unit of added complexity becomes more expensive and at the same time less effective, until at some point you get negative returns. This means that adding more complexity makes everything worse, not better.

He compared seventeen different examples, from the western Roman Empire to the Ik (a tribe in Northern Uganda 'who live at what must surely be the extreme of deprivation and disaster', as he put it). As a society grows in size, starts to develop technically and may need to trade with its neighbours or defend itself against aggression, it becomes more functionally differentiated and develops more complex social and political forms. The process soon becomes self-perpetuating, as the society gets used to adding more complexity to deal with new problems whenever they arise. For example, to defend itself it needs an army. The bigger the army gets, the more it has to be trained, armed, fed, housed, paid and kept in line by officers, guards, artificers, caterers etc., all paid for by domestic taxes and/or tributes from conquered people.

There's a neat description of how complexity builds up

until it reaches an unsustainable level by Dmitry Orlov in *The Five Stages of Collapse*[22]:

Modern societies rely on the government to defend property rights, enforce contracts and regulate commerce. As the economy expands, so do the functions of government, along with its bureaucratic structures, laws, rules and procedures and – what expands fastest of all – its cost. All of these official arrangements show an accretion of complexity over time. Each time a new problem needs to be solved, something is added to the structure, but nothing is ever taken away, because previous arrangements are often grandfathered in, and because simplifying a complex arrangement is always more difficult and initially more expensive than complicating it further. But socioeconomic complexity is never without cost, and once the economy crests and begins to contract, this cost becomes prohibitive. In the context of a shrinking economy buffeted by waves of escalating crises, an outsized officialdom comes to exhibit ever greater negative economies of scale, while the arduous task of reforming it so as to scale it down and simplify it cannot receive priority due to a lack of resources.

The NHS is an interesting example of negative returns on increasing complexity. It probably reached this point several years ago, which is one reason its costs are escalating so fast. The bottom line is that medical techniques have become more and more complex as scientific research reveals more about the biochemical mechanisms of disease. As a result, given the cost restraints in a tax-based system, administrative functions have also become more complex, especially with the creation of artificial devices like the so-called 'internal market' and enormously costly schemes like the Private Finance

Initiative, which load the benefits onto private firms and the costs onto the public sector[23]. Some of these inefficiencies can be offset by sophisticated information technology, but that in itself brings problems with enormously complex IT systems that frequently add work rather than subtracting it because they are so sophisticated that no-one knows how to use them properly. (Ask the admin staff in any doctor's surgery!)

Tainter's book was published more than thirty years ago. Even then he pointed out that: *Patterns of declining marginal returns can be observed in at least some contemporary industrial societies in the following areas: agriculture; minerals and energy production; research and development; investment in health; education; government, military and industrial management; productivity of GNP for new growth; and some elements of improved technical design.* (p.211)

He was not making subjective judgements; these are all areas for which statistics were available that showed how greater levels of investment had yielded fewer improvements per dollar spent on them.

Industrial agriculture provides a good analogy for this. You get greatly improved yields when you first start adding chemical fertilisers and pesticides to the soil but, as the years go by, you find yourself having to add greater and greater amounts of these additives in order to get the same results and you end up with severely degraded soil. This is a familiar pattern with any kind of addiction. It has become a familiar theme in the world of economics, too, especially where the cost of providing new jobs is concerned.

Tainter also observed that the situation we're in is one of 'peer polity competition', where competing groups of societies (thirty years ago, and still to a great extent now, this meant the capitalist and communist halves of the world) '*tend to evolve towards greater complexity in a lockstep fashion as, driven by competition, each partner imitates new organisational, technological and military features developed by its competitor(s).*' (p.214)

The most familiar version of this is the so-called arms race, which means that neither bloc can afford to allow itself to collapse, no matter how much it costs to maintain that competition. This is ironic, in view of the fact that the Soviet Union went through a partial collapse only one year after Tainter wrote these words in 1989, but it applies just as much to techno-industrial competition as it does to military confrontation. Since 1989, the role of chief competitor in both these fields has been increasingly taken up by China, so his conclusion still stands:

Collapse, if and when it comes again, will this time be global. No longer can any individual nation collapse. World civilisation will disintegrate as a whole. Competitors who evolve as peers collapse in like manner. (p.215)

Prodigious efforts have been made to keep the system running, especially since the 2008 recession. The enormous cost of these efforts has mostly been borne by the poorest people in the world who are the least able to afford it. The 1% who control the levers of power and have profited enormously from this process might be able to keep it stumbling on for a while yet, but the longer they manage to keep it going, the more certain we are to head towards a systemic breakdown even if we survive the next financial collapse. Both runaway climate change and accelerating ecological damage will see to that. Either way, unless something miraculous happens, we're fatally compromised.

References

1 https://www.apa.org/news/press/releases/2017/03/mental-health-climate.pdf

2 Including a recent (2021) study funded by the campaigning organisation Avaaz, and carried out by several researchers under the leadership of Caroline Hickman. They surveyed 10,000 young people aged 16–25 in ten countries, 59% of whom said they were 'very or extremely worried' about climate change; 64% said that governments were not doing enough to avoid catastrophe. Available at https://papers.ssrn.com/sol3/papers.cfm?abstract_id=3918955&fbclid=IwAR0QqH5KQBEMXq-sZvsS0BVQiRbN1L2zEy6vtkbXcUjxqiJAQzJHDkSgJWU

3 The best account of the background to this that I have seen is *The Crash Course*, a video series produced by the American financial journalist Chris Martenson. See https://www.peakprosperity.com/crashcourse

4 From the Berkshire Hathaway annual report, 2002.

5 See, for example, Richard Heinberg, *The End of Growth* (New Society Publishers, 2011).

6 See Gail Tverberg's excellent blog at https://ourfiniteworld.com for a series of very clear analyses of this fundamental problem.

7 See John Michael Greer, *Dark Age America* (New Society Publishers, 2016).

8 A recent book, edited by Jem Bendell and Rupert Read, goes into this scenario quite thoroughly. See Bendell and Read, *Deep Adaptation: Navigating the Realities of Climate Chaos* (Polity, 2021).

9 A point repeatedly made by John Michael Greer. See *The Wealth of Nature: Economics as if Survival Mattered* (New Society Publishers, 2011), for a full discussion of this issue.

10 E.F. Schumacher, *Small is Beautiful: A Study of Economics*

*as if People Mattere*d (Vintage, 2011).

11 Search 'global energy demand' on the Internet; there are many sources for this assertion.

12 See Meadows, Meadows, and Randers, *The Limits to Growth: The 30-Year Update* (Earthscan, 2005)**.**

13 A recent (July 2021) study by Gaya Herrington, commissioned by KPMG, confirms that the 1972 'worst-case' scenario is still the best fit for current global economic data (*The Guardian*, 25.07.21). See also John Michael Greer's blog, Ecosophia, where he recently wrote about the same subject. This is available at https://www.ecosophia.net/a-prayer-for-nonbelievers/

14 See 'Carbon Capture & Storage' by Gabriel Levy in *Ecologist* magazine, 13 Nov 2020 https://theecologist. org/2020/nov/13/carbon-dioxide-removal-sucks

15 Chris Martenson, 4 October 2019, at https://www. peakprosperity.com/getting-real-about-green-energy/

16 For comparison, after sixty years of development there are now only 450 operating nuclear power plants in the world, plus about fifty currently under construction.

17 See Jason Hickel, 'Why Growth Can't be Green', in *Resilience* magazine, September 2018. See also George Monbiot, 'Green Growth doesn't exist – less of everything is the only way to avert catastrophe', *The Guardian*, 29 Sept 2021.

18 See Ellen Hodgson Brown, *The Web of Debt* (Third Millennium Publishers, 5th edn., 2011).

19 John Michael Greer, *The Long Descent* (New Society Publishers, 2008).

20 See Arnold Toynbee, *A Study of History* (Abridged edn., Thames & Hudson, 1972).

21 Joseph A. Tainter, 'The Collapse of Complex Societies', *New Studies in Archaeology*, (C.U.P., 1988).

22 Dmitry Orlov, *The Five Stages of Collapse* (New Society

Publishers, 2013), p.105.

23 See John Pilger's excellent documentary about what's really been happening to the NHS, available at https://www.youtube.com/watch?v=Jl JGL8Z52YE&fbclid=IwAR1uL52e2FDvC-vOvc5e_ rNL8lcCp4Me7Rsdeqve4Zy7NqD6sj6tlY8lvCl

- 7 -

Conrad

28 JULY 2017

THE THIRTIETH OF July is designated annually by the United Nations Office on Drugs and Crime (UNODC) as World Day Against Trafficking in Persons (better known as 'human trafficking').

An article by Baher Kamal on the Global Issues website today[1] quotes some shocking statistics from the 2016 Global Report on Trafficking in Persons. Up to a third of all victims of trafficking are children, and nearly half are women. The ILO estimates that about 21 million people have been forced to work in conditions of slavery or servitude, including many millions of sex workers. People are also forced to work as beggars, or in pornographic movies, or have their organs harvested for sale. More than 500 different 'trafficking flows' (routes) were detected between 2012 and 2014, involving citizens from 137 different countries. Reports have appeared in the mainstream news about migrants from all parts of West and Central Africa, trapped in Libya waiting to cross into Europe, who are being openly sold in slave markets.

These are some of the statistics but behind each one there's a personal tragedy: another family torn apart; another childhood ended; another woman's life ruined and laid to waste by the power of toxic masculinity that is rampant all over the world. People are trying to escape from terrible situations in their home country, only to find themselves trapped in even worse conditions wherever they turn.

The UK, with its 'hostile environment' policy, is very much part of the problem. We are a rich country, but the casual racism of the right-wing press has led to a situation where many thousands of vulnerable migrants are subjected to danger and destitution to satisfy the righteous indignation of their readers.

If we don't succeed in at least reducing the ongoing disruption of our normal patterns of global climate, it won't be long before this situation becomes much worse. Resource wars and extreme weather events have already made conditions in some parts of the world very difficult. As the climate becomes more unstable, more harvests will be ruined, more poor countries won't have the resources to cope; before long whole populations will be forced off their devastated lands to seek food and shelter in neighbouring countries already swollen with refugees from previous crises.

On the whole, we prefer not to think about any of this. It sounds too alarmist to be true. But, like many deep-seated conditions, the longer we leave it, the worse it will get. And the worse it gets, the more difficult it will be to change.

🍃

The months roll by and Lizzie doesn't get any better. That's usually the way with dementia; once it's got its claws into you, it doesn't let go. Indeed, it can't let go because the changes in your brain are irreversible.

Sophia goes back to Romania for a few weeks at the end of May, and her colleague Valentina takes over. Valie is less experienced but she has an irrepressible sense of fun and knows how to use Lizzie's penchant for drama to invent some ingenious scenarios to distract her when she gets obsessive. There's never a dull day at 36 Darnwood Avenue.

In July, Sophia returns. They are supposed to do the handover in two hours, according to EuroCare's rules, but Valie stays on for a week while she's waiting for her next assignment. This allows each of them to cover for the other and take a day off to go shopping and sightseeing in Bath, which is just up the road from Radstock, with me as their guide. EuroCare would have a corporate fit if they knew what we were up to.

🌿

I'm spending most of my spare time working with Lightning Tree. Since the Fire Valley community folded, Max and I have been trying to revitalise our training course for activists and bring it to the city, but we have found this much more difficult than we expected.

It was relatively easy to run a course like this with a highly motivated group of people who were already living on the land, because they could integrate the training with their daily lives and support each other's learning, but things are very different in the city. For example, if we want to do what we call 'nature immersion', we have to hire a piece of relatively unspoilt countryside for the purpose. Then, when we assemble the group there, we find that no-one wants to do any psychological work, they want to enjoy being in Nature instead because they need a week to get the city out of their system. Then the week is over and they have to go back to the city again.

Our main problem is that no-one has heard of us and, although we aren't earning any money out of it, we still have to hire venues and provide food and equipment. We can't get enough people to pay even the small amounts we're asking for because they don't know if they can trust us yet. We can't point to a long history of successful training courses with endorsements from people who've done them and thought they were wonderful. It takes a while to acquire a good reputation.

Meanwhile my commitment to the enterprise is being undermined by the sense that it's time I let go of this obsession with trying to save the planet. I don't know where this sense is coming from, but it haunts me as I doggedly pursue our dream. The only reason I don't abandon Lightning Tree is that it would feel like a terrible failure and a betrayal of my colleagues, not to mention the Divine Feminine, with which (as a principle) I've had a certain fixation for a while. Probably it's all mixed up with my mother, so I can't let go of it.

I'm also struggling with the group process in our team, which I find frustrating. Everyone has their own ideas about what we should be doing, and I'm finding it very hard to let go of mine to make room for somebody else's. This, of course, is a familiar problem with groups of idealistic people who are trying to change things. It's ironic because this kind of intra-group tension is one of the very things we're trying to *address with our training course. Physician, heal thyself!*

🌿

One evening I come home brimming with frustration and talk about it with Sophia, not for the first time. She listens for a while, then she looks at me with her insouciant Transylvanian smile and says, 'My dear, I think you are tryink too hard.'

I sit down and pour myself a glass of Jim Beam. 'Maybe you're right,' I say. 'I'm obsessed. Just like Lizzie! Why is it so hard to let it go when it obviously isn't working?'

'Is like it is,' she says. Sophia doesn't waste words.

That night I can't sleep. I wake up at 2am after dreaming about my friend and mentor Conrad, who died twenty years ago. In this dream, I'm with a woman who somehow isn't what she seems. Conrad is trying to tell me something, but I'm not paying any attention to him. Then I realise that he's saying something important about this woman but, just as I realise it, I wake up. I lie there for a long time, wondering what he was trying to tell me.

🌿

When I was younger, I enjoyed many adventures with Conrad, not only out there in the world but also adventures of the mind. He was extraordinarily well read and a real inspiration to people like me who didn't buy into the current consumerist world view.

Although we agreed about many things, he approached life in quite a different way. He was much more at home in the mythopoetic world than he was in my practical world of 4x2s and VAT returns, so we often ended up getting frustrated with each other. When I tried, as I often did, to dislodge him from his imaginal world and return him to the forensically 'real' one in which I felt more at home, he would lecture me: 'The trouble with you, Chris, is you always have to be *right*.' And that, I reflect, is exactly what I'm now doing with my faithful group of eco-warriors in Bristol.

I suppose I'm not much different from poor old Lizzie in this respect. If you argue with her interpretation of reality, it's because you're a cruel, unfeeling person who wants to do her harm. If you argue with mine, you're an idiot who just doesn't 'get it'. We're very black and white; there are as few grey areas in my world as there are in Lizzie's. She just has a few more holes where her brain should be.

Somehow, for me, Sophia's casual remark becomes a kind of turning point.

🍃

Conrad was born and brought up in a terraced house in a working-class area of Middlesbrough where they didn't have very much, and what they did have was useful rather than beautiful. Back in the sixties, he introduced me to the wild part of the Dales where he had his hideaway. Jane and I ended up living off-grid in a cottage about a mile away. I was with him a few years later when he died, and the experience of his death helped me to lose my own fear of dying.

Towards the end of the Second World War, when he was only nineteen (and I was three), he served as a tail gunner in Lancaster bombers. He was a prime target for the Me109s which came roaring down on the lumbering bombers as they approached their targets in the Ruhr. Tail gunners had a notoriously high casualty rate but, by the grace of God, he survived. He went on to win a scholarship to Cambridge University, where he studied what was then called Moral Sciences with the great philosopher Ludwig Wittgenstein.

After graduating, he dropped out for a while and lived on his own in a forest on a mountain in the Lake District. He took me there once to show me what it was like, and to demonstrate how he managed to keep a low profile and successfully avoid the gamekeepers. I must confess that I was in awe of him, and felt flattered that he counted me as a friend. Later he worked for my building company in London, where he distinguished himself by his ability to drink four pints at lunchtime and still go back to work and build a stud wall that was almost straight. Or at least straight enough to survive a casual glance.

He was a scholar of what he called 'cosmology', by which he meant that esoteric area which embraces philosophy, mythology, religion and occultism. He taught me how to cast horoscopes and read astrological charts, which I did with great enthusiasm for many years. He had worked with Jung's close collaborator (and lover) Toni Wolff, and he taught me to take my dream life seriously (or at least, to watch out for 'serious' dreams amongst the usual surrealist entertainment) and to be aware of 'signs' and synchronicities in my life.

He was also an awkward bastard who alienated many of my middle-class friends (including my first wife, bless her cotton socks), and he didn't care if he upset people. But that was a small price to pay for our friendship. I

168

admired his single mindedness, although I was never able to emulate it, and at times he scared me shitless with his truculent dismissal of everything 'ordinary' as being unworthy of his attention. But there's always a downside to every good thing.

⬥

At this point in my life, I remembered and envied Conrad's spirit of ruthless determination, obsessed as I was with my project and worried as I was that it would be diluted and weakened by anyone who didn't understand it 'properly' (by which I meant 'in the same way that I did'). Consequently, I decided to honour Conrad with an all-night vigil at my 'sit spot' in the Coombe. I would invoke his spirit by ritually burning the last of his unfinished works, which had lain untouched in an old file on my bookshelves for twenty-five years waiting for me to do something with it. It would never be published now, as it had 'gone cold' many years earlier and I had no enthusiasm for it, nor had I ever understood what he was really aiming at by writing it. Rather than just throwing it away, I thought it would be best to make a fiery sacrifice of it at the very spot that I'd made special with hours of love and attention.

I chose one night in July when the moon was new because I wanted this to be the start of a new phase in my work. I prepared for it by buying a small tarp, nicking an old galvanised rubbish bin lid off a skip for a firepit, and some offcuts out of the same skip for fuel. I took my fold-up camping seat because my bones are old and cranky and they wouldn't survive a night sitting on a log. I took the fuel and the firepit up there a week in advance as it was a long way to carry it all in one load.

You're supposed to fast before a vigil, so on the chosen day I had nothing to eat. I was in my spot by 8pm, ready for whatever the night would bring. I strung up the tarp, laid the fire and found a place to sit comfortably where the breeze wouldn't blow the smoke into my face. (That never works, by the way; the smoke always knows where you're sitting.)

By 10pm it was quite dark and I could see a whole cloudless sky full of stars through the treetops. I heard the owls talking to each other up and down the Coombe; as usual, their conversation lasted about an hour, then they fell silent and all I could hear was the rustling of the leaves in the gentle breeze. I told myself I'd start the ritual at midnight and settled down to wait.

I was about to start the proceedings about an hour later, when I was startled by an owl calling very loudly. He couldn't have been more than twenty feet away. He called just once, *Tow-wooo!*, but there was no answering call from any of his mates. 'Oh my God,' I said to myself. 'That's Conrad,'. As I said it, I felt an urgent need to shit. At first I thought it must be fear, but I wasn't showing any of the usual signs of fear; my heart wasn't racing, my breathing was normal, and I felt quite relaxed. Then I realised what the cunning old bastard was signalling.

Years ago, when a group of us used to go up to his cottage in Swaledale for a few days, to get away from London, the first thing I would do was stride up the hillside and have a good old country crap. I'd take a trowel with me and bury it, then come down the hillside again feeling like I'd got rid of London and was ready for rebirthing in the clean air of North Yorkshire. Most people who knew about this were mildly amused, but Conrad regarded it as a significant ritual. As I'm sure he realised, on this occasion forty years later in the Burrington Coombe I had no trowel with me, I could no longer squat properly because of my artificial knee, and I hadn't brought any toilet paper.

'Fuck you, Conrad,' I said, divesting myself of my trousers and heading for the branch I usually sat on when I came up to my 'sit spot'. Projecting my rear end as far as I could over the edge of the chasm, I let fly into the darkness. Fortunately I had a couple of old tissues in my trouser pocket, which I carefully tore in half and used for what Rabelais called a 'breech-wipe'[2].

Now I was ritually prepared for a spot of book-burning. I lit the fire, made a solemn invocation and started feeding the pages of his *magnum opus* into the flames, one page at a time. There were 228 of them (I counted), so it took quite a while.

When I'd finished, after about two hours, I sat back in my folding seat and contemplated the darkness beyond the fire, which was still burning merrily in front of me. I must have fallen asleep because I had a dream in which I was climbing up a barren hillside towards an old house (which in the dream was my old house) when I became aware that there was water coming up out of the ground in hundreds of little springs all over the hillside. As it flowed down the hill it was carrying away my house, piece by piece.

I woke up with a start. The fire had burned down to the embers, which were still glowing red in the pitch darkness. I thought I could see a strange shape about six feet away on the other side of the firepit and I fancied it looked very much like Conrad, sitting on one of my kitchen chairs in the cottage that Jane and I had shared in North Yorkshire, just like he used to do thirty-five years earlier when he came to see us. He'd lean back in the chair and I'd worry that he'd break it if he leaned back any further. He was gazing at me thoughtfully as if he was wondering what all those years had done to me.

'Conrad,' I said, cheerfully, almost as if I'd been expecting him. He looked real, but at the same time there was a certain numinosity about him. If I tried too hard to see him clearly, it was difficult to be sure that he was really there, but if I relaxed my relentless need for certainty and looked at him indirectly so he appeared in my peripheral vision rather than head on, I could see that he was, indeed, present.

'That was well done,' he said. 'I'm surprised you kept it that long.' His voice sounded a bit weird, as if it were coming from inside me, but it was definitely his voice and not mine.

'You mean the manuscript?'

'Yes,' he said, this time with a trace of irony 'My *magnum opus*'.

'Yeah. Sorry, um – but I thought it was time for me to let go of it.'

He smiled and nodded. I felt a bit awkward. 'I carried it around for years, not knowing what to do with it...'

'Yes, of course. Was it burning you up?'

He was being ironic, of course – referring to something he'd asked me to do about a week before he died. He'd asked me to make a bonfire of all his *Golden Dawn* books, because they were 'burning him up'.

'No, I just did it to invoke you. Or maybe to provoke you.'

'I'd been wondering when you'd get round to it.'

'I hope you didn't mind...'

'Of course not! I owe you a favour anyway, because you chose to witness my ... departure. I was glad you were able to sit with me. It made a difference.'

'I learned a lot from that, about... you know, death.'

We sat for a while in silence. Part of me was thinking, *'This can't be happening! You're sitting here talking to a dead person.'* Another part said, 'Shut the fuck up, and pay attention.'

'That was a stupendous shit you sent me just now,' I ventured.

'That's your speciality, isn't it, getting rid of shit? Usually the kind that comes out of the back end of a bull.'

'Thanks, Conrad'.

We fell silent again. I was wondering how to ask the big question.

After a while, he said very quietly, 'So what brings us here?'

I sighed with relief, and told him all about my work, my colleagues, my frustrations, and my desire to access a bit of his ruthless spirit of detachment so that I could do the job properly.

He thought about it for a while. 'So this is *your* work?' he asked.

'Well, I think so! I've been trying to do it for three or four years now.'

'What made you take this up?'

I told him about Fire Valley and my obsession with the Divine Feminine.

'Ah,' he said. 'So you've been seduced by the Goddess. And what do you think she wants you to achieve?'

I heard the hint of irony in his voice again – he never could resist a bit of irony – and tried to ignore it. Instead, I told him how I saw the situation, the dire need for people (especially activists) to cultivate some self-awareness so that their activism would be more effective and they wouldn't be so prone to burn out, etc., etc.

'Yes, I see what you mean,' he said, dropping the irony. 'But what makes you so sure that you'll get better results by being ruthless?'

'Oh, I dunno, it's just how I feel,' I said, and immediately regretted it.

'Oh, it's how you *feel*, is it?' Conrad laughed.

I sat there feeling uncomfortable, wishing I hadn't got myself into this bizarre situation. I had forgotten how good he was at catching me out.

He let me stew in my discomfort for a few minutes. I had the impression he was actually puffing away at his pipe, like he used to when he sat in our cottage all those years ago. After a while, he continued. 'I'd be inclined to ask myself if I have to act like this just because I have a feeling?'

I thought about how many times I'd said that to one of my clients. The ones who wanted to murder their wife, or give up hope, or run away with their secretary? *First sit with this feeling, and you might find out what it's telling you about yourself.*

'I mean, it's very hard to be ruthless to order, unless you're very sure of yourself or terrified of losing. Most "ruthless" people are either psychopaths or they have a gun at their back. Psychopaths are deeply unconscious of their own terror, as you know. But you're not a psychopath, are you? And no-one is making you do this work. Not even the Goddess!'

'True,' I said wearily. 'So you think I shouldn't really be doing this?'

'You have to be the judge of that,' he said. 'The thing is, it seems to me you're assuming that this situation – this collapse you keep talking about – you're assuming that it can be understood in terms you are already familiar with, so it can be addressed by methods that are also familiar. Like meditation groups, self-awareness workshops, that kind of thing.'

'Why not? They're pretty basic, aren't they?'

'Yes, but are you really sure the situation you're trying to address can actually be changed by the kind of action you're preparing for? Maybe it's not that kind of situation. Maybe it's more about people being compelled to undergo a certain kind of experience.'

'There have been collapses before...'

'You keep talking about a "collapse".'

'Surely that's what it is, isn't it?'

'If you're convinced that's what it is, then obviously that's how you'll experience it. But if you don't keep on putting it into that particular box, there may be more to learn from it. The word "collapse" conceals more than it reveals. I mean, obviously from the point of view that you're inhabiting right now, then of course it's a collapse.'

'Oh.'

'Maybe you should think about it a bit more? There are other sources of information you could look at before you jump to conclusions. Steiner, for example.'

Conrad had introduced me to Rudolf Steiner's work way back in the seventies. It flashed across my mind that he was talking about Steiner's vision of the confrontation between humanity and the dark power known as Ahriman.

'But don't stop thinking about it the moment you feel you've got "the answer",' he continued. 'Keep the whole thing alive, question everything. Come on, you're not such a bonehead as you once were. You've matured a bit since I knew you.'

'Thanks,' I said. *Patronising bastard! Just like you were when you were alive.*

'Quite so,' he said with a wry smile, as if he'd read my thoughts again. 'And maybe pay a bit more attention to *how* you think. You tend to be a little too ... literal, if I may say so. Working with symbols isn't the same as working from an architect's drawing.'

'Of course not,' I said indignantly. 'Anyway I'm a bit better at working with symbols these days. At least, I hope so.'

'Yes, you are. But you still have a tendency to become a bit, shall we say, dogmatic.'

Unlike you, I thought, and gave him a cheery smile.

'Unlike me,' he acknowledged, and smiled back.

We sat in silence a bit longer. *The confrontation with Ahriman!* I was thinking, with some excitement. *It can't get much more interesting than that.*

As if in agreement, a sudden flurry of wind rustled the leaves all around us, then there was a long moment of silence. When Conrad spoke again, his voice was very quiet so I had to really strain to hear him. 'You need to learn how to live with one foot in each of the Two Worlds.'

There was a commotion in the undergrowth on my left, as if some small animal were being attacked. I looked round, but couldn't see anything. When I looked back, wanting to ask Conrad a few more questions about what he'd just said, there was no-one there.

In that moment I felt more alone than at any other time in my life. Something in me wanted to dismiss the whole experience as a feverish dream. I started talking to myself about psychosis, but my efforts to normalise everything just sounded a bit silly, and I had to laugh.

I piled some more wood on the fire and sat for a long time watching the red sparks flying and dancing in the heat. *You need to learn how to live with one foot in each of the Two Worlds.* Why did that resonate so strongly? And what on earth did he mean by 'the Two Worlds'?

*

At about four in the morning, just as the sky began to get a bit lighter, the owls started calling each other again like they usually do.

'Fuck you, Conrad,' I said cheerfully, for the second time that night. This time I really meant to say 'thank you', but it didn't quite come out like that.

References

1   www.unodc.org/documents/data-and-analysis/
    glotip/2016_Global_Report_on_Trafficking_in_
    Persons.pdf.

2   From his *Gargantua* and *Pantagruel* tales where he
    discusses the question 'What is the ideal breech-
    wipe?' He considers many possibilities but in the end
    he decides it's 'the neck of a goose'.

- 8 -

Stories

TUESDAY 8 AUGUST 2017

PRESIDENT TRUMP, WHO has been sparring with North Korea's leader Kim Jong-Un for a while and calling him rude names like 'Little Rocket Man', finally threatens to bomb his impoverished country off the face of the Earth. 'North Korea best not make any more threats to the United States,' Trump says, speaking from his golf club in Bedminster, New Jersey. 'They will be met with fire and fury like the world has never seen.'

They've been met with fire and fury before, back in the early fifties, when the USA dropped 635,000 tons of bombs on them to stop the Communists from taking over in the south. They bombed the country so thoroughly that by 1953 there were no substantial buildings – factories, transport infrastructure, schools, hospitals or blocks of flats – left intact in North Korea for them to destroy.

Many people aren't aware that they've already done it once before. Perhaps even President Trump himself does not remember; if he did, I'm sure he would understand why the North Koreans are deeply suspicious of him and

179

his country. They have been through the most dreadful suffering under their obscene autocracy, but this isn't just a question of competing ideologies. There's also a deep historical wound that has never been allowed to heal properly.

🍃

Lizzie is not particularly bothered by Mr Trump's bloviations. She was thirty years old when the United States last bombed the crap out of North Korea, her daughter was ten years old, and her first husband had just left her for another woman. Knowing Lizzie, I doubt if she had much awareness of what was happening on the other side of the world.

In her own tiny world – the one she inhabits at 36 Darnwood Road – she spends most of her time alternating between her two favourite characters, Poor Little Miss Alone-and-Bereft and Lady Elizabeth. Sophia doesn't take either of them seriously, so Lizzie develops a new drama, in which she's so ill that she's almost dead. Sophia calls it 'the coma drama', and invents a new name for Lizzie, 'The Mumia'.

'What's a momiya?,' I ask.

'Like in Egypt,' she says. 'When they take the dead people and put the bandages.'

From then on, poor old Lizzie is known to us and our small circle of friends as 'The Mumia'.

🍃

When she's not worrying about her health, Lizzie's default obsessions – 'going home' to one of the 'other houses', or finding out where 'they' are keeping her poor dead daughter

180

– are always liable to reappear.

One day I'm working quietly in my room upstairs when she knocks on the door. 'Chris!' she says. 'Can I have a word with you?'

'Of course, my dear,' I say, and invite her in.

'Thank you, dear,' she says. It's quite unusual for her to call me 'dear'. She sits down and takes a while to collect herself, then she launches into a long speech about wanting to go home to the 'other house'. She sounds urgent, pleading almost. Surely there must be something I could do to help her go home?

An idea occurs to me. 'Which of the houses do you want to go back to?' I ask as gently as I can manage. 'Can you describe it?'

'Oh, yes,' she says. 'It's got a green front door, and there's a cherry tree growing in the front garden.'

She's talking about the house she's living in now, of course. 'I think I know that one,' I say. 'Is there a pub on the corner of the street called the Waldegrave?'

'Yes, there is,' she says. 'A big pub with a car park behind.'

'Yes! That's the one. And can you see the church tower from the house, behind the trees?'

'Yes!' she says, excitedly. 'St James Church. I was there only the other day. A friend of mine died and I went to the funeral.'

I walk over to the window and point. 'Well, I think you're in luck, my dear! Look, there's the church tower, it's just over there. And if I look in this direction, I can just about see the pub sign. There it is! The Waldegrave. And just down there, in the front garden, there's a cherry tree. Look, you can come over here and see for yourself.'

Lizzie's excitement suddenly evaporates. On her face I see

only dismay and bewilderment. 'What?' she quavers.

'It's exactly as you said, Lizzie. I think you're already there, in your special house. Come and have a look!'

But Lizzie only becomes tearful and distressed. 'You don't really want to help me,' she wails. 'It's no good asking you for help. You just don't listen!' She breaks down, sobbing.

After all this time, I still haven't got used to the logic of dementia. The poor woman is consumed with anxiety and it has to attach itself to something – anything – as long as it's not the fact that she's losing her mind. Hence the stories. If you take away the stories, there's just a deep pool of anxiety and nowhere for it to go. No wonder she doesn't want to face 'reality'.

So she clings to her stories with terrible desperation because they are all she's got left to separate herself from the awful truth. In some respects we're all quite similar, clinging on to our stories about progress, democracy and so on. We may think that Lizzie's stories are a bit wacky, but they're no wackier than some of the conspiracy theories in which many people find meaning these days (QAnon, Bill Gates's nanobots, the Illuminati, 'Covid is a hoax').

If you don't believe what Lizzie says, it's because you are a cruel and heartless person who doesn't want to help her; if you don't believe the conspiracy theorists, you're one of the sheeple, the ordinary idiots who just don't get it. In these days of fake news and 'alternative facts', something like this was bound to happen.

❧

It is often said that we live our lives through stories, and on the whole it seems to be true.

You can sometimes get the essence of a person's story just by watching their body language. The Victim, for example, with his slumped posture, his sad eyes and his downturned mouth – he literally, physically inhabits his story. Anyone can get a sense of his unhappiness, even though he doesn't verbalise it. He wants people to feel sorry for him and they very often do. Or maybe they feel like kicking him repeatedly in the nuts, which is probably something to do with their own victim story, the one they suppressed a long time ago. They don't like him because he reminds them of it.

Being repeatedly kicked in the nuts would confirm his story about himself, which is why he's unconsciously trying so hard to get someone to do it.

I've often noticed myself acting (and feeling) as if life's a struggle and things are against me. For example, I used to catch myself plodding tiredly up the stairs when I had to fetch something. Perhaps I inherited this persecution story from my mother, because I remember it as being one of her favourites. 'Oh, what a nuisance!' she would exclaim, at least twenty times a day. It's still easy for me to fall into this kind of story, but it's also quite easy to get out of it again as long as I'm alert enough to notice how my Victim has taken over. This has the almost automatic effect of shifting me into a different story, where I wake up and find I've actually got plenty of energy after all. Suddenly I'm bounding up the stairs, two at a time. Where did all that energy come from? It wasn't there two seconds ago.

When I was a therapist, I occasionally used to recommend something similar to my clients. 'Try walking differently and see what effect it has on how you feel about yourself.' Change the personal story. Walk like a cat, for example, or a millionaire. A simple practice like this can teach us a lot about ourselves if we're interested and flexible enough to move a little way out of our comfort zone[1].

❧

We often inhabit a story based on rage, defeat, envy or one of the other negative emotions we're plagued with on a semi-conscious level. Eckhart Tolle calls this 'inhabiting the pain body'[2]. If you catch yourself falling into one of these states, it's worth noticing what it feels like in your body. There's an emotional pain somewhere, if you let yourself feel it for a moment. As Tolle says, the only way to heal this pain is to cultivate self-awareness. Then, even if we can't eliminate stories altogether, it's possible to find one that supports a healthier life.

This doesn't mean we can choose whatever version of 'reality' happens to appeal to us, though. Positive Thinking, insofar as it promises this kind of fantasy heaven, is an interesting example of the confusion produced by a culture that's mesmerised by 'success'. It can work very well when it's properly applied, but this doesn't mean that we can just make up a story that we'd *like* to inhabit and *insist* that it will come to pass. Some Posi-Think practitioners seem to believe that the universe is somehow magically bound to 'manifest' whatever we choose to imagine, regardless of the laws of *karma* or the limits of what's actually possible for us, wide though these are.

As a therapist, I once worked with a man who was completely sold on Positive Thinking. He'd been fine when things were going well for him, but now that they weren't going so well you could sense his barely-suppressed panic.

I guess he came to see me because he imagined I'd be able to show him how to try harder. I suggested it might be better for him if he made friends with his fear rather than keep on trying to push it away, but it was literally impossible for him to do this while continuing to inhabit his Positive Thinking story. Poor guy; he eventually told me I was useless and he'd rather spend his money on another intensive course in Posi-Think because he obviously couldn't have been doing it right. It stands to reason, doesn't it? If he'd been doing it right, things would still be going well for him, wouldn't they?

I hate to say it, but the story of the Green New Deal (GND) sounds to me suspiciously like Posi-Think. People believe in it for the best of reasons, but this doesn't necessarily mean it's going to work. I wish it were otherwise because I have great respect for those few politicians who are trying their hardest to make it happen. They are interested in social justice just as much as in reducing CO_2 emissions, and God knows we need a bit of that after forty years of cold-hearted neoliberalism.

If enough people take the GND seriously, it might lead to a reduction in the use of fossil fuels and keep the faltering economy going a bit longer. But to what end? More of the same, but with a cleaner energy source? That's a bit like saying we can continue with our war on Nature, but we'll use nice clean bombs instead of the nasty dirty ones we've been using up till now. Of course, as ever, the devil will be in the detail, so we can only hope that if some version of a GND does see the light of day it will have been thoroughly researched before it is rolled out.

🍃

It seems like we can't really avoid living in some kind of story, even though we're not always fully conscious of it, because that's how we human beings give shape to our lives. The stories we live in tend to give their characteristic shape to every situation we encounter, including one that threatens to bring our entire civilisation down.

Here's what writer George Monbiot says about it:[3]

When we encounter a complex issue and try to understand it, what we look for is not consistent and reliable facts but a consistent and comprehensible story. When we ask ourselves whether something 'makes sense', the 'sense' we seek is not rationality, as scientists and philosophers perceive it, but narrative fidelity. Does what we are hearing reflect the way we expect humans and the world to behave? Does it hang together? Does it progress as stories should progress?

...A string of facts, however well attested, has no power to correct or dislodge a powerful story. The only response it is likely to provoke is indignation; people often angrily deny facts that clash with the narrative 'truth' established in their minds.

The only thing that can displace a story is a story.

A good example of this is the story that led 52% of the Brits who voted in the 2016 referendum to vote to leave the EU. Readers of the *Telegraph*, the *Sun*, the *Mail* and the *Express* had been bombarded for years with negative 'news' about the EU, in accordance with the wishes of their billionaire owners, so this was a story with which they were already thoroughly familiar. After winning the vote, large numbers of them turned their protest into a self-righteous crusade, complete with heroes, villains, betrayals and at least one glorious rebirth. The Remainers had plenty of reasoned argument on their side but no heroic story to match, so they were always at a disadvantage.

How we respond to the ecosystem crisis depends very much on what story we choose to frame it with. For the futurists, it's just another inconvenient obstacle on the journey towards a glorious techno-Utopia, where all our problems will be solved by a combination of artificial intelligence, space travel, transhumanism and wishful thinking. For the climate change doomsters, it's a story of inevitable near-term human extinction.

My own 'story of the world' always tended to emphasise the shadow side of our supposedly enlightened civilisation, so I chose to see it as an apocalypse and found plenty of evidence to support my bias. Lately I've come to see it in a more nuanced way, but I still think the most powerful stories about it – like the Extinction Rebellion manifesto – are not ones that try to paste a layer of Positive Thinking over the top of a decaying corpse. They say, quite rightly I think, that the only way we're going to at least limit the damage is through mass civil disobedience, and this involves a large element of personal risk. Not perhaps as deadly as the risks that indigenous people have to take to save their threatened homelands in the Amazon rainforest, for example, but nevertheless very real.

*

For the last three or four hundred years, as Monbiot points out in his book, our common foundational story has been 'The Story of Progress'. Those who uncritically inhabit this story nowadays tend to assume that whatever new arrangement we invent is obviously better than the traditional arrangement it replaces, especially if it involves a more hi-tech (or 'smart') approach. This leads many of them to look for purely technical solutions to the problem of climate breakdown, like massive renewable energy or geoengineering projects, so that we can keep on 'making progress' without any major changes in our recklessly wasteful lifestyle. Others might see this as dangerous nonsense, especially if they feel that it's our slavish reliance on technology (what James Kunstler calls Techno-Narcissism) that's responsible for the mess we find ourselves in[4].

But there's another, deeper story that underlies the story of progress, a story so fundamental to our way of living that it's hardly even noticed. *If you want to 'make progress' in a technical sense, you have to understand the world as a collection of things that can be taken to pieces and put together in a new way.* So, the basic idea that underlies our story of progress is what Charles Eisenstein, in his monumental work *The Ascent of Humanity*, calls 'The Story of Separation'[5]. This story tells us that we are all separate from one another and from the natural world around us, enclosed in a boundary called 'myself' which ends with our skin and relates to the outside world as a complete, self-sufficient unit.

We've met this already; it corresponds to the left-brain mode of perception we were discussing in Chapters 2 and 4, which I ended up calling 'machine mode' because it has allowed us to radically change the world in a way that's been largely determined by the specific technologies we have developed. We are saturated with this story to such an extent that we just call it 'common sense', i.e. for most of us, it's an unquestioned statement about the absolute nature of reality.

As we have seen, this is a relatively recent development which has led over the last three or four centuries to the establishment of the rational, science-based world with which we are familiar today. We find it almost impossible to see the Story of Separation as 'just another story' because it has been enshrined in our language, which is geared towards making logical statements that relentlessly separate subject from object. That's the trouble with stories: until we become more conscious of them, it's impossible for us to question the assumptions on which they are based. And it's often quite difficult to persuade people that there are limits to what they call 'common sense'.

But as we saw earlier, this coin has two sides. The Story of Separation is balanced 'on the other side' by what Charles Eisenstein calls the Story of Interbeing. The word 'interbeing' sounds a bit strange (it's a name coined by the Buddhist monk Thich Nhat Hanh), but it could equally well be called 'wholeness' or 'relationship', or even 'universal love'. It corresponds much better with the right-brain mode of perception outlined in Chapter 2. As a story, it has been with us throughout recorded history, and the most ancient versions of it (which we call 'myths') are still kept alive by indigenous people. It lies behind all spiritual teachings; it has even been adapted by secular humanism and applied in areas of social justice, political reform and, more recently, environmental protection.

This balancing mode of Interbeing has always seen the natural world as one essential wholeness, grounded in a spiritual reality rather than a material one. It may or may not derive from a supreme being (for some of us, it feels more like an inherent quality of the universe itself) but it's described as 'spiritual' because it is the active expression of a much more subtle *meaning*, not just the deterministic outcome of the interacting properties of material *stuff*.

🍃

These two foundational stories, derived from different but complementary modes of perception, are both 'true'. It's not difficult to see how closely they correspond to the preferential ways in which the world is seen and understood by the two hemispheres of the brain, as described by Iain McGilchrist in *The Master and His Emissary*[6]. Separation, which is more the province of the left hemisphere, has become the foundational mode in which Western civilisation now recognises (*re-cognizes*) the world. But they are not rival stories (or modes of perception) in the sense that one of them is 'right' and the other one 'wrong'.

We couldn't deal with the external world if we weren't able to identify separate parts of the whole, so our sense perceptions have to be organised to give the impression of separateness. But our inner sense of the world has never been organised like that; inwardly, in our subjective world, we see things in a much more holistic way through feeling and intuition as well as intellect. This is just as true now as it was several thousand years ago, although we don't necessarily think about this wholeness in the same religious/mystical/mythical way as we did then.

But there are still crucial ways in which the wholeness that we see (or visualise) is more important, or more fundamental, than the separateness of its identifiable parts. Think of a piece of music, a beautiful landscape, a bottle of wine, a good friend, a love affair, or a sense of community, for example. Wholeness encapsulates not just complexity, but also *value*, *significance* and *meaning*.

Above all, it's this mode of seeing that lies behind our capacity for caring. If we genuinely value and care for each other and for the natural world in which we live, it's not because we've made a calculation but because we feel some kind of empathic connection.

In recent years this has become increasingly difficult. As psychoanalyst Sally Weintrobe has pointed out, our natural capacity to make these connections has been deliberately undermined by those who set the agenda for our consumer societies, especially the so-called Neoliberal agenda that has been so active since the Reagan/Thatcher revolution of the 1980s. In her book *Psychological Roots of the Climate Crisis*[7], she shows how this has led to the disastrous state of affairs we now find ourselves in – because although there have been unmissable signs of climate change for a long time, the so-called 'masters of the universe' have almost succeeded in suppressing the real story through their control of the media, while keeping us in a kind of trance state where most of us prefer not to know too much about it. They have done this using yet another story, the modern equivalent of a fairy story, which says that our security, our happiness and our fulfilment as human beings depend on our enthusiastic participation in the consumer economy. This fairy story assumes that the magical consumer economy is capable of limitless growth that Planet Earth can support forever without suffering any harm.

❦

We may have a natural feeling for wholeness, but it's not so easy to describe what 'wholeness' actually is. We can't really understand it by logical thinking. Instead, as Jeremy Naydler has pointed out in his study of the Machine[8] (quoted in Chapter 4), we need something more like what we used to call 'contemplation'. That's a more subtle and inward process that requires time, patience and a certain humility. Nowadays we may find this difficult because we are so thoroughly oriented towards *doing* (i.e. manipulating the external world) rather than *being* (i.e. inhabiting, understanding and participating in it through our own inner world, which includes feeling as well as cognition). The best we can do with logical thinking, as in the scientific study of ecology, is to understand how the separate things we see 'out there' interact with each other so as to make up a whole.

This difficulty is well described by Henri Bortoft, in his seminal work on holistic science, *The Wholeness of Nature*[9]: *Our everyday awareness is occupied with things. The wholeness is absent to this awareness because it is not a thing among things. To everyday awareness, the whole is no-thing... When this loss happens, we are left with a world of things, and the apparent task of putting them together to make a whole. Such an effort disregards the authentic whole.* (p.14)

In other words, the whole that we construct is not the authentic whole. Bortoft describes wholeness as an 'active absence' because, although we can't identify it in the same way we identify a thing, we are nevertheless aware of it as a meaning or a quality which has a definite resonance in our feeling nature. We can easily recognise this, at least implicitly, despite our reliance on the story of separation.

But we still seem reluctant to understand the natural world in this way, probably because we have lost our feeling for the sacredness of our Mother Earth that was pervasive until a few centuries ago, and replaced it with soulless categories like 'natural capital' or 'the environment'.

Interviewed in *Emergence* magazine recently, the writer and ex-activist Paul Kingsnorth made this comment[10]:

Increasingly, it seems to me that the kind of spiritual void, if you want to use that word, at the heart of our culture is the essential thing. If you don't hold anything sacred at all, if you don't believe as a society or as an individual that there is anything greater than you, whatever that thing is, then everything is about you. If you have a society that doesn't believe anything is greater than itself, then it becomes— what we've become I think—narcissistic and materialistic, really almost a society of what Buddhists would call "hungry ghosts", wandering around and eating the world.

...I was always very struck with the meaning of the word "holy." It is an Old English word—the original word is hālig, which also meant whole, as in not separated, not divided. If you see the Earth as whole, you have a very different relationship to it than if you see the Earth as a collection of separate parts which you can use and manipulate. I think that we as a society don't hold anything sacred anymore, and, as you say, even using words like sacred or spiritual will invite derision in a lot of quarters. We've convinced ourselves that everything that matters can be measured.

I think that's the heart of the crisis that we have... That old animal, emotional, spiritual connection to the natural world—we just pretend it isn't there anymore, or that it's just a bit of fluff that doesn't really matter, but it does. I think it's the heart of things.

So the way we actually experience 'interbeing' or one-ness is very different from the way we experience separation. We can't access it by any process that can claim to be objective or by logical thought; it's only accessible through inner sensing or intuition. This is unique, wordless and direct, a kind of psycho-spiritual 'coming-into-presence'.

In the inner, experiential world of one-ness, everything exists through relationship. If you really experience a tree, for example, it's as if you can feel its tree-ness inside yourself. This is what I mean by saying that this world 'exists through relationship'. If you haven't done this little exercise before, try it next time you go for a walk in the woods. Of course the tree also exists as a separate object, but your inner relationship with it means you are now giving it a kind of personal value. It means something to you, even if it only lasts for the brief interval of time when you actually make the connection. This makes your perception of it essentially different, especially when some corporate vandal wants to chop it down to make way for a 'development' (as the famous Cubbington Pear was chopped down recently to make way for the HS2 line)[11].

And if we contemplate it seriously – if we take the time to let it really sink in – we may find that since everything in the natural world is related to everything else, all relationships must spring from some primordial one-ness, whether that is conceived as God, or emptiness, or the Great Spirit. This is like saying that there is something of God in every human being, or every tree, or even (to misquote William Blake) every grain of sand.

For believers in scientific materialism, the primordial one-ness is still there but it has been reduced to a single point in pre-historical time, known as the 'Big Bang'.

194

Hence, from this point of view, *all relationships appear to be ultimately causal*, although believers in scientific materialism may not always behave as if they were. The fact that science has banished the primordial one-ness to a particular point in time 13.8 billion years ago, says a lot about its relationship with the sacred. 'God' has been made to disappear from our experience of the world, only to reappear in the form of the original event that set it all up. Perhaps they think he was the one who lit the fuse.

Scientific materialism (that is, classical or nineteenth-century science) fits extremely well with the experience of separation. The newer sciences developed in the twentieth century (for example, quantum physics) don't fit nearly so well, so we are finding them much harder to grasp. But their appearance at this point in time says a lot about the place which humanity has reached in its collective evolution.

One of the best introductions to the 'new science' is still Gary Zukav's 1979 book, *The Dancing Wu Li Masters*[12]. Zukav is very clear, not just about the details but also about the meaning and significance of this new science. We're so used to thinking in separation mode (which is the way that classical science operates) that our entanglement with what we are observing (which is a feature of the new science) can seem to us like a mystery. It's not amenable to logical explanation.

It's worth taking a longer look at this, because there is a surprisingly close analogy between the duality revealed by the new science and the duality revealed by our study of the two different modes of perception.

❧

The new science tells us that light (or indeed, any other manifestation of radiant energy) can be seen either as a wave phenomenon or a particle phenomenon, depending on the way we set up our experiments. Do it one way and light (for example) behaves like a 'field' made up of 'waves'; do it another way and it behaves like very small particles (photons) that travel in straight lines through space.

This gives us an interesting analogy with the two modes of perception outlined in Chapter 2. In left-brain mode, our perception of reality shows it to be atomised, separated out into individual 'things' that interact in quasi-mechanical ways, just as light does when it behaves as separate photons or 'packets'. But in right-brain mode, our perception of reality is more like a field phenomenon, where everything is intimately related to everything else and ultimately cannot be separated.

On the level of human interaction, we could say that most bureaucratic transactions (e.g. getting your passport stamped) are analogous to particle phenomena because they are set up specifically to avoid any relationship between the parties. However, most normal human interactions are more like field phenomena, which set up a relationship between the participants even if it's only a temporary one. The same applies to relationships between people and Nature, for example, the relationship between the indigenous Shipibo person and the forest they live in, or between 'the old man and the sea', or between the mountaineer and the mountain. All these examples are intense, interpenetrating, and can sometimes be highly emotional; they are never just transactional or objective.

I must emphasise that this is just an analogy but, if we want to, we can play with it and see where it takes us. What if reality itself is as malleable as our holistic perception of it? This would mean that our perception affects the way that 'reality' behaves, in the same way that the relationship between a woman and her pet cat (for example) changes both of them. This is what Paul Levy means when he says that we 'dream up' our reality[13]. This can just as easily take the form of a collective dream; it doesn't have to be personal. A well-known example of this is the so-called American Dream, which animated the USA for most of the twentieth century until they were collectively mugged by reality during the twenty-first.

Taking this a bit further, can we put ourselves in touch with a reality that isn't even there yet? After all, this is what innovators do when they bring something radically new to the market. For example, we can be fairly sure that a way will be found to connect people's brains with the so-called Cloud, because so many engineers are working their socks off to dream it up. Whether this is a good idea or not is beside the point; something like it is probably going to happen. What sort of experience that will turn out to be is anyone's guess.

Or we can start to visualise (imagine, dream up) a much healthier reality, such as the one which Charles Eisenstein characterises as *The more beautiful world our hearts know is possible*[14], a more balanced, slower, more intimate, less materialistic world, in which human beings re-learn how to live in harmony with Nature without being compelled to destroy her in the name of industrial growth. And by nurturing this vision (for that's what it is, a vision) we can perhaps bring it closer to reality and act from inside it so that one day, when the engineered visions of a hi-tech future have been buried in the rubble of our decayed civilisation, it can become mankind's new home.

*

Sometimes people fall deeply into the perception of one-ness more or less by accident and describe it as a profound mystical experience. Claire's story in Chapter 2 is like that. Mother Nature can do this for us on the rare occasions when we become totally absorbed in her.

Here's another example, from Fritjof Capra, author of *The Web of Life* and *The Tao of Physics*: *...I had a beautiful experience which set me on a road that has led to the writing of [The Tao of Physics]. I was sitting by the ocean one late summer afternoon, watching the waves rolling in and feeling the rhythm of my breathing, when I suddenly became aware of my whole environment as being engaged in a gigantic cosmic dance.*

Waking up to one-ness can have the impact of a mystical experience because, as we've seen, it's essentially an inner world; by this I mean that the one-ness we're experiencing isn't 'out there', separate from the person who is experiencing it. On the contrary, we experience ourselves as being part of it. This is why such an experience is often characterised as 'deep'. Indeed, it can have potentially infinite depth, whereas the World of Separation has almost infinite *extent* but very little *depth*. This is a crucial distinction because we commonly refer to this external world as the 'real world', which implies that we see our inner subjective world as unreal. The story of separation has been powerful enough to separate us even from ourselves.

Before the story of separation got such a hold over

us, life was experienced very differently. Indigenous (pre-civilised) people, who live closer to the land, saw themselves as an integral part of the natural world. This (as they saw it) was not in any way separate from what we now call the 'spiritual' world, so their inner lives (and their foundational stories) were very different from ours. Dreaming was an important activity (or rather, state of being) for many indigenous people, some of whom still retain this ancient way of relating to Mother Earth. Their stories, for example the song lines of the original Australians, tend to be specifically structured around their own natural context (forest, desert, mountain, savannah), but there are structural similarities across many different so-called 'primitive' mythologies that point towards common origins and suggest a time when human beings were constituted very differently from the way we are today.

Carl Jung characterised the 'primitive' or pre-civilised consciousness, from which these alternative stories are derived, as a *participation mystique*, deriving this notion from the French philosopher Lucien Levi-Bruhl[15]. In this mode of perception, nothing is completely separate. Everybody participates in the same one-ness, which is given its story-like character by the symbolic or mythological attributes of every living being and, indeed, every observable natural formation as well.

This world of symbolism can be brought to a high art as it was, for example, by the ancient Egyptians. For them, a falcon wasn't just a common bird of prey, it was an embodiment of Horus, God of the Sky, whose right eye was the Sun and whose left eye was the Moon. An ibis wasn't just an elegant wader, it was an embodiment of

Thoth, God of Magic and Science, whose gift of language enabled them to understand the way the world worked[16]. This world of symbols was as real to them as our world of external perceptions is to us. For them, the falcon *was* Horus; it didn't just remind them of him.

It's quite hard for us, in our flat, levelled-out world of facts, to understand what it was like to live in a world as alive and vibrant with meaning as that.

Participants in the Story of Oneness, like those ancient Egyptians, naturally see themselves as being part of the story. They don't see the story as something separate from themselves that they 'believe in'. This is how we talk about such stories nowadays because our story is one of separation, so we assume that their story can't possibly be real. 'It's just a primitive belief,' we say, using this description in a pejorative sense, meaning childlike, naïve, uncultured. 'We got rid of superstitions like that ages ago.'

Jung did indeed characterise this way of seeing the world as 'primitive', but I don't think he was using the word in a pejorative sense. On the contrary, he was well aware that the ancient wisdom embodied in it was becoming more and more relevant in the modern age as our destruction of the natural world around us becomes more frenzied and unstoppable.

According to Jung, we never really discarded those primitive beliefs. What we actually did was to assimilate the spiritual world around us into our own subjectivity, so it has mostly taken up residence in the inner world we now call 'the unconscious'. It has been given this name, obviously, because we're not normally aware of it, but it still speaks to us in symbols, dream images and subtle intimations of another reality whose demons plague us, and whose angelic beings bring us comfort. But most of all, it still brings us *meaning*, which is very poorly represented in the World of Separation.

The more we hide ourselves in our separateness, which is devoid of deep connection or intrinsic meaning, the more inwardly hungry we become. The more we try to avoid feeling our inner hunger for wholeness, the more we crave all the substitutes that the World of Separation provides for us, like power, status and the ownership of property. Thus we try to replace *being* with *having*, which will never work no matter how hard we try.

&

In the ancient wisdom traditions, the World of Separation was regarded as a kind of clever illusion – *maya*, the World of Appearances in Vedantic philosophy[17]. Nowadays it's regarded as the only 'real world'. It seems that we have grown so used to believing that only one of these stories can be true that we now find it hard to hold both of them in balance, but above all this is what the world needs now. For example, we need good science, but not in service to the consumer economy. Rather, we need it in service to the Earth, to help us regenerate and care for the natural world that supports us instead of filling it with junk.

On a more personal level, perhaps we also need to abandon 'common sense' for a while and take stock of our lives to see if there are ways we can resist or avoid the influence of the ubiquitous Machine. Do we really need to live such complicated lives? Do we really need to keep buying more *stuff*? Can we be more in touch with ourselves, more sensitive to the needs of others, more caring? These are questions that can only be answered from a right-brain perspective, which means from 'inside'. It's no good looking at them logically, turning them into a to-do list, or making them into a program. They need to be pondered, contemplated, lived in.

This means that we have to hold both ways of seeing the world in balance, which is quite an art. I guess this is what Conrad meant when he talked about 'living in the Two Worlds'. Rudolf Steiner was also referring to this balance with his two 'devils', Lucifer and Ahriman[18]. For him, they weren't really devils at all in the sense of evil beings; they were more like twin pillars of reality. He said we needed to be in an equal relationship with both of them, even though they pull in different directions. They are only devils insofar as either of them on their own, if taken to an extreme, will lead us into a land of dangerous illusions.

Lucifer (which is Latin for 'bearer of light') wants us to become spiritually omnipotent, but Ahriman wants us to become omnipotent in the material world. For Steiner, the way they are reconciled – the third pillar of reality, the point of synthesis in the dialectic – is embodied in the figure of Christ. In this triad, Christ stands as a symbol for self-awareness, which doesn't come naturally but needs to be cultivated deliberately. Self-awareness doesn't just happen on its own, like physical growth. Many very successful people, including those in positions of power, appear to have almost zero self-awareness. This is one of the reasons why it will be very difficult to avoid the worst effects of climate breakdown.

Depending on our state of mind, one of the two (usually Ahriman, for us moderns) tends to dominate. When we are anchored firmly in the external world (as most of us are most of the time because of our cultural conditioning), it's hard to hold onto the inner one. We usually have to sit somewhere quietly and take ourselves into a more reflective state where we can allow the inner world to come into being in its own way and its own time. We can't use force on it in the way that we can on the external world.

This, more than anything else, is the task that confronts us now as Ahriman threatens to take us over completely with his hideous hi-tech world of robotics, artificial intelligence and pervasive control.

If we don't have the patience for this task, we may live our lives almost completely immersed in the World of Separation, and then it becomes very hard for us to acquire the necessary perspective that enables us to really change anything. Our soul life simply disappears underground and reappears, as Jung said, in the unconscious. And if we take no notice of that too, it externalises itself in the form of 'luck' (either good or bad), chance events, accidents, illnesses and so on. What's inside is always manifested outside[19] in some way, and our fascination with technology is manifesting now in a particularly dangerous and suicidal way.

We can't fight this as if it were some kind of psychological war; all we can do is to be more self-aware, which means being present to our inner experience, watching it unfold, and maintaining a degree of detachment from it. This is nothing like the kind of heroic quest to overcome evil that we love to see acted out in the movies, but it's what we need right now because it will open the door to the deep transformation that our world needs.

In its simplest form, being present means keeping part of our attention 'at home', anchored in the body, rather than allowing it to wander about in a way that makes it available for capture by whatever stimulus happens to be around. The advertising industry (including platforms like Facebook) has become adept at grabbing our attention so that it can steal our energy and use it to feed the infinite appetite of the voracious Machine.

Charles Eisenstein's view is that we will eventually break free from the dominance of the story of separation for two main reasons. One is that the disastrous consequences to which it has given rise will soon become so obvious that we'll *want* to change before it's too late; the other is that we already know, deep down in our hearts, that a very different world is possible. In this respect he's similar to Eckhart Tolle, who makes essentially the same prediction about our blinkered consciousness in *A New Earth*[20].

I want them to be right, even though I'm sure this transformation won't be easy. The story of separation has bccn stamped indelibly on practically every artefact, institution, concept, habit and way of life that our civilisation has ever produced, with the honourable exception of some of the great art (music, painting and sculpture, architecture, poetry, theatre), the occult, and mystical traditions associated with the various religions. Short of some kind of miracle, it seems to me quite possible that only a really big, world-wide disaster will shake us enough to change our ways – one that will leave us in such a state of grief and helplessness that only then will we be receptive enough to take in something radically new. A financial collapse or a state of endless war might not, on their own, be drastic enough; we've experienced those already, and nothing changed.

Maybe it will take nothing less than the collapse of our entire civilisation. Or rather, as Conrad suggested, let's stop calling it 'collapse' and use a more apt description like 'unravelling', because that's how it is being presented to us. Complex supply chains as well as bureaucratic systems are starting to fall apart, and we will very likely find it too risky, or too expensive, to replace them. That's what 'collapse' actually looks like, in the early stages.

*

If our civilisation is finally unravelling, as many of us believe, it may provide exactly the right conditions for the kind of spiritual rebirth that will lead us out of this dilemma and open up some different possibilities for the future.

Our humanity is always there just under the surface, waiting for a chance to express itself. Life gives us plenty of these opportunities but they are especially abundant when there's a disaster, whether it's natural or man-made. At such times, human beings tend to do what human beings do best and behave in ways that enhance rather than diminish our humanity – that is, we help each other out. It's what most of us do when there's a disaster; we cease to bother about the differences between us and we all pitch in to help each other out.

There are so many stories about this that it hardly needs saying. Some of them are recounted in Rebecca Solnit's remarkable book, *A Paradise Built in Hell*[21]. A well-known recent example was the devastation in New Orleans caused by Hurricane Katrina in August 2005, where local people –

mostly poor black families – worked tirelessly to help each other out, while the federal authorities mostly got in the way and tried to prevent them from doing anything useful for themselves. There will be no shortage of disasters like this now that climate breakdown is starting to bite. A more recent, less dramatic example has been the phenomenal increase in the provision and use of volunteer-led food banks during the Covid crisis.

XR has something of this spirit in the way it is continually organising and re-organising itself to confront the climate emergency. Being in XR can feel like being part of a new tribe, a community with a strong moral purpose, something very different from the usual game of looking good, competing with each other and buying *stuff*. In this sense, it seems to me that XR is a real product of the Age of Aquarius as opposed to some of the *ersatz* ones we've been enjoying since the sixties. Perhaps this will be the age when human beings start learning to co-operate with each other on a global scale for the sake of the Earth which nourishes and sustains us.

It's in our hands. If that's what we want, we can start preparing for it now by embodying as much as we can the change we want to see. 'Be the change', as people often say. This means taking our inner life much more seriously and living from our deepest values rather than just mindlessly serving the Machine, living our lives from a different vision of the future, as if we really could be part of 'the more beautiful world', and caring for each other rather than just looking out for number one.

The simplest version of this is to spread loving kindness wherever we can, and not take part in the shouting, blaming and the vilification of those with whom we disagree. The younger generation already understands this much better than us oldies, and their voices will be heard more and more as the unravelling progresses.

It sounds too simple to be true. But the world of wholeness is, in its essence, just like that. Simple.

References

1 My favourite story in this vein was told to me more than twenty years ago by a woman I worked with. She was a timid soul but she had a wolf inside her. Normally she kept her wolf hidden, but she used to enjoy 'walking her wolf' on the way to work in the morning, as her route took her across two parks. One day she had an interesting confrontation in the lift at work. A man who'd always enjoyed teasing and mildly bullying her got into the lift with her and started playing his usual games. 'So I just let my wolf out,' she said, 'and kind of snarled at him. And to my surprise, he just stopped, and he's never done it again.'

2 Eckhart Tolle, *The Power of Now* (Hodder & Stoughton, 1999).

3 George Monbiot, *Out of the Wreckage* (Verso, 2017).

4 James Howard Kunstler, *Too Much Magic* (Atlantic Monthly Press, N.Y., 2012).

5 Charles Eisenstein, *The Ascent of Humanity* (North Atlantic Books, 2007).

6 McGilchrist's work was anticipated fifty years ago by the work of Robert Ornstein and others in the 1970s. See R. Ornstein (Ed.), *The Nature of Human Consciousness* (Freeman & Co., 1973).

7 Sally Weintrobe, *Psychological Roots of the Climate Crisis: Neoliberal Exceptionalism and the Culture of Uncare* (Bloomsbury Academic, 2021).

8 Jeremy Naydler, *In The Shadow of The Machine* (Temple Lodge, 2018).

9 Henri Bortoft, *The Wholeness of Nature: Goethe's Way of Science* (Floris, 1996).

10 https://emergencemagazine.org/story/the-myth-of-progress/

11 Check out 'The Felling of Cubbington Pear' by singer-songwriter Amy Naylor on YouTube. I never saw the

208

tree when it was still there, but her song made me cry.

12 Gary Zukav, *The Dancing Wu Li Masters* (Fontana Paperbacks, 1980).

13 See his website, https://www.awakeninthedream.com/

14 Charles Eisenstein, *The More Beautiful World Our Hearts Know is Possible* (North Atlantic Books, 2013).

15 C. G. Jung, 'Psychological Types', (*Collected Works*, Vol. 6).

16 See E. A. Wallis Budge, *The Gods of the Egyptians* (2 vols., Dover, 1969).

17 The word *maya* has a long history. The ancient Vedic sages saw it as a kind of miraculous power, the power of the spiritual world (the world of emptiness) to reveal itself in the manifest world of form.

18 See Rudolf Steiner, *The Influences of Lucifer and Ahriman* (Rudolf Steiner Press, London, 1954). There is not sufficient space to go into this properly here, but it's well worth some serious study.

19 This looks like an argument for Positive Thinking, but 'what's inside' includes everything, both conscious and unconscious. If our Positive Thinking depends on suppressing something, the suppressed truth will manifest just as much as the one we want to promote.

20 Eckhart Tolle, *A New Earth* (Penguin, 2009).

21 Rebecca Solnit, *A Paradise Built in Hell: The Extraordinary Communities that Arise in Disaster* (Penguin, N.Y., 2009).

- 9 -
The Good Old NHS

12 SEPTEMBER 2017

'THE GLOBAL LAND Outlook', a report issued today[1] by the UN Convention to Combat Desertification (UNCCD), gives an alarming view of the pressure on the land due to intensive agriculture. 'Each year,' it says, 'we lose 15 billion trees and 24 billion tons of fertile soil.'

It points to the increasing competition between the human demand for food, water and energy, and the so-called 'ecosystem services' that regulate and support all life on Earth. It says that during fifteen years, from 1998 to 2013, about 20% of the Earth's vegetated land showed persistent declining trends in productivity. Land degradation, it says, leads to competition for scarce resources, and hence insecurity, migration, and increasing inequality.

The report acknowledges that the modern system of industrial agriculture has resulted in huge increases in short-term productivity but it's based on monocultures, GM crops, fertilizers and pesticides, all of which seriously undermine long-term sustainability. It's the same old problem of declining marginal returns on increasing complexity (i.e. you solve a problem by using a techno-fix, but that creates six new problems that you don't notice at first but they turn out to be even harder to solve, and so on *ad infinitum*).

The agronomists tell us that industrial agriculture is the only way we're going to be able to feed the ever-increasing human population of the world. Traditional farming just won't cut it, they say; it's too small-scale and too labour-intensive. But that's only because farming has benefited so much from industrial machinery powered by cheap oil, and from the huge variety of chemicals designed to increase the productivity of otherwise depleted and damaged soil. It also depends on the capitalist dogma that bigger is always better, and efficiency is more important than any other economic value.

People get turfed off the land and forced to find work in the factories. Then the factories get automated, but the people can't return to the land because it's now owned by international agri-businesses whose sole aim is to make the maximum amount of profit out of it. They're only interested in feeding the world if, by doing so, they can make a lot of money for their shareholders and their senior managers.

Back in 2013 the Trade & Environment Review, a report by the UN Commission on Trade & Development (UNCTAD) written by sixty international experts, came to the conclusion that small-scale organic farming is the only viable way to feed the world in the long term without causing massive collateral damage to the Earth. Experts in regenerative agriculture have also shown that organic farming, if sufficiently widely practised, will generate enough bio-enriched soils to absorb a large proportion of the additional CO2 emissions that industry is pumping into the atmosphere. Why is no-one listening?

✿

Lizzie is not greatly concerned about land degradation caused by intensive agriculture. As far as she's concerned, food comes from Tesco, and Tesco has never let her down. So far.

Sophia has established a daily routine. It's essential to have a routine, she says, otherwise dementia patients get anxious and upset. They have chaos in their heads; they need order in their lives. Underneath their sometimes bizarre behaviour is a terrible fear that undermines everything they do.

Lizzie tries to create her own crazy sort of order by keeping her attention fixed on her obsessions, which is actually a cunning way of exporting her chaos into the external world. (She's not unlike ex-President Trump in this respect.) The daily routine is a way of grounding her so that she doesn't get too carried away by her fantasies. Unfortunately, no-one has yet found a way of imposing that kind of discipline on Donald Trump.

Most of her low-level obsessions are about pain and illness, and they always include a demand to see the doctor. Usually she thinks she has cystitis, because she has a pain somewhere in the region of her belly. 'I've got the most terrible cystitis!' she cries, clutching her stomach. 'It's agony!' If she's clutching her stomach it's more likely to be her perennial diverticulitis than cystitis, but we regularly take urine samples down to the surgery to be analysed, just to be sure. Getting her to provide a urine sample is a hit-and-miss affair, so to speak; even if Sophia succeeds in getting her to perform, the bathroom usually needs a spring clean afterwards. The lab never finds anything, and the 'cystitis' usually vanishes by lunch-time.

Lizzie uses pain, real or imagined, like Trump used Twitter before they stopped him, as a device to get attention. This sometimes makes it difficult to know how to respond. Sophia has learned not to react immediately but to make careful observations before she does anything. It's not hard to tell whether the pain is real or not.

❧

Something that keeps coming up is Lizzie's fear that she's going to have another heart attack. She had a minor heart problem a few years ago, for which she's taking the anti-coagulant drug Apixaban, and she thinks any pain in her chest is going to kill her. This perennial anxiety often makes her feel a bit panicky, which increases her heart rate, but it seems like the end of the world to her.

Sophia has witnessed heart attacks, she knows the symptoms, and whatever Lizzie is experiencing is not life-threatening. 'Calm down, Lizzie,' she says. 'You are just anxious, is not heart attack. Sit down and breathe a bit.'

Lizzie thinks that Sophia isn't taking her seriously, so she escalates the drama. 'I'm very ill!' she cries. 'Why don't you call the doctor? You want me to die!'

To which Sophia calmly replies, 'I am not impressed of your drama, Lizzie. Come and sit on your bed, and calm down.'

One day, when Lizzie is talking on the phone with her

well-meaning but equally anxious friend Mervyn, she tells him that she is terrified of having another heart attack, but 'the girl' won't do anything about it and doesn't care if she dies. Although Mervyn is well aware of Lizzie's tendency to dramatise everything, and he doesn't know anything about her medical condition, he instructs her that if she EVER feels a sharp pain in her chest area, she should ignore what 'the girl' says and IMMEDIATELY dial 999: no ifs, no buts.

By sheer coincidence the same afternoon, Lizzie imagines a sharp pain in her chest area, so she does what she's been told to do and dials 999. She tells the call handler that she's on her own, and she even manages to recite the address correctly, so experienced is she by now with making 999 calls. However she doesn't tell us what she's done, so we are very surprised when the ambulance stops outside and the paramedics knock on the door.

They are very professional. While they examine her, Lizzie seizes the opportunity to morph into the gracious Lady Elizabeth, and makes the most of it. She's charmed and suitably flattered when one of them says, 'Well, I hope I'm as fit as you are when I'm ninety-six.'

They interview Sophia and study the so-called 'care plan'. This is a document full of medical jargon, which looks very professional but doesn't convey much useful information about Lizzie's actual condition. For example, it describes her as having 'mild cognitive impairment' instead of telling the unvarnished truth that she's suffering from a serious and progressive mental derangement for which there is no known cure. It's possible to extract some sense out of it if you're used to all the euphemisms but, as 'the client' is supposed to be able to read it and challenge anything in it that she doesn't like, it can't say very much that's really useful.

The paramedics spend two-and-a-half hours of their precious time checking Lizzie out before they depart satisfied that there's nothing to worry about. After they've gone, I hear Sophia upstairs, instructing Lizzie in broken English not to call the ambulance next time, but please to call the carer.

'Why should I call you?' asks Lizzie with impeccable logic. 'You don't care if I live or die'.

That same night, Lizzie wakes up as usual in the wee small hours and lies there for a while feeling sorry for herself. Eventually she's rewarded by another sharp pain in the chest area, but she hesitates to call Sophia because a little voice inside tells her she'll get much more attention if she dials 999 again. So she reaches for the phone...

We are woken at 2am by someone banging on the door, ringing the bell and shouting.

'Ce dracu s'intampla!' I hear from the next room, as Sophia falls out of bed. I stumble out and collide with her on the landing. While she checks what's happening with Lizzie, I limp downstairs on my rickety-rackety legs, let the second pair of paramedics in, and give them a brief sitrep. Sophia reappears on the landing and calls downstairs, 'She just have panic, is nothing serious.'

The older paramedic sends the younger one upstairs while she takes some details. Lizzie greets him with a charming smile but he's not impressed. They spend about twenty minutes in the house. As soon as they've seen that she does indeed suffer from dementia, and that this is the second heart attack she's imagined in one day, they go away on another call.

Sophia instructs me to give Lizzie a stern warning (in unbroken English) that if she dials 999 again without calling us first, we will make sure she gets taken back to the

215

care home, immediately and forever. I carry out Sophia's instructions in a suitably loud and firm tone of voice. Lizzie listens, stony-faced.

She doesn't do it again, not because of my warning but because after this episode we disable the phone system at night. But she's impressed with the ambulance service. They have taken her seriously and given her a lot of attention, which she feels she doesn't normally get either from Sophia or from her GP practice.

Lizzie has no idea of the strain that the NHS is under. She was reared in a household where the doctor came whenever he was called, because he was expensive, so he knew that he would only be called when he was really needed. Maybe he stayed for half an hour, had a cup of tea and wore a cheery smile. Now the doctor only comes when he thinks there's a good reason, he stays ten minutes, looks as if he's in a bit of a hurry and occasionally prescribes another pill. Lizzie thinks he's useless, and nobody (except the nice ambulance people) has ever really cared about her.

🍃

In the so-called 'real world', the heroic practitioners of the beleaguered NHS struggle with this kind of thing all the time. The NHS stands as a symbol for our deeply ambiguous pursuit of modernity and all its manifold blessings. It was a brilliant idea at the time, when the economy was growing and we could afford to spend some of our taxes on a universal healthcare system. It has been brilliant during the Covid pandemic, when its practitioners have been compelled to work harder, and in more difficult conditions than most of us are capable of even imagining, just to keep us safe. But it has its limits. Even before Covid-19 struck, it had become almost unmanageably complex and difficult to control, and its costs were escalating faster than we could keep up with.

One of the main reasons why the NHS has become so overburdened is that we're growing a lot older, mainly because of public health improvements in areas like diet, sanitation and housing. However, a large proportion of us 'oldies' are living with chronic health conditions which are 'managed' (but not cured) by various constantly evolving and very expensive drug therapies. In other words, we're not really getting any healthier because our health has been compromised, at some level by the stressful, competitive, alienated society that progress has given us. Obesity, cirrhosis of the liver, cancer, heart disease, diabetes, depression, dementia ... so many kinds of debilitation, many of which only need one small external trigger (like the coronavirus) to become deadly.

Medical science is a good case study of the successes and failures of our left-brain, Story of Separation thinking. It is very good at identifying cause-and-effect relationships, as long as they can be understood straightforwardly as 'mechanisms'. It has understood Covid-19 in this way and managed it very well, despite the awesome complexity of the disease. It's also very good at prosthetics. I have two artificial hips and one artificial knee, remarkable pieces of engineering inserted by very competent surgeons, and I'm very grateful to the NHS for enabling me to continue walking about for so many years.

But our materialistic science is not quite so good at comprehending multi-level systemic relationships because it takes everything to pieces instead of contemplating the world in its wholeness. At the same time, it's hyper-rational, and pays very little attention to the information that we can derive from an imaginative engagement with our own felt senses. As John Michael Greer put it: *To deal with the psychospiritual roots of many common health conditions is to threaten the foundations of the scientific-materialist point of view*[2].

Worse than this, the GP service in the UK has been increasingly constrained by the adoption of standardised and bureaucratically monitored procedures and practices to save money. This has given GPs less and less scope to act as real doctors who know their patients and can see them sympathetically as human beings. Instead, they have been inexorably pushed towards seeing them as a collection of symptoms to which they must apply standardised, evidence-based treatments that are more or less the same for everybody.

This is the medicine of the Machine; indeed, the NHS is already using sophisticated computer programs to diagnose illnesses without any human doctor being involved. Dr David Zigmond, author of several books on the subject[3], calls this 'industrialised medicine', which sums it up very well.

*

Medical science has been brilliant at identifying the particular bacterial or viral agents that cause infectious diseases where they can see a one-to-one relationship between cause and effect. As a result, almost all these have been eliminated, at least from the richer parts of the world, apart from the most rapidly evolving ones like some of the zoonotic viruses. But illnesses with a stronger psychosomatic component, like arthritis or asthma, don't respond so readily to this approach. The symptoms can often be alleviated or suppressed, but when they are systemically related to our hyper-individualistic and competitive way of life (as many psychosomatic illnesses are), modern medicine often remains bewildered and powerless to make a real difference.

Asthma, for example, is usually understood as a biochemical response to atmospheric pollution, but it can also be understood as a psychosomatic response to deeply-held fear, especially in children with a particular sensitivity to criticism or a fear of being shamed. My father was asthmatic and, as a child, I was well aware of the anxiety he felt, although he tried very hard to conceal it. A clue to his fear of being shamed was the fact that he was prone to projecting it onto his children by shaming us. I could *feel* his anxiety in the way his breath got caught up in his chest, especially when things weren't going the way he wanted them to. His diaphragm wouldn't relax as it should have done in a normal breathing cycle, so he was having a panic reaction that locked the distorted breathing in place and made it worse in a kind of positive feedback loop. Asthma is a bit like a mild but never-ending panic attack.

What can modern medicine do about this? It can provide the sufferer with chemical inhalants that have the effect of relaxing the diaphragm at the cost of several potentially dangerous side effects, one of which eventually killed my dad. But it can't eliminate the underlying somatised anxiety, which will come back again and again however often these chemicals are inhaled. The asthma had been bred into my dad's body/brain system, and was impossible to shift by physical means. No doubt air pollution made it worse, but I doubt very much that was the root cause. When he was a child, there wasn't much pollution in the air; when he was born in 1912, there were hardly any vehicles on the road and he lived in a village many miles away from any factories.

The connection I made between asthma and deeply-suppressed fear is, of course, totally unscientific. I didn't even get there by a process of deductive reasoning but by feeling into it. I'm not particularly good at doing that, but in this case it just presented itself to me because I was curious about my father.

The clincher for me was my first therapist. I was the client from hell for a while because I questioned everything he said and tried hard to sabotage the 'therapeutic container'. I noticed that when I challenged him really strongly he started to exhibit mild signs of asthma because he felt stressed by my awkward behaviour. Whenever this happened, I was reminded of my father.

I made a similar connection when I became curious about my own arthritis. Someone with a Jungian background suggested I go into a trance-like state while sensing into my arthritic knees and see what images came up. What came up for me was a powerful image of a mad dog with blood all over its muzzle, held back by a strong steel chain.

The physical causes of my knee trouble were the sports injuries I suffered when I was seventeen, but there was something else as well. When I contemplated the image of the dog and the chain, it became clear how well it fitted with my experience growing up. I was already aware that because of the way I was shamed in childhood (not just by my father but by my experiences of being bullied at my first boarding school, which were much more damaging), I had turned my anger inwards and developed a strong internal bully whose task was to make damn sure I didn't ever attract the same kind of attention again. My internal bully did this quite successfully by mercilessly attacking every manifestation of 'weakness' that arose in me.

As a result of his efforts, I developed a tendency to go looking for trouble, a kind of 'fuck you' attitude that didn't serve me too well in an argument. You might describe it as an 'inflammatory' attitude. I developed arthritis, not just in my injured knees but in several other places as well. Arthritis is an inflammation of the synovial fluid in the joints and it has no cure in the medical sense. I believe mine at least is related to the kind of ruthlessness with which I tried to suppress my own 'weaknesses' in an effort to dominate all potentially difficult situations.

You could say that the mad dog was my anger, and the strong steel chain was the way I held it in my body.

❧

Many gifted and sensitive people have recognised the power of these psychosomatic connections and have become healers. Some of them, like the American writer and therapist Louise L. Hay, have become very well-known especially in New Age circles. Louise traces almost every dysfunctional pattern in her clients' bodies, feelings and external lives to patterns of negative belief that they hold about themselves, especially resentment, criticism, self-hatred and guilt[4]. As a basis for healing, Louise Hay recommends the constant use of positive affirmations to shift these negative thought patterns and has helped many thousands of people to change their lives.

This doesn't work for everybody, but it does work well for those people who are open to a strong belief that it *will* work for them. Louise consolidated her journey as a healer by curing herself of cancer, which is no small thing.

Another healer/teacher who cured herself of a serious cancer using her own psycho-spiritual energy is Brandon Bays. Her self-cure story was quite striking, and led directly to the healing method she has been teaching for the last twenty years, known as The Journey[5]. On her two-day 'Journey Intensive' course, assisted by numerous volunteer helpers, she seeks to guide large groups of people through essentially the same experience she went through as the basis for her own self-cure. Her helpers are all people for whom The Journey has made a big difference in their lives.

I took the course a few years ago, and found that Brandon – although she was clearly speaking her own truth and wasn't faking anything – couldn't overcome my long-standing scepticism about motivational speakers. However, the experience had a beneficial effect on many people who were there and I've no doubt that her method can change people's lives if, like Louise Hay's clients, they are open enough to let it work on them without putting any obstacles in its way. Unfortunately I find it very difficult to let go of the habit of critical thought, so I wasn't able to let it work on me.

❧

Conventional science is compelled to deny that any of this is 'real' but, given that it works for some people, we have to acknowledge that there must be energies and connections that science simply can't see. Science is a belief system, just like any other framework for explaining the workings of the universe, but as such it has many weaknesses. One of them is that it can't fully comprehend the energies and structures that maintain life, which don't just work as causal mechanisms but as holistic systems. Most so-called 'complementary' therapies, from osteopathy to acupuncture, recognise this and work well for large numbers of people.

The limitations of scientific medicine are well illustrated by the curious case of the placebo. We all know about the so-called 'placebo effect', whereby people can be 'cured' by a pill containing nothing but sugar and chalk if they believe it contains an effective drug. This effect can be taken much further. It's now recognised that people have healed themselves from the most catastrophic physical conditions using only the power of visualisation.

There are many ways of approaching this; the framework I'm most familiar with is the one described by Dr Joe Dispenza[6], an American chiropractor who had six vertebrae in his spine badly crushed in an auto accident and healed himself by learning how to use the power of his own mind to reconstruct his damaged body. It sounds outlandish, but he was so convinced it could work and so determined to make it happen that he succeeded in completely rehabilitating himself by working very intensively on it for three months (*only* three months!). He spent the next few years studying neuroscience to find out more about the mechanisms that had enabled him to do this.

Since then he has run hundreds of meditation and healing workshops, as a result of which large numbers of people have cured themselves of conditions which were not responding to conventional medicine.

In his placebo book, he describes a plausible mechanism which, he says, makes this process scientifically understandable. He explains that the would-be self-healer has to engender a heightened emotional state in him or herself that will affect their thought patterns in the way that is necessary to bring about the complete conviction that it's going to work. This is not, strictly speaking, a scientific explanation in the usual reductionist sense but a straightforward empirical observation. As far as I know, there's no scientifically verifiable mechanism behind this; it's really a bit of a mystery, rather like 'the power of prayer'. But that wouldn't go down well with a sceptical readership.

If we turn to the work of Rudolf Steiner, we can find there a conceptual framework that gives us a more comprehensive view of these phenomena[7]. Steiner called this conceptual framework 'spiritual science', to distinguish it from the materialist-reductionist framework we normally call 'science'. He described the human being as having not just one but four interpenetrating 'bodies' of various levels of subtlety. The heaviest and most solid – the only one that materialistic science can 'see' – is the physical body. This, said Steiner, is interpenetrated by the etheric body, which is made out of the subtler energies that keep the physical body functioning as a whole and enable it to repair itself. (Then there's the astral body and the 'I' or ego, but they need not concern us here.) The etheric body exists at the level of thought forms, so the physical body can be directly affected through the practice of visualisation.

To a conventional scientist this sounds like superstitious nonsense, but if we engage imaginatively with Steiner's framework it comes to life in a remarkable way. I have some experience of this having (at Conrad's suggestion) cured myself of a bad attack of 'tennis elbow' in about a month solely by using visualisation techniques.

Such ideas as Joe Dispenza's are never going to be accepted in an organisation like the NHS because, like any other organisation of the State, it is constrained by the limitations of the Machine. The people who work in it may (and, thank God, when they can they usually do) come in with their own more human values, but the bottom line has to be dictated by the Machine, which can only understand and support machine-like concepts. These include ideas like efficiency, cost effectiveness, and evidence-based practice.

It's interesting how they make a big thing out of evidence-based practice because, although it can work very well in a case like Covid-19, it has its limits. The statistical evidence for the effectiveness of scientific medicine can sometimes appear very thin, while evidence for the effectiveness of various complementary medical models (osteopathy, for example, or homeopathy or acupuncture) is often equally as good or better. However, the practitioners of these modalities have a hell of a job trying to persuade the NHS to adopt them because they aren't 'scientific' in the usually accepted sense, even though they often produce very good results in the patients they treat.

It would be unreasonable to expect anything else from official institutions at the present time, but that's ultimately how the Machine looks after itself. This has its origins in a hidden process that has nothing to do with evidence or science, but is the result of a collective agreement at the unconscious level based on a need for every decision to be based on some kind of indisputable authority. This affects the evidence we are prepared to accept as being 'proper evidence', which has at least to pretend to be based on quantitative data and on a mechanism that can easily be explained within the separation paradigm. The pursuit of external knowledge through the exclusive use of left-brain thinking has led us into a minefield of unresolvable ambiguities, and we cling to our experts like children clinging to Daddy in an uncertain world.

⌀

We are social beings. On one level, everything we think, believe or do emerges as an adaptation to the social matrix in which we grew up. Systemic conditions, such as asthma, arthritis and many others, can perhaps be understood not just as physical ailments but also as different ways of somatising the psychological damage that can result from our unbalanced pursuit of individualistic and very masculine-oriented goals.

In our Western-style societies, many of us (me included) are haunted by the fear of being a 'loser'. At all costs we must conceal our weaknesses – or else the polar opposite: some of us prefer to make a theatre of them and throw ourselves on the mercy of others. (People tend to do this if it was the only way they could get the love they needed when they were children. I suspect our Lizzie knows all about *that*. Maybe she was aware on some level that Daddy's love was an *ersatz* thing, a family script, conditional on her playing her part as his little princess.)

'Staying strong' has become one of the most durable messages we give to our children in this time of fear and dislocation; it has to be when the world around us is seen as a competitive arena in which we're compelled to act as rivals for scarce resources on every scale from the personal to the national. By staying strong, we cut ourselves off from the intelligence we could have found in our own sensitive bodies if we had been prepared to pay attention. Instead, we look for intelligence in the abstract language of our heads.

All too often, by staying strong we avoid opening up to the love we could find in ourselves as well as each other. We find a substitute in the comfort of our own stubbornness and, of course, our secret addictions. By staying strong, we cut ourselves off from the healing we could find in Mother Nature if we remembered how to relate to her with respect; instead we are condemned to seek healing in the cold embrace of science.

I've no doubt that my need to stay strong has been as much of an obstacle as a strength in my own life's journey, including my experience a few years ago on the Brandon Bays course. It's no wonder that the mental and physical health of so many of us is so badly compromised.

It's also no wonder that we're hardly aware of this; we're so used to the situation we're in that we find it hard to imagine a different way of being. Even if some of us agree that it would be nice if people trusted each other and lived together in peace and harmony, the cynics are always keen to assert that human nature is basically nasty and brutish, and we need some kind of inner bully to keep us in order or we'd all revert to a state of primitive savagery. (When someone is voicing this kind of opinion, notice how strongly attached they are to this way of thinking. That, in itself, says a lot about where it's coming from.)

This belief in the 'inner bully' has always been closely

associated with the moral teaching of the Christian Church, although I don't think it has much to do with anything that Jesus Christ actually taught when he was alive.

Freud called this inner bully the 'superego', deriving his image of it from the repressive authoritarian rule of the nineteenth-century Austrian state. He saw it as a civilising influence that was needed to keep the unruly lower self (which he called the 'id') in order lest it break out of its cage and do some damage. This superego, or inner bully, is commonly called the 'inner critic' by psychotherapists, or sometimes the 'persecutor' or the 'Controller'. Philip Shepherd calls him the 'inner tyrant':[8]

The tyrant's fantasies live in us all. They show up in every urge we feel to assert a special status in ourselves; in every harsh judgement of another that raises or defends our worth by comparison; in every thought that we stand apart from nature, or need to control it; in every instance in which we harden against the Present, or withdraw from it; in every attempt to impose a top-down solution on our lives. Each of these tendencies is an urge to turn away from wholeness; any such urge is a contraction towards self achieved independence; and any such contraction is an attempt by the inner tyrant to exert control.

To accurately assess the threat posed by our identification with the tyrant, you might appreciate that, on a global scale, our alienation from the wholeness of the world and the anxieties stirred up by that alienation could justifiably be deemed the deepest crisis of our age – for it leads to a corrosion of our social support systems (family, community, society), the despoiling of the natural world and the heedless destruction of other species. It keeps us from seeing that the world's wounds are our personal wounds, just as it inclines us to try to heal our personal wounds by concentrating on the self and seeking to manage it, rather than by softening into the wholeness that is held by the harmonies of the Present.

'The anxieties stirred up by that alienation' is a phrase that resonates with me. When I was in my mid-fifties and wanted to make some changes in my life but did not quite know how to do it, I did a bit of volunteering, working one day a week in a rehab centre for homeless drug and alcohol users in Bristol. This place had been set up by a small group of Catholic monks who heroically raised half a million pounds to build it and keep it going, but the staff were all secular therapists. None of them (as far as I knew) were Catholics, or even religious at all.

Their 'clients' were brought in full of angry defiance (or in the case of the alcoholics, a kind of soggy defeat), but within three or four months those who had managed to stay the course were transformed into the most thoughtful, kind-hearted, sensitive people you could ever wish to meet. Essentially, the therapy had uncovered the vulnerable human being underneath all the aggression and the victimhood. It had also provided the conditions within which their newly-rediscovered humanity could flourish in a safe environment until it was sufficiently established for them to go back into the world with some chance of surviving without the drugs or the alcohol.

They had originally become addicted not because they were in some way inadequate or 'bad', but because their need for sensitive attunement to the world had been brutally violated, usually by their insane family lives. Some of the stories that came out during group therapy sessions were shocking, truly heart-breaking accounts of abuse and

229

neglect. No-one can survive that kind of treatment and grow up to behave like a 'normally adjusted' citizen.

The insanity in such families comes from repeated violations that were suffered by their ancestors and passed down from generation to generation. In Britain, for example, we had historical violations like the Enclosures of the Commons between the seventeenth and nineteenth centuries, when large numbers of people were forced off the land to face the brutal living conditions in the early industrial economy. Then we had the mass slaughter of the First World War, when the young and the brave were told a pack of lies and fed wholesale into a monstrous killing machine. This kind of trauma lives on, newly embodied in each subsequent generation. No wonder we, as a society, have become so polarised by the symbolism of Brexit.

Having for the first time in my life seen this kind of patient healing at work in the rehab centre, and having inherited some money from my poor old mum, I decided at the ripe old age of fifty-five to retrain as a psychotherapist. I suppose I wanted to use Mum's money to learn how to heal some miniscule part of the world's wounds instead of just staying aloof and feeling smug.

Although I've never had a serious drug problem, I could see that the only real difference between me and some of those rehab clients was that I had somehow managed to conceal my own wounding more successfully than they concealed theirs. I could easily identify within myself the same anger, defeat and alienation that they were manifesting when they arrived; in many respects, despite all the training and at least ten years of receiving therapy, I still can.

In my time as a therapist, I worked with many kinds

of psychological difficulty. In almost all cases, the most powerful source of my clients' distress was their own inner tyrant because it was always there inside their head (or more often their body, disguised as feelings of inadequacy or worthlessness) and it never left them alone.

Louise Hay says exactly the same thing, although her method of dealing with it is different. In my view, the most honest and thorough way to deal with this distress is to establish a relationship with the tyrant, but it's the one thing that most of us don't want to do because it means we have to accept the pain and sit with it for a while instead of reacting against it.

When we do manage to communicate with our own inner tyrant, we may see that his (or her) mission was originally to protect us from being bullied, shamed or otherwise attacked, but he became over-zealous in his protection and now he can't let go. This is a common dynamic in abusive relationships, although it's hard for us to imagine what that's like if we haven't been close to one. But it is possible to establish a relationship with one's own personal tyrant that may allow him to loosen up bit by bit. To do this, we have to stop being a victim and become a compassionate observer.

Maybe we need to re-establish our relationship with the Earth as well and ask for her forgiveness, because we're the abusers and she's the victim of our abuse. We could try sitting with her, recognising the awful damage that has been done, feeling her pain, and acknowledging that we are all responsible for it as active members of the consumer society.

I find this very difficult because, whenever I do manage to do it as a kind of exercise, the feeling of sadness is almost overwhelming. As a practice, it needs to be balanced by our enjoyment of such remnants of wild Nature as are still left for us to enjoy. In my experience, Mother Nature can be infinitely forgiving. It's a comfort to know that she retains this power, even though we've done our best to turn her into a toxic waste dump, a chemically-degraded food factory or a popular theme park.

References

1 https://knowledge.unccd.int/glo/GLO_first_edition

2 Blog post, 'Delusions of Omnipotence', in *Ecosophia*, May 29, 2019.

3 See David Zigmond, *If You Want Good Personal Healthcare – See a Vet* (CreateSpace Independent Publishing Platform, 2015). The three volumes in this series are made up of essays written by Dr Zigmond over a forty-year period, which are beautifully written case studies describing how the NHS has gradually been compromised by a management programme that prioritises efficiency and standardisation at the expense of a more humane, balanced approach.

4 Louise L. Hay, *You Can Heal Your Life* (Eden Grove, 1988).

5 Brandon Bays, *The Journey* (new edn., Harper Element, 2012).

6 See Dr Joe Dispenza, *You Are the Placebo: Making your Mind Matter* (Hay House, 2014).

7 See Rudolf Steiner, *Occult Science: An Outline*, trans. George & Mary Adams (Rudolf Steiner Press, 1963).

8 Philip Shepherd, *Radical Wholeness* (North Atlantic Books, 2017), p.148.

- 10 -

Yoo-hoo, World!

25 OCTOBER 2017

ONE YEAR ON from the destruction by the French authorities of the infamous Calais 'Jungle' camp, refugees are still gathering in the area, sleeping wherever they can find a bit of shelter. Today, *Sputnik* magazine publishes an interview with Marta Wallander, Director of the Refugee Rights Data Project, about their plight[1].

'The current conditions are really dire,' she tells them. *'They're characterised by intentional sleep deprivation, ... with police officers waking refugees up in the middle of the night ... to chase them away from their sleep location. Spraying sleeping bags with tear gas or pepper spray, and ... confiscating sleeping bags, clothing, shoes and anything that keeps refugees remotely warm ... [This] drives people further towards traffickers and smugglers ... The situation needs to be de-politicized, de-securitized. We need to see it for what it is. It is a humanitarian issue, with individuals really suffering in their current context, without any viable alternative.'*

For many migrants, the suffering starts much earlier in

their journey. For example, reports have been emerging since May about slave markets in Libya. Migrants, who travel there from all over North Africa in the hope of crossing the Mediterranean and finding a new life somewhere in Europe, are being fleeced by people smugglers and then systematically betrayed when they arrive. Many end up being sold into slavery.

And then there's the awful lottery of the journey across the Mediterranean, crammed into small boats that are towed out to sea by the traffickers and then abandoned, with little hope of rescue, in the middle of the night...

*

By now, I've become obsessed with the forthcoming apocalypse. I don't talk about it very much because it's not the sort of thing people want to talk about, but one day I regale Sophia with my current theory. We're in this mess (I say) because we've spent the last 2000 years suppressing the Divine Feminine. On the whole, she agrees with this assessment, although no-one has yet succeeded in suppressing Sophia for very long.

Meanwhile she has also been nursing her own obsession, which is about going to Peru and sampling the delights (or terrors) of Ayahuasca. When I mention the Divine Feminine, she has a brilliant idea. If I were to go to Peru and take Ayahuasca, she says, I could have a real encounter with the Divine Feminine instead of just reading about it in a book! (She thinks I spend far too much time reading books, or thinking. Especially thinking.)

She explains to me that Ayahuasca isn't just a random high, it's part of an ancient holistic tradition of plant medi-

cines that embodies the ideas I yatter on about, like the wholeness of experience, and the balance between masculine and feminine principles.

'For you,' she says, 'is just interesting idea, but for them is part of the life. Come on,' she says, appealing to my sense of adventure. 'I want to do it for long time but not on my own, and no-one did had the cojones to come with me. Why we don't go together?'

I have never taken hallucinogens; just like poor old Lizzie, I don't much like doing anything that makes me feel I'm not in control. But I'm surprised to find myself getting intrigued by the idea. Maybe this will be a more direct way of experiencing the 'two worlds' that Conrad talked about.

My inner octogenarian shakes his head sagely and whispers, 'You're far too old for that kind of caper,' but my sense of adventure goes, 'Oh, yes, please!' and elbows the old geezer out of the way with no trouble at all. The thought of diving into the Amazon jungle and hanging out with this crazy Romanian witchy woman is just too spicy to resist.

Any such conspiracy between the carer and the client's relative would be strictly against EuroCare's ethical rules, of course, but that just makes the dish taste even spicier.

Before long, we're spending much of our time figuring out what's the best way to do it. She says we should just go there and trust that the universe will provide us with the experience we need, but my inner octogenarian digs in his heels and advises us to book something worthy and predictable, because otherwise it's too much of a risk.

I find an outfit called The Temple of Shamanic Healing, with a comprehensive plant medicine programme, which looks like they take the whole thing very seriously. They also sound like they look after their 'pilgrims' quite well. Sophia looks disdainful, but I point out that I'm seventy-five, not thirty-five, and I need a bit of comfort.

She says, 'Well, in that case, why you don't just go on cruise ship?'

Then she reads the prospectus, which says that the temple offers an eighteen-day retreat with no less than nine Ayahuasca ceremonies. She decides that a bit of comfort might not be so bad after all if it's accompanied by nine ceremonies, so we book to go on their winter programme.

The retreat isn't cheap, so I have to sell my beautiful big green van, which I converted lovingly into a little home on wheels and then lived in for three years down in Devon. The poor thing has been languishing for the past year in a friend's field. I'm sorry to see it go because I did an enormous amount of work on it, but I can't afford to insure it so I have to let it go.

*

While we're busy plotting our Peru adventure in her dining room, Lizzie's bowel function becomes more and more unpredictable. Gradually this becomes her principal obsession. She begins to stay upstairs where she's not too far from the loo. She can't use the downstairs loo, because it's too narrow for her to get into and turn around with her Zimmer frame.

It's not just that she's worried she might have another Accident. The poor old thing also has a haemorrhoid and she thinks she has to keep pushing really hard to get rid of what she calls 'the lump I can feel inside me'. Which only makes it worse, of course.

We keep suggesting that we get her a commode so she can

come downstairs again and still be near a loo, but whenever we make the suggestion she changes into Lady Elizabeth and reacts with horror and indignation. 'I wouldn't want one of THOSE things in MY house!' she says, with a haughty expression on her face.

Lizzie's predicament is that she's terrified of being left in the house on her own; she needs to be constantly reassured that there's someone there to look after her. But as soon as she knows someone is there, she wants them to spend their time sitting with her, listening to her endless complaints about the world. Unfortunately it's difficult to stay with her for very long without getting the feeling that you're being used. That would be OK if it actually helped to improve her situation, but it soon becomes obvious that it doesn't.

Amy doesn't mind being used like that because she's in it for Jesus, but for anyone else sitting with her in the bedroom quickly becomes a kind of torture. You don't want to leave her on her own, but neither do you want to see her determinedly amplifying her victimhood and wallowing in her distress. Most of us simply can't put up with that kind of inner conflict for longer than half an hour.

Now that she's more or less permanently upstairs, Lizzie has a problem: how to get the attention she wants when we are no longer within striking distance? She can no longer shuffle into the dining room (which Sophia and I now use as a den) and announce that one of her precious possessions has been stolen.

And so, stranded upstairs on her own, she develops The Yoo-hoo.

Neither of us remembers when she utters the first of these appeals for attention, but it soon becomes an everyday thing, then it's every hour and finally sometimes every ten minutes.

For the musically minded, the call is a descending minor third pitched about an octave above middle C, repeated at least four times, thus: Yoo–oo–oo–oo hoo! Yoo–oo–oo hoo! Yoo–oo–oo–oo hoo! Yoo–oo–oo–oo hoo! She has a surprisingly steady musical warble, considering she's ninety-six years old. We are impressed.

At first, that is; after a while we cease to be impressed, and after a further while we are beginning to be annoyed by these impromptu arias because she does them for silly reasons.

'Someone has taken my hairbrush!'

'No they haven't, Lizzie. Look, here it is in your drawer.'

'That isn't my hairbrush! I've never seen it before!'

'Well what does your hairbrush look like, then?'

'It's a bit like that one, only bigger.'

'It's a bit like that one, only bigger' becomes a running gag below stairs, in all sorts of inappropriate ways.

Soon Lizzie is deploying the Yoo-hoo at night as well. She's usually active between 2am and breakfast time, and she Yoo-hoos on the landing, right outside our bedroom doors. Sophia counsels me on no account to respond. 'If the Mumia call Yoo-hoo in the night and you come, she will never stop,' she says with great conviction.

'What if she's having a heart attack?' I say.

'If she really need me, I will go,' says Sophia haughtily. 'What you think, I am stupid?'

I re-tune my FM radio to a spot between stations to pick up some white noise and leave it on all night. Sounds a bit like a waterfall, and masks the Yoo-hoos just enough to enable a good night's sleep.

❧

Looking after someone with dementia can present both the carer (who has the skills) and the client's relatives (who normally have the power) with ethical issues every day, several times a day. As far as Sophia and I were concerned, plotting to go to Peru together wasn't one of them, although it would have been regarded by most care agencies as a major ethical issue. As with most ethical questions, it depends on your point of view.

Sophia regarded her ethical responsibilities as a matter of personal integrity rather than a corporate code of behaviour, so she took responsibility for her decision by making sure that Lizzie would be reliably well looked after while we were away. She did this by persuading her most trusted Romanian colleague, Valentina, to act as relief carer once again for the duration of our six-week 'holiday'. EuroCare were happy with this arrangement, because it saved them a lot of work looking for a temporary replacement.

Valie had already looked after Lizzie while Sophia was away on her summer break, so she knew what to expect. She was very young, not yet thirty, but as Sophia said, 'She have a good soul and she is very smart, not like some of the idiots who train with me when I come in England.'

EuroCare addresses all ethical issues by imposing strict rules, which didn't surprise me. Their ethical dilemma is a quite a familiar one in our society due to our obsession with issues of control and reliability. For understandable reasons, every time something goes wrong in the social care system, the cry goes up: 'This must never happen again!' And so we commission a bunch of experts to develop a comprehensive rule book that everyone has to follow rather than picking good people, educating them well and then trusting them to do the best they can in the circumstances. The devil is always in the detail, so 'doing it by the book' tends to be a very restrictive way of working. Reliable, but not very creative.

There was a big debate about this issue while I was a psychotherapist. In the mid-2000s the government came up with a plan to set up a bureaucratic machine to monitor the ethical behaviour of counsellors and psychotherapists.

This was vigorously opposed by the more independent-minded practitioners amongst us. We argued that any bureaucratic system would have to depend on legally enforceable standards, which would have to be specified to a large extent as unambiguous rules. Therapeutic practice would then become increasingly risk averse, but we pointed out that the essence of good practice is the ability to take well-judged risks with our clients because they needed us to help them to take those kinds of risk with their own lives. Thus therapeutic practice would lose its teeth and descend into a dull, formulaic kind of mush. We made such a fuss that the government got fed up with us and delegated the policing role to the professional organisations, which could afford to be a little more subtle in their approach.

The care organisations are in a different situation. Caring for mentally or physically disabled elderly people is a 'Cinderella' occupation in the UK, mostly farmed out to private contractors and given minimal funding that limits the amount they can spend paying their staff or training them. It's a low-pay occupation; agencies like EuroCare 'train' their workers with five days of theory and a long list of assessments, rules, paperwork and procedures. Then they give them a multiple-choice paper test and send them out to look after vulnerable people with challenging behaviour and complex needs.

Caring for these people depends very much on skills (or rather qualities) like empathy, patience, humility and kindness. But there's no NVQ in empathy, no 'A' Level in patience, and no university degree in kindness. These qualities are just assumed or taken for granted, and carers are paid as little as their employers can get away with. I guess the only reason the carers put up with this is because they are, on the whole, very much appreciated by the people they care for.

Sophia, with her twelve years of experience in Germany, is scathing about our attitude towards live-in carers here in the UK. In Germany, she says, the agencies treat you more like a professional. The doctors ask for your opinion when they make decisions, and the agencies trust you to make your own decisions and to consult them if you have any problems. Here in England, she says, they don't really trust you, nor do they give you any real support. They certainly don't let you make your own decisions. They treat you more like a semi-skilled worker who has to follow a strict set of rules. These are specified by so-called 'risk assessments', procedures designed to categorise the client's situation and make sure all the officially recognised safety issues are seen to be covered because the Care Quality Commission is breathing down their necks enforcing standards.

Every patient presents their carers with their own small, everyday, ethical dilemmas. Each carer has her own way of resolving them, and each agency supervisor will have their own attitude to what their carers are doing. Mostly they try not to get involved, but woe betide the carer if something goes wrong and someone makes a big fuss about it. The agencies can't afford to be very supportive, so it's always the carer who ends up in trouble.

The more we try to define ethical behaviour by rules and procedures, the closer we get to the ethics of the Machine. The Machine doesn't take into account the personal factors, the ambiguities of the situations to which its rules apply. Real situations lose their uniqueness and become 'examples of this type of situation' or 'examples of that type of situation'. And then of course – as with the French police at Calais – if it's too difficult for you to deal with a humanitarian issue, you can just re-label it as a security issue so it becomes OK to give your unwanted refugees a good kicking instead of helping them to stay alive. Or, if you're the UK Home Secretary, you classify them as 'illegal', as if there was a viable legal route that they could and should have taken instead of making the perverse decision to arrive here at night in a dangerously overcrowded rubber dinghy.

*

There is something of an analogy here with the dire situation we're in as regards climate breakdown. For any government, this is replete with ethical dilemmas. It's one thing to declare a climate emergency and talk about achieving various CO_2 emission targets, but quite another to ensure that anything useful actually flows from this.

Democratic governments work by balancing the demands of various different interest groups according to the stated values of the party in power, and the 'climate change lobby' can only be treated as another interest group, albeit one that is urgent, vocal and rapidly growing. But the bottom line for democratic governments has always been to ensure (or at least, to promise) a steady increase in the standard of living of their voters. Because the demands of the climate change lobby can only be met fully by rowing back on this sacred bottom line, this makes it difficult for governments and creates a huge ethical dilemma.

So the fallback position (as with any difficult problem) is to produce a lot of window dressing, play around with statistics and make it look as if something is happening, rather than actually doing anything.

Governments are happy that climate change has been narrowly defined in terms of CO_2 emissions because it has been possible to devise 'cap and trade' or 'net zero carbon' schemes, which are designed to work within the existing market-based system so they can easily be gamed to ensure that no-one has to do anything real[2]. Meanwhile, they can say that they are 'tackling the problem', without having to affect the sacred bottom line.

There are plenty of expert critics who can demonstrate that these cap and trade schemes are not much more than window-dressing, but of course it takes a while to do the research, assemble the arguments, present a case and get it heard. Fortunately organisations like XR now have a sufficiently large membership, backed by expert opinion, to keep pointing at the reality and exerting real pressure on governments, otherwise they might get away with it. But governments are adept at window dressing, having had decades of experience, and there are plenty of other clever ways they can delay things.

If our elected representatives really wanted to take some responsibility for the welfare of the citizens who voted for them, in other words if they behaved in an ethically defensible way, they would be presented with some difficult choices because almost anything they could do about climate breakdown would be against the interests of one or other powerful group.

At the very least, they could put more effort into making sure that the population was properly educated about the dangers of inaction. But – judging by recent Australian experience – this would put them into conflict with media empires like Rupert Murdoch's News Corp, which might endanger their billionaire support; that's not a risk they might be prepared to take. Or they could strengthen the basic environmental protections we already have and make them much more comprehensive, but this would put them in conflict with a number of big polluters who contribute to their funds, like the agribusiness corporations, so once again they probably won't risk it.

Above all, they could act immediately to stop subsidising the fossil-fuel corporations, and curb their power, but the FFCs would complain loudly that this would threaten our extravagant lifestyles and put jobs and growth at risk. So they end up finding themselves rather limited in what they actually can do without causing themselves a great deal of discomfort. Besides, many of our elected representatives have skin in the game, especially in the USA, whose so-called 'democracy' was bought and paid for a long time ago. It's a very difficult dilemma, and it's the main reason why I think we're heading for trouble rather than for any meaningful change.

Of course, not all MPs in the UK are beholden to the corporations, but those who have real vision (beyond the usual Westminster power games) seem to be pitifully few and far between. Even the radical Left, although they say they are keen to tackle climate change, seems to suffer from a kind of reality blindness.

Traditional socialism (which is where they are coming from) relies for its state spending on taxes derived from the same wasteful, extractive economy as ordinary free-market capitalism, so it's hamstrung on climate change in pretty much the same way. It's painful to watch a socialist politician with real heart, like the wonderful Jess Phillips, declare her support for the environmentally disastrous HS2 railway because, she says, it will bring 'jobs and prosperity' to her Birmingham constituency. Given that climate change and ecological devastation are part of the same picture, we have to ask whether the tiny increase in 'jobs and prosperity' that HS2 might bring makes it worth spending such astronomical sums of money on the destruction of yet more green acres, more rare habitats and more irreplaceable ancient woodlands, especially when the coronavirus pandemic has given such a body-blow to the whole economy that it's hard to see how we can afford such huge, complicated infrastructure projects.

It's an ethical problem, but in our value system jobs and prosperity are still considered much more important than the damage and devastation we are visiting on the natural world that sustains us. Thus the pain and distress of animals used in scientific experiments, or dosed to the eyeballs with hormones and antibiotics in industrial food factories, are considered unimportant compared with our access to new drugs or cheap food. In the same way, the survival of the Indonesian rainforest is considered unimportant compared with our need for more palm-oil products to make more processed foods to make us even less healthy than we already are.

Change has to come (and is already coming, in a variety of ways) from the bottom up, not the top down. As ecological disaster comes closer, those who are concerned about it are adopting bolder strategies to put pressure on the politicians. Extinction Rebellion is perhaps the boldest player in this drama so far, organising mass civil disobedience against governments where it has been previously used only against corporates like the fossil fuel industry.

My friend Max has been very active in this because he has always regarded our predicament as a moral failure on the part of senior politicians who ought to be taking their ethical responsibilities more seriously. He has been arrested more times than I can remember, and still he's out there stopping the traffic by lying in the road or talking to cynical journalists about the stand XR is taking. He's not in danger of losing his life, like many environmental activists in countries like Nigeria or Brazil who are confronting the private armies deployed by the corporates (or the state), but he's certainly in danger of losing his freedom, which is no small thing[3]. Hats off to these guys for putting themselves in the firing line when most of us don't dare to go further than signing a few petitions or joining a few officially sanctioned, well-marshalled, orderly, middle-class protests.

🍃

We are creating multiple ethical dilemmas, or predicaments, in the world right now. Many of these look more like system problems (unpayable debt, soil depletion, increased resistance to pesticides and antibiotics, reliance on more and more expensive sources of energy and, of course, the 'big one' climate breakdown) but they are actually ethical problems as well. We know that they will affect our children and our children's children far more than they will affect us. If nothing else, this should make us pause and take stock but on the whole it doesn't; indeed, it won't until we can no longer ignore the fact that it's happening. Hopefully that won't take forever, as it's already in front of our faces in the form of increasing wildfires, storms, floods, droughts and all the other obvious signs of climate breakdown.

The response to Greta Thunberg's *skolstrijk* was very interesting. She seems to have made her protest in just the right way, and at the right time, to hit a raw nerve in the body politic, as if mainstream politicians were aware on some level of their guilt in failing to do anything to stop the escalating climate crisis. She quickly became a big star; on the whole, the school kids' Climate Change Strikes before we were hit by Covid-19 provoked much less of an authoritarian backlash than we might have expected. There is a dawning sense that we've let the children down, that something is wrong with a society that can no longer deny that something drastic is happening to the global climate but is still unwilling to do anything effective about it.

The younger generation are also aware of this and they aren't going to take it lying down.

❧

Perhaps the most difficult ethical dilemma is about mass migration.

Numerous studies have shown that the world is becoming a less hospitable place for humans, indeed for all life forms. This is partly because of climate breakdown, as vividly illustrated in Mark Lynas's terrifying book, *Six Degrees*[4]. But it's also due to our foreign wars, our ruthless imposition of neoliberal economic policies, and the ecocide and social disruption associated with our insatiable demand for oil and other commodities.

Large numbers of innocent people have been (or will soon be) displaced, exploited or traumatised. Many of them, especially from war zones, are trying to find sanctuary in rich Western countries like our own, which historically have been responsible for creating the conditions that have led to this mayhem. Migration pressure is growing and will continue to grow, and we will all be affected one way or another.

At the moment, this tends to be seen in terms of the tired old Right/Left argument. The Right says, 'Stop all this immigration! We can't take any more of them, they are overwhelming our social services and some of them are bad people.'

The Left says, 'These people are refugees fleeing from various kinds of oppression. Many of them have been seriously traumatised and deserve to find a place of safety. We are a rich country that professes Christian (or at least humanist) values; moreover, we helped to create most of the trouble from which they are now forced to flee, so we should welcome them.'

Obviously both of these arguments have some truth in them, even (it has to be said) the dangerous argument that 'some of them are bad people'. (I've occasionally worked with refugees, and some of them do behave badly. This is often because they have been brutalised by the traumas they have been through in their country of origin, but you have to know them quite well before you can know this about them. People who make these judgements often don't know anything about them at all.)

Once again, it's very hard to balance these arguments if you have to make a policy decision, so it becomes an unresolvable issue and we tend to gravitate towards extremes. The whole Brexit shambles is, in part, an unintended consequence of this dilemma.

How are we going to reconcile these extreme positions? Throughout history, the answer has been that we usually can't. Once things have gathered enough momentum, it's hard to stop them. As the climate becomes more volatile, the global food system starts breaking down and the rich nations go to war over scarce resources, millions of people will be displaced and try desperately to migrate to the more fortunate parts of the world. The more they do it, the more people will see them as 'the problem' and try to keep them out.

Fascism is already rearing its ugly head and the migrants (especially those who come from Muslim countries) will be increasingly demonised. It's already happening across Europe, in the USA and in Australia, as well as here in the UK.

We know how *that* ends up because we've seen it before.

❧

As immigration is such an emotive issue, the UK government has devised ways of dealing with it that are characteristically devious and underhand. Perhaps the most devious is the so-called 'Hostile Environment Policy', which was formally introduced a few years ago by the Home Secretary, later to become our esteemed

Prime Minister, Theresa May. Given the injustice, trauma, heartbreak and misery that this policy has caused for so many innocent people, I don't know how we in the UK can still claim that we're a 'tolerant' country with a 'long tradition of welcoming refugees fleeing from oppression' (to quote a Home Office statement issued in response to a recent news item).

A recent article in *The Guardian*[5], written by an anonymous informant whose work in the Home Office was to make asylum decisions, spells out some of the ways in which his job had been deliberately made as difficult as possible by management pressure to produce quick results. The informant says that in their initial training, decision makers are told that if they want to be regarded as 'successful' in the job, they would be 'expected' to produce more refusals than approvals. That clearly implies that the actual merits of the refugees' cases are less important than the business of keeping them out of the country. This is similar to the well-documented management pressure on Department of Work and Pensions staff who deal with benefit claimants, and is a clear example of what I am calling 'the ethics of the Machine'.

Perhaps even worse than this was the informant's account of the Home Office's internal propaganda machine. '*Our office intranet*', it says, '*was plastered with departmental propaganda featuring our minister, Priti Patel, grinning next to Home Office employees, supposedly enacting the "People's Priorities" – priorities that apparently did not include access to adequate housing, or addressing the internment camp conditions at the Napier and Penally barracks, or responding adequately to the rash of suicides among asylum seekers.*'

Personally, I would have more respect for the Home Office if they just came right out and said, 'Our job is to make it as difficult as possible for any refugees to be allowed into this country, no matter what they are fleeing from. We don't give a toss about ethics, we just want to please our voter base.'

❧

I signed various protest petitions when the Windrush scandal emerged, but nothing changed. Not long afterwards, I read that some quite highly skilled, highly paid immigrants were being deported, even if they had lived here for a long time and were doing valuable work, because they made minor mistakes in their tax returns. The Home Office appeared to assume that any such mistake must mean that the person was a potential terrorist.

I emailed Mr Javid again, and suggested to him that this was an abuse of power, and couldn't be considered ethical in a civilised society. Two months later I received this reply, which is a brilliantly worded example of bureaucratic deflection:

Dear Mr Wilson

Thank you for your email correspondence of 21 May to the Home Secretary about people being deported due to making errors on their tax returns. Your enquiry has been passed to me to reply.

Please be advised that all applications must meet the requirements of the rules in the category in which they have applied. I would advise that in order to safeguard an individual's personal information and comply with the Data

Protection Act 2018, we are limited in what information we can provide when the request is made by someone who is not the applicant.

If you do have any further questions, please contact us at: www.gov.uk/contact-ukvi-inside-outside-uk

Yours sincerely
T Farquhar
Customer Performance and Improvement
UK Visas and Immigration

Notice how Mr Farquhar dodges the question about ethics and re-casts it as a narrow legal issue. This is another way in which the ethics of the Machine manifest themselves. Iain McGilchrist refers specifically to this aspect of narrow left-brain thinking in *Ways of Paying Attention*, which I quoted in Chapter 2.

Our bureaucracy is supposed to embody what we call 'fairness' – to treat everyone equally – but fairness depends on the assumptions that are built into the system. These are often made deliberately opaque so that they can be used as a means of political oppression. They become a weapon that the state can use against people they don't like because they are a bloody nuisance, such as climate change protesters, trade unions, nomadic communities, migrants, squatters, animal rights activists, human rights lawyers, and so on. The rules can be made to look 'fair' on paper, or justified by assertions about 'What The People Voted For', but in practice the ethics of the Machine allow the system to be used for whatever nefarious purpose the government decides.

I have to ask myself, who is more to be pitied? Is it Mr

Farquhar, who spends all his time doing an unutterably bleak and soulless job lying to people to cover up the crimes committed by the Home Office? Or is it me, for expecting a man in Mr Farquhar's position to be able (or willing) to give an honest answer?

References

1 https://sputniknews.com/analysis/ 201710251058519716-refugee-crisis-calais-camp

2 See, for example, Carbon Trade Watch (2009): *Carbon Trading – How it works and why it fails*, published by the Dag Hammarskjold Foundation. See also *Climate Scientists: Concept of net zero is a dangerous trap*, by James Dyke, Robert Watson and Wolfgang Knorr (The Conversation, April 22 2021). Available at https:// theconversation.com/climate-scientists-concept-of- net-zero-is-a-dangerous-trap-15736

3 In April 2021, Max and five co-defendants were tried on charges of criminal damage after an action they carried out in 2019 where they caused £25,000 worth of damage to the Shell headquarters building on the South Bank in London to draw attention to the fact that the company knew that its operations were causing serious climate harm and damage to ecosystems, as well as damage to the lives and livelihoods of the indigenous human communities on whose lands they were drilling for oil. By causing so much damage, the XR group were taking a deliberate risk, because it meant they would have to be tried by a jury in a Crown Court where they would be able to speak to the jury in their defence. Despite the judge's ruling that they had no defence in law, the jury deliberated for seven hours and finally acquitted them.

4 Mark Lynas, *Six Degrees: Our Future on a Hotter Planet* (Harper Perennial, 2008).

5 'The Home Office is failing refugees. I've seen it from the inside' (*The Guardian*, 8 Oct 2021).

- 11 -

Shadows

AN ARTICLE IN *Global Issues* magazine today[1], quoting the Stockholm International Peace Research Institute SIPRI, gives sobering details of the current sales volume of major arms (tanks, APCs, aircraft, ships, etc.) across the world.

When the Cold War ended in the early nineties, there were hopes of a 'peace dividend'. This meant that the money spent on arms (which had been increasing steadily since the 1960s) would start falling, so more money would become available for civil development of the world's poorest countries. Arms sales did fall somewhat during the nineties, but in 2002 they accelerated again, reaching $374.8 billion in 2016, most of which went to US companies like Lockheed Martin ($40.8 billion).

The largest buyers were India (which is home to about one third of the world's 'abject poor', defined as living on less than $1.90 a day), and Saudi Arabia (which is currently using its huge stockpile to murder large numbers of innocent civilians in the Yemen). The UK also has blood on its hands in this appalling conflict with its Saudi Arabia arms sales and its maintenance teams which keep the Saudi Air Force flying.

Meanwhile President Trump, influenced by his then National Security Adviser, the mildly unhinged John Bolton, announced that the USA will withdraw from the INF (Intermediate-range Nuclear Forces) treaty with Russia, which has helped to keep a fragile peace in Europe for the last three decades.

America maintains about 600 military bases around the world, as well as more than 4,000 in its own country. Its Department of Defence budget for 2019 was agreed at $686 billion, the highest in America's history. America spends more on defence than the next five countries *combined.* I guess it really does feel threatened in some way, but it almost looks as if it *needs* to maintain a wide variety of 'enemies'. Perhaps that's because these 'enemies' give it a convenient place on which to project its own violence, its unresolved trauma and (some would say) its guilt for a long list of war crimes, from the extermination of its own indigenous people right up to the so-called 'War on Terror'.

Right now, the future doesn't look very safe. Ever since the Second World War, the US government's relentless desire for 'security' (or what they call 'full spectrum dominance') has cast a long shadow over the world, and the shadow is getting longer all the time.

Lizzie isn't greatly concerned about the forthcoming demise of the INF treaty. She's more interested in the worthy babblings of her stepson, Jolyon, who is playing an increasingly important role in her life.

When he first appeared in our lives back in February, Lizzie didn't remember who he was; however, as he obviously knew Jane, she enjoyed talking to him on the phone. She often talks to him about Jane, complaining that she's being held prisoner somewhere in a basement.

Jolyon tells me that he's trying to get her to understand that Jane is in the Kingdom of Souls, and that she's waiting for her dear mum to join her in that blessed place. If Jane is indeed waiting for someone to join her, I'm absolutely certain it's not her mum. But I don't let him in on the secret; I just wish him well with his efforts to educate her.

Over the next few weeks, he keeps telling us he thinks he's at last managed to get the idea of the Kingdom of Souls across to her, and while she's talking to him it does almost seem that way. But as soon as their conversation is over, she forgets all about it. She's much more comfortable with her usual obsession about Jane being somehow still alive than she is with Jolyon's worthy attempts to explain the Afterlife. She pesters both Sophia and me to find out about this Kingdom of Souls. Why are they keeping Jane there? Can you get to it by bus or by train? Could I take her there in my car? Is it very far away?

She keeps begging Jolyon to come and see her. He says he doesn't like driving long distances, and his partner Steve isn't very well, so it will be a major undertaking, but he'll come 'as soon as he can'. He tells me that Steve has very bad arthritis, which means he can't travel far without a lot of pain.

Meanwhile he sends Lizzie a long letter full of details about the afterlife and the Kingdom of Souls, and how lucky she is to have such good care, and what a wonderful mother she was to Jane, and how he can't wait for the day when he

258

can come and see her. Lizzie gets us to read it to her every day, often more than once, until we're heartily sick of it.

I find it impossible to keep on reading the bits about what a good mother she was because Jane gave me numerous examples of how abysmally awful Lizzie was as a mother, and Jolyon's attempts at flattery make me feel sick.

'Why you think he say those things?' Sophia demands. 'He want that she like him so he can get the money. Why you can't see?'

❧

The other person Lizzie calls nearly every day, sometimes three times a day, is the dreadful Amy. We're not sure why we feel so negative about her, it's just an elusive 'something'. It's a shame, because Amy is one of the few people who bothers to come and see Lizzie regularly. She comes faithfully once a week on Thursdays, sits with her and massages her hands. She still comes even when Lizzie tells her she's useless because she can't help her find 'my other houses'.

'But she keeps telling you you're useless,' we protest.

'Yes,' smiles saintly Amy, 'but she can't help it.'

Sophia thinks Amy also wants to get her hands on Lizzie's stuff when she dies because she's being such a 'good girl', and she often talks about Lizzie's beautiful sewing machine and Lizzie's elegant tableware. That doesn't seem like a good enough explanation to me. I think Amy really wants to save Lizzie's soul for Jesus.

Amy tells us she's noticed that Lizzie often talks about 'somebody called Jolyon who tells her that he knows where Jane is'. Who is this Jolyon, she asks?

Sophia gives her a quick run-down. 'He is the stepson

from Lizzie, but she is not remember. He tell us he is gay, he have a partner who is call Steve, and he live in a place I think is call News Cassel. He write a letter to Lizzie which say that Jane is in Kingdom of Souls, and will meet again when is Lizzie pass away.'

'Well if he's homosexual', *says Amy, pronouncing the word as if she were holding up a particularly revolting creature for Sophia's inspection,* 'I don't know why he's talking about the Kingdom of Souls.'

'Why he shouldn't talk about?'

'Because he'll be headed straight for hell,' *she says, simply.* 'He's the Antichrist.'

'He is *what?' asks Sophia, hardly able to believe her ears.*

But Amy turns away with a prim little smile on her face and makes it clear she doesn't want to discuss it. Later, Sophia tells me about her conversation.

'Ah!' *I say.* 'Amy shows her true colours.'

'Is something of darkness in Amy's soul', *says Sophia.* 'I am not surprise she say those things.'

This time, I'm inclined to agree with her.

⌀

Amy's pious and somewhat rigid exterior belies the confusion and lack of self-worth that I suspect she probably feels inside. She keeps herself under strict control and covers it up with a thin layer of bonhomie, like an attractive-looking cream cake full of processed shite that will cause chaos in your digestive tract so you'll wish you hadn't eaten it.

This kind of self-control is a powerful obsession for us as a civilisation. It's not just the righteous who suffer from it, I'm afraid; we all do, because our society tries very hard to condition us into it from an early age. Most of this conditioning is quite unconscious, which probably makes it a lot more effective than it would be if we tried to do it deliberately.

It's not that controlling our behaviour is always 'wrong' – far from it; social life would be impossible without some sort of control. But we don't always choose our targets very wisely. For example, many (perhaps most) of us in this 'culture of uncare' are terrified of being judged as needy, so we try not to behave in a way that displays any kind of vulnerability. This constant judging, and constantly being judged, is incredibly damaging, unhelpful and unnecessary. If we could control our behaviour more impartially, without always having to stifle our legitimate personal needs or judge ourselves and other people as 'bad', our quality of life might be very different.

A good perspective on this is given in Carl Jung's concept of the Shadow. The more our behaviour is controlled so that we conform with the emotional numbing required by our machine-driven society, the more our natural impulses (especially the ones we've been told we shouldn't have) are relegated to this shadow area, where they continue to work on us in an unconscious, disruptive way.

According to Jung, there's both a personal shadow and a collective one. The Collective Shadow works in a variety of ways, and can play an important part in any situation where people find themselves divided into warring factions where one or both sides encourage hatred for the other one, such as war, civil strife, social unrest or collapse. It is through this psychological mechanism (often called 'othering') that people are able to channel and focus their anger and violence. It can be especially active at a time of rapid and destabilising change, so it's worth pausing to take a good look at the Shadow on every level to see how it works and what damage it can do.

❧

This is what the American poet Robert Bly says about what he calls the 'shadow bag'[2]:

When we were one or two years old we had what we might visualise as a 360-degree personality. Energy radiated out from all parts of our body and all parts of our psyche. A child running is a living globe of energy. We had a ball of energy, all right; but one day we noticed that our parents didn't like certain parts of that ball. They said things like, "Can't you be still?" or "It isn't nice to try and kill your brother." Behind us we have an invisible bag, and the part of us our parents don't like, we, to keep [their] love, put in the bag. By the time we go to school our bag is quite large. Then our teachers have their say: "Good children don't get angry over such little things." So we take our anger and put it in the bag.

...Then we do a lot of bag-stuffing in high school. This time it's no longer the evil grownups that pressure us, but people our own age... I lied all through high school automatically to try to be more like the basketball players. Any part of myself that was a little slow went into the bag...

In my own shadow bag, it's a terrible crime to be branded a loser. This was mainly the result of my boarding school education, which turned me into a rebel – not a quiet rebel, like my dear brother, but the kind who feels an inner compulsion to rub it in people's faces in case it isn't noticed and appreciated. This hasn't changed much since I was a teenager, although I've learned not to make such a big deal of it now that I'm getting older. Such is the power of the entity known as the 'inner tyrant', whom we met earlier (in Chapter 2).

This entity is always trying to control our behaviour. It has various names: Freud called it the superego; many psychotherapists call it the inner critic, some call it the 'controller' or the 'saboteur'. It not only tells us how we should behave, but also makes us terribly afraid of how others might see us if we don't.

This is the result of years of conditioning, not all of which results from what people actually say to us. Much of it depends on negative attitudes that parents, teachers and others project onto children without saying a word, just by disapproving looks or meaningful silences. This is examined in detail by Daniel Goleman (author of the world-famous book *Emotional Intelligence*) in his follow-up study, *Vital Lies, Simple Truths*, where he shows how this kind of wordless communication leads to all kinds of cognitive and emotional distortions in later life[3]. Shaming is a much more powerful method of control than physical punishment because as children we have no defence against it, whereas beatings at least evoke some degree of defiance. It's mostly shame that feeds the inner tyrant.

What Robert Bly calls the 'shadow bag' is the stinking dungeon into which the Tyrant throws everything about us that he doesn't like.

No wonder we disavow anything that's hidden away in our own private dungeon. 'Oh, I'm not like *that*,' we say. Then, because we're deeply sensitive to it, we keep finding all around us the awful things that our Tyrant has thrown down there, only now we see them not in ourselves but in

263

other people, other groups and other cultures. This what Jung called 'projecting the shadow'. What the Tyrant is actually trying to do is to protect us from the pain caused by our secret feelings of shame and worthlessness. The most effective way he can do this is by encouraging us to project onto other people everything he's taught us to despise in ourselves, and to make moral judgements about them which show ourselves in a better light.

The trouble is that we're conditioned by our culture to conflate people's moral behaviour with *who they are*. If someone fails to come up to our own imagined standards, we judge them to be a 'bad person'. Why? Because only bad people behave, or think, or look like that. You only have to sit in a court of law for an hour to appreciate the significance of this conflation.

Those of us who are alarmed by ecocide, for example, tend to identify people like Donald Trump and his supporters as being very bad people indeed, because they actively pursued policies that would ensure that our beautiful planet would be harmed irreparably.

As the pressure gets worse, people on all sides of the current ideological debates have shown an increasing tendency to identify each other as bad. Thus, Trump's supporters are fed up with being told by enlightened liberals (also known as 'snowflakes') that they are 'bad people', because they sense that there's a big dollop of hypocrisy behind the accusation. Which there often is.

When we identify someone as a bad person, by implication we become the good people, the ones who would never stoop so low. As a recent example from my own life, there was a Tory MP whom I absolutely detested. He is an arch-Brexiteer with a very upper-class background, widely regarded as a bigot. It felt good to accuse this man of bigotry because it made me feel better in some obscure way. I was aware that my accusations didn't make any difference, except to increase the amount of righteous anger floating around in the conversation space, but this didn't stop me from detesting the man.

I became curious about this and asked myself whether there was some 'shadow' reason why I persisted with this attitude. What was it about him that was so bad that I had to find a way of asserting that I'm completely free of it? Was it perhaps my own inner bigot that I was so ashamed of? (Don't worry, we all have one, only most of us don't like to admit it.)

One evening I see him talking to a reporter on TV and discover that his alleged bigotry isn't what really irritates me; it's actually his sanctimonious aura of upper-class superiority. I spot this out of the corner of my eye as it tries to creep stealthily back into my own shadow bag.

Oh dear! That'll be me trying to disown my own sense of superiority, then. Not quite so 'upper class' but essentially the same thing. Years of conditioning by the British public-school system made sure of that - despite my best efforts to reject it, having had it used against me on numerous occasions as a boy.

I worked for half my life as a carpenter in deliberate defiance of my expensive, middle-class education, and thoroughly enjoyed playing the part of a 'jolly builder'. But my natural home in the wretched British class structure remained unchanged. All I succeeded in doing was adding a surface layer of expletive-rich, imitation working-class bad behaviour. As they used to say, you can take the boy out of the middle class but you can't take the middle class out of the boy.

Strangely enough, once I'd seen this I could even feel a certain sympathy for the man, constrained as he is by his dreadful upbringing. I could feel a hint of the fear that lurks unseen behind the convincing veneer of effortless superiority that is commonly affected by the English aristocracy. The poor buggers are deeply terrified of their own vulnerability. The place where most of them learn to feel this kind of terror is the English so-called 'public school' (which most other societies would call a 'private' or 'fee-paying' school).

These patterns of like and dislike, attraction and repulsion, are like a huge dammed-up energy grid that runs under the surface, connecting us all in an invisible network of semi-conscious relationships. It's always there, always active, and always ready to spring into action, as it did (for example) in the 1992–95 Bosnian war, in which the Serbian Christians, who had lived together with their Muslim neighbours more or less peacefully for centuries, suddenly turned into genocidal murderers and mass rapists.

The more unaware we are of the existence of this energy grid, the more power it has to push us into mutually antagonistic sub-cultures that waste their energy hating each other instead of learning how we might co-operate to change our world for the better. It's one of the tragedies of being human, at least in this stage of our evolution. We're desperate for a feeling of belonging but all too often we can only achieve it by 'othering', i.e. stoking up our dislike of the common enemy. We should remember that the external embodiment of the inner Tyrant is the populist leader, who convinces us that the threat we're feeling comes from 'those others', and then offers to protect us from them.

On the activist end of the social media spectrum, this kind of negative projection is hard to avoid. There's plenty for us to hate out there amongst the politicians and the corporates who are conspiring to wreck the planet. There you are: I just did it myself.

🌿

Bayo Akomolafe has an interesting take on racism as an example of this habit of ours to form 'hate tribes'. Responding to the notoriously violent white supremacist rally at Charlottesville on 12 August 2017, where a peaceful *antifa* protester was killed by an avowed Nazi sympathizer running her over in a car, he writes[4] about how we usually understand the people we brand as racists:

As subjects of a modern arrangement of things, we tend to see things as independent from other things, not as intra-acting agencies. To explain the emergence of an object and why it behaves in the ways that it does, we look within the object, cutting it open, hoping that by means of isolation, distillation, reduction, extraction or abstraction, we might arrive at the secret ingredient within the object – the essential core that lies behind the fleeting form of its materiality. The structure behind the appearance.

As an example, ... the racist is the unfortunate psychological product of the choices s/he has made in times past – the unit of racism. A glitch to be fixed. What we fail to notice is that ... the efforts to pinpoint the trouble of racism in the racist is an effect of a dualistic, Enlightenment (Judeo-Christian) philosophy – the same one that hopes to arrive at the essence of an onion by stripping away layer after layer.

It's a radical thing to say and a most dangerous notion to admit: that in some non-mystical way, I am practically entangled with those people I would rather demonize as white supremacists and Nazi sympathizers. The dual framework permits us to separate the 'racist' from the 'non-racist', to instal a fundamental distinction between their absolute depravity and our detached moral coherence, and to defer and deflect responsibility. There are not too many places to go from there... [The cost] must be that it further represses what wants to be expressed, and does not allow healing to happen.

Bayo outlines the deep history behind the recent resurgence of white supremacist values in America: the way European countries, especially England, sent their unwanted poor off to the New World to get rid of 'the problem'; the promises that were made to them and not kept; their temporary rescue by the industrial economy, their subsequent betrayal when the corporates exported their livelihoods to China, and their final abandonment by the political elite. All of this, and more, goes into the social conditions that have given rise to a white supremacist backlash as the legions of those left behind search for a sense of identity and agency to replace what has been stolen from them by those who have the power.

It bears repeating, he continues, *the heart of hate is the universe of relationships it excludes... [H]ealing is not a matter of banishing monsters but of embracing our alter egos – the wilds we often exile beyond our fences.*

When we dismiss and vilify the people we disagree with, or the scapegoats we blame for our own troubles, we both reify their 'badness' and, at the same time, express our unconscious dismissal and vilification of the parts of ourselves that we don't like. For the white supremacists of Charlottesville, this was their barely conscious sense of themselves as being somehow historically worthless and powerless, mere pawns in a game that successful people play all the time – the game of using people to make money. They project the worthlessness they feel inside themselves onto 'those others': foreigners, Jews, black people, 'snowflakes', whatever.

I am reminded of the Joe South song which was made famous by Elvis Presley in the 1970s: 'Walk a Mile in My Shoes'. And until you've done that, don't assume that you know anything at all about me.

The Shadow also has an opposite side, which I suppose we should call 'The Light' although that doesn't really describe it. This is our tendency to put people on a pedestal and worship them if we see in them qualities that we admire, as the white supremacist might worship someone like Donald Trump because he can feel a sense of belonging within the Trump 'tribe' that he hasn't felt anywhere else for a long time.

This is a big part of the dynamic that makes populist leaders into such powerful figures. One thing they all make a song and dance about is their (alleged) rejection of establishment or technocratic values. Trump, for example, continually rails against the Washington 'establishment' and refuses to be seen as part of it, although as President he served quite well the interests of the plutocracy that owns it. His followers just love the way he pokes the middle finger at 'The Swamp' and defies the established protocols of good government. He does everything his followers would love to be able to do if they were in his place and didn't feel so victimised and disempowered. Make America Great Again! Lock Her Up! Build That Wall! And so on.

They are doing what we might call 'projecting the ideal'. This isn't always a bad thing; in fact it's one way (beyond pure imitation) in which all children relate to their parents. By extension, it's also one of the traditional ways in which the pupil learns from the teacher, or the disciple from the guru.

This is one of the reasons why, for example, the supporters of ex-President Trump will never change their minds about his refusal to accept the 2020 election results, despite all the evidence and the failure of every legal attempt to overturn them. Their view of him exists up there in the world of ideals, not down here the world of facts. Their belief in his moral superiority, which is widely shared and vehemently defended, has become an essential prop for their own personal well-being.

'Projecting the ideal' is something we all do in our romantic relationships, but it can be just as unhealthy in a close relationship as it is in politics. I saw this once in a guy who used to work for me when I was a builder. He was a reformed ex-con, who'd fallen in love with – and married – his social worker. He used to call her Princess, and he was utterly devoted to her. In effect, he was using her as a 'goodness bank' – a safe place where he could put his rather vulnerable inner Good Boy. He'd been a very bad boy, she had rescued him from his badness, and now she was his Angel of Light. This might have worked well when he was with her but he could still be quite a bad boy when she wasn't around, as we found to our cost.

Perhaps she, in turn, was using him as a safe place to stash her unconscious desire to be a disorderly, reckless trollop. Who knows? But I found myself, somewhat uncharitably, wondering how long it would last.

*

There's a widely shared (but mostly unconscious) agreement within any culture about what Carl Jung called the 'collective shadow'. In a sexually repressive culture like that of Victorian Britain, for example, every kind of sexual behaviour was stuffed into the collective shadow bag. During my lifetime it has been fascinating to see how most of it has been allowed to creep out again, following landmark battles like the *Lady Chatterley's Lover* trial in 1960, the decriminalisation of homosexuality in 1967 and the Oz trial in 1971.

In this age of social media, the shadow bag has become more heterogenous because there is less and less agreement about what should go into it. Greed and anger, for example, have begun to crawl out of the bag and are becoming quite commonplace and even acceptable in the age of grossly overpaid executives, Facebook politics and the 'culture of uncare'. So is our native British racism. I can remember many conversations (or rather, banter sessions) with my mates in the building trades where they experimented with letting their racism peep cheekily out of the bag like a pet ferret to see how others might react.

Now that professional racists are being made into folk heroes as part of the fallout from the Brexit vote, I'm not surprised that we're seeing our native British racism migrate from cheeky banter to mainstream, unabashed hatred and vilification. This acquired quite a nasty edge following the notorious interview that Oprah Winfrey did with Meghan Markle, which revealed the suppressed racism within the venerable institution of the British monarchy. It was made even nastier by some of the media commentators who have enjoyed vilifying her and her husband ever since.

Maybe there are as many different shadow bags as there are identifiable sub-cultures in our uncertain society. In most of them, racism and homophobia are still banned. Nevertheless, in some of them, like the evangelical Christian group that my mother-in-law's friend Amy inhabits, homophobia is actually encouraged, ignoring the cultural changes that have occurred over the last fifty years.

To fulfil our need to feel morally superior in any contentious situation, we (like Amy) tend to identify with the 'good group' and project the things we collectively don't like onto 'the bad group'. The things we collectively don't like can be an enormously elastic category, which has allowed (for example) people here in the UK who wanted to leave the EU to be venomously offensive towards people who disagreed with them (and vice-versa, of course), and literally split families apart on account of a difference of opinion. We may manage to get on perfectly well with them under normal conditions and even laugh about our disagreements, but when things start getting difficult we can suddenly start finding the devil himself in 'those others'.

Jung saw a large-scale example of this in the way that the pre-war Nazi propaganda machine demonised everybody who wasn't a 'pure-bred Aryan' (whatever that means), especially the Jews. Interviewed just after the German army surrendered at Rheims in 1945, he compared their fantasies to those of a therapy patient of his who believed that her husband was a devil in human form[5]:

One day a woman comes to me and breaks out into the wildest accusations against her husband: he is a veritable devil who torments and persecutes her, and so on and so forth. In reality the good man is a perfectly respectable citizen, quite innocent of any such demonic intentions. Where does this crazy idea come from in this woman? It is the devil in her own soul that she is projecting; she has transferred her own wishes and her own rages to her husband... Exactly the same thing happened on a large scale in the history of Europe. For primitive man the world is full of demons and mysterious powers which he fears; the whole of Nature is animated by these forces, which are nothing but man's own inner powers projected into the outside world. Christianity and modern science have de-demonized Nature, which means that the European has consistently taken back the demonic powers out of the world into himself, and has steadily loaded his unconscious with them. Out of man himself the demonic powers rise up in revolt against the supposed spiritual constraints of Christianity. The demons begin to break out in Baroque art: the columns writhe, the furniture sprouts satyr's feet. Man is slowly transformed into an uroboros, the 'tail-eater' who devours himself, from ancient times a symbol of the demon-ridden man. The first perfect example of this species was Napoleon.

In another example of a similar kind of projection, the British who colonised large parts of Africa in the nineteenth century saw the indigenous people as child-like, undisciplined, primitive, stupid and ungodly. This wasn't surprising in a society where the elites were so

273

determined to coerce their own poor people into being sober, disciplined factory workers who would obey orders and fear God's retribution if they failed to comply. These values were indelibly imprinted on the collective British subconscious as we tried relentlessly to force the inhabitants of our African colonies into serfdom and a kind of infantile Sunday-School Christianity.

I can still remember an 'important person' who visited my boarding school at its so-called speech day in 1956, when I was fourteen years old, referring to 'the Africans' as 'hewers of wood and drawers of water' (which I guess is a Biblical description, although I haven't been able to find it in there), and impressing upon us that it was our destiny to bring civilisation to these benighted places[6]. Within twenty years or so, we had lost all our colonies in Africa so I'm afraid I never did get to fulfil my destiny.

Likewise, the early settlers in North America regarded the indigenous people as 'savages', not only because they obstinately refused to believe in the one true God, but also because they fought back when the colonisers insisted on stealing their land and subjecting it to exclusive and individual ownership. The Native Americans were treated as human vermin, and the colonisers tried as hard as they could to eliminate them altogether.

Christian civilisation, with its God of Love, has a record of projecting its angry, murderous shadow onto any and all cultures it regards as uncivilised, and has committed the most horrendous atrocities on many of them, especially in the Americas[7].

There's a remarkable passage in Jung's *Modern Man in Search of a Soul*[8] where he describes a conversation he had with a Native American friend, who he reports as saying:

'We don't understand the whites; they are always wanting something – always restless – always looking for something. What is it? We don't know. We can't understand them. They have such sharp noses, such thin, cruel lips, such lines in their faces. We think they are all crazy.'

Jung comments: *My friend had recognised, without being able to name it, the Aryan bird of prey with his insatiable lust to lord it in every land... That is how the European looks when he is extricated from the cloud of his own moral incense. No wonder that to unearth buried fragments of psychic life we have first to drain a miasmal swamp...*

'Buried fragments of psychic life' and 'a miasmal swamp' both describe very well what we find in the shadow. Funnily enough, 'the swamp' is how Donald Trump described the Washington political establishment. Could this be the supreme irony of the much-maligned Trump presidency? Or was he describing something much closer to home? I can't help wondering.

🍃

The descendants of those who stole the North American continent from the indigenous people have proved themselves worthy successors to their rapacious European ancestors by spreading mayhem all over the world, sometimes directly but usually by proxy. Writers like Naom Chomsky have meticulously documented these activities over the last sixty or seventy years in Indonesia, Vietnam, Africa, the Middle East and central and south America[9]. Sometimes, as in Vietnam and more recently in Iraq and Afghanistan, this has involved the American military machine directly, but more often it has been carried out through covert economic warfare and by supporting local right-wing reactionaries (Suharto in Indonesia, Pinochet in Chile, *Svoboda* in Ukraine, etc.) rather than by actual conquest[10].

As this book went to press, the current tragedy in Ukraine was just unfolding. The Western media establishment has typically treated this as an unprovoked attack by 'the mad dictator Putin'. He may well be a bit unhinged, and his army is carrying out a particularly brutal attack on the civilian population of Ukraine, but it's not entirely true to say that it was unprovoked. The CIA has been just as active in Ukraine for the last twenty years, as it has everywhere else, exploiting the deep divisions in that troubled country and financing pro-NATO, anti-Russian politicians and far-right movements like *Svoboda*. The veteran journalist John Pilger wrote an article in *The Guardian* newspaper as far back as 2014, during the Maidan revolution, in which he actually predicted that this unnecessary and dangerous provocation would very likely lead to another war in Europe[11].

The NATO leadership must have known how Putin would react if Ukraine was allowed to join the organisation, but they went ahead with the preparations for it anyway. Russian concerns about NATO expansion are quite legitimate – just imagine how America would react if, say, Mexico negotiated a mutual defence pact with Russia, and was then armed to the teeth with Russian weapons, under Russian control – but these concerns were repeatedly dismissed by the West, despite the well-known promise made thirty years ago that NATO would expand 'not one inch to the East'. How has it come to this?

In the West, especially the Anglo-American West, we tend to idealise Freedom and Democracy, perhaps to disguise the fact that we are heedlessly sacrificing both of them to the economic and political demands of the Machine. But the Machine, whether its servants are Russian or American, has very little interest in freedom and none at all in democracy. The Russian people have a justifiable cynicism when it comes to such notions, but we still seem to believe our own propaganda, and the American *mythos* with its ideal of absolute individual freedom, has given rise to a collective shadow which sees the Devil in anything even mildly 'socialist'. Russia, because of its communist history and its unrivalled track record in suppressing all dissent, fulfils this role to perfection. Long before his invasion of Ukraine, Vladimir Putin, with his KGB background and his tendency to advertise himself as the strong man of Russia, had already made himself into the ideal 'monstrous Shadow' for us to hate.

This kind of 'othering' underpins endless wars, whether they are fought in the name of 'security' (Chechnya, Ukraine) or 'freedom and democracy' (Iraq, Afghanistan). War serves the interests of the Machine in so many ways, not least of which is the enormous and very lucrative global arms trade. And now in Ukraine, tragically, the ordinary people are again paying the price, and there's no going back.

*

Another example of the same kind of inversion is the so-called 'War on Terror', whose chief bogeyman is that hate-filled character, 'the terrorist'. At the same time, one of our favourite movie characters is the maverick freedom fighter, trying to save his country (or his community or the human race) from some oppressive power. In the real world, one man's terrorist is another man's freedom fighter; likewise one man's 'freedom-loving, democratic country' (Israel, for example) is another man's terrorist state. It all depends which side of the fence you're standing on. If I were a farmer in Afghanistan whose extended family had just been destroyed in an American drone strike, or a Palestinian Arab farmer whose 200-year-old olive trees had just been gleefully torn out of the ground by the Israeli Army, I'm sure I'd feel the same way.

After the Twin Towers were destroyed in September 2001, an American humanist psychology forum I was involved in hosted an online discussion about what could have motivated the perpetrators to do what they did. They seemed to be genuinely puzzled about the cultural roots of such extreme violence, as if they were so far outside their view of the possible depths to which a human being could descend. The men who did this dreadful thing must have been *so angry*, these good people opined. What kind of socio-cultural background could possibly lead them to experience so much anger?

Perhaps naively, I commented that they might take a look at American foreign policy rather than wasting their time speculating about the terrorists' cultural background. I was immediately inundated with the cries of the injured innocents. One of them even suggested that my remarks had 're-traumatised' her. How could I suggest such a thing? We only want to bring good things into the world! Why do they hate us so much[12]?

Why, indeed.

As Adam Curtis has shown so graphically in his documentary work[13], the War on Terror is as much a device for controlling the domestic population as it is an actual battle with actual terrorists. Since it creates many more angry people than it destroys, it ensures that the terrorists will keep on coming. This provides a convenient distraction from the fact that the economy is crumbling (not the fake economy of financial trickery but the real economy of production and jobs). People are feeling less secure, less optimistic and a lot less in control than they did even ten years ago – but they tend to go along with their chosen media outlet and blame its favourite scapegoats rather than making the effort to think clearly about their situation.

*

As our civilisation starts to unravel, and people's lives become more and more difficult, old enmities are being revived and new ones formed. The elites, through their media friends, are pointing the finger at our favourite bogeymen, *those others*, who are trying to undermine our democracy, steal our secrets, or invade our societies and live off our generosity. This goes down well with a population that's becoming more and more alienated, impoverished and stressed out because all kinds of badness can easily be projected onto them. When he was in power, President Trump and his Republican backers put a lot of their energy into painting 'the illegals' as sub-human, disease-ridden criminals who harbour terrorists and threaten the peace and stability of the USA.

As the people become more restless, particularly in the USA, the surveillance state is trying, with increasing determination, to maintain control. The political elites are becoming more and more paranoid and obsessed with national security. This, as journalist Chris Hedges has pointed out[14], is characteristic of empires in decline. It's also characteristic of a human culture that's grotesquely out of balance, as we saw earlier. Gradually, essential democratic rights like freedom of the press and the right to hold peaceful protests are starting to be eroded. This is all grist to the mill for the Machine, because of its heavy reliance on surveillance technology.

It may well be that the pressure-cooker situation in the USA will be relieved by yet more warfare, despite the country's recent humiliation in Afghanistan. The ongoing obsession with Iran may yet provide a convenient outlet for this. Potentially much worse is its obsession with the old Communist heartlands of Russia and China, both of which are armed to the teeth with nuclear weapons. If the US were to get involved in a war with either of these big boys, it's not hard to imagine how quickly and how thoroughly the world would be destroyed. We can only hope that Joe Biden keeps a cool head when the Ukraine conflict turns into a protracted guerrilla war, and he comes under pressure to get more directly involved.

This progressive breakdown of 'normal' political stability is not much different from the kind of psychological breakdown my mother-in-law is going through as the dementia gets progressively worse. She struggles to maintain control, knowing at some level that she can't, and as she does so, she lives more and more in her obsessions.

Fortunately she isn't in a position to enforce her demands, but if she were (for example, if she were very rich, like most members of the political elites) she probably would. Then we'd all be running around like demented rabbits, trying to pretend that there's a logic to our madness, very much like they were forced to do in the White House while Donald Trump was in charge. And in our own sad, incompetent, Brexit-obsessed UK government in the days of Theresa May and Boris Johnson.

*

As the civilised world starts to crumble around us, its shadow side is becoming more and more evident, and the dangers it poses more and more real.

The prelude to this was 1914, the convulsions of the 1930s and 40s were the dress rehearsal, and now we are looking straight into the dragon's eye. He still seems a fair way off because most of us haven't yet woken up from the hypnotic spell of the story of Progress, but it won't be long before we feel his hot breath on our faces.

As Carl Jung anticipated, the future of our civilisation may depend on whether or not we wake up to our own shadow side and become aware of its potential power to make us destroy each other rather than face up to the fundamental issues that are really driving our discontent. It's not 'those others', it's we ourselves (on both sides) who need to change.

For poor old Lizzie, it's already too late. I hope that's not true for us. One of the things we can all do is to practise a measure of detachment from the cheap drama that characterises so much of the commentary in the media, especially on social media. Or we can go further and practise seeing the situation from the point of view of 'those others' – the ones we love to hate.

References

1 www.globalissues.org/news/2017/12/14/23798

2 Robert Bly, *A Little Book on the Human Shadow* (Harper San Francisco, 1988), p.17.

3 Daniel Goleman, *Vital Lies, Simple Truths* (Simon & Schuster, 1996).

4 Extract from Bayo's essay ' Icarus: The Depreciating Value of Whiteness and the Place of Healing', accessed at www.bayoakomolafe.net/

5 Posted by Leah Cohen at https://medium.com/@lenabloch/carl-jung-on-psychology-of-fascism-in-his-famous-interview-werden-die-seelen-frieden-finden-52c2b6be0d5c

6 I have to say that a few of us thought his remarks were grossly offensive and said so loudly and clearly to whoever would listen. We weren't all as meek and conformist as they perhaps expected us to be.

7 Christians are, of course, not alone in this. Muslims are doing the same to their own brothers in various part of Africa and the Middle East, Hindus are doing it to Muslims in India, and Buddhists are doing it to Muslims in Myanmar, to mention just a few.

8 C. G. Jung, *Modern Man in Search of a Soul* (ARK edition, 1984, p. 246).

9 See, for example, *The Washington Connection and Third World Fascism*, by Naom Chomsky and Edward Herman (Spokesman, Nottingham, 1979).

10 See, for example, John Perkins, *Confessions of an Economic Hit Man* (Ebury Press, 2006) and Naomi Klein, *The Shock Doctrine* (Penguin, 2008).

11 John Pilger: *In Ukraine, the US is dragging us towards war with Russia* (*The Guardian* newspaper, 13 May 2014). Available at https://www.theguardian.com/commentisfree/2014/may/13/ukraine-us-war-russia-john-pilger?CMP=Share_iOSApp_Other

12 This is a rhetorical question often voiced by Israelis about their Palestinian Arab neighbours. Evidently they haven't been told about the *Naqba* (the expulsion of nearly a million Palestinian Arabs from their ancestral lands by Israeli militias in 1948), or if they have, they've been told it wasn't as bad as it's made out to be, or they think it was in some way justified.

13 Especially *Bitter Lake* (BBC, 2015).

14 See, for example, his book, *America: The Farewell Tour* (Simon & Schuster, 2018) and the video of his talk, 'Fascism in the Age of Trump' at https://www.youtube.com/watch?v=BMYjroVIDLA

- 12 -

The Kingdom of Souls

6 JANUARY 2018

ACCORDING TO TODAY'S piece by Kelly Levine on the Global Issues website[1], it's clear that 2017 was a year of record-breaking extreme weather and other events related to climate breakdown.

For a start, it was one of the three warmest years in the 138-year record. (The warmest year was 2016, the second warmest was 2015.) In the US, there were fifteen weather disasters costing more than $1 billion each, including three hurricanes with a combined cost of nearly $300billion. California had its largest-ever wildfire. In Australia, more than 260 heat and rainfall records were broken. East Africa suffered from a terrible drought.

Scientists found that the extent and rate of decline of the Arctic sea ice has been much greater in the last forty years than in the previous fifteen hundred. They also found that carbon dioxide concentrations at 403.3 ppm., were the highest in 800,000 years, and 45% higher than pre-industrial levels. Meanwhile, deforestation and land degradation have led to the world's forests changing from a net carbon sink, which takes CO_2 out of the atmosphere, into a net carbon source, which puts it back in again.

And finally, permafrost temperatures were the warmest ever recorded.

All is not well with our suffering planet. At the same time, the Trump administration in the USA worked hard to ensure that all references to 'anthropogenic climate change' were removed in all the reports produced by its many agencies. For many of the authors of such reports and the teams that worked to produce them, this meant that years of careful and dedicated work were being summarily trashed, because their politically appointed bosses were more interested in pleasing the insane criminals in the White House than they were in preserving whatever personal and professional integrity they may once have possessed.

*

Christmas comes and goes. Sophia and I don't make a big deal out of the celebrations, as Lizzie will only convert them into another alone-and-bereft drama.

As the new year rolls round, she loses more and more of her already depleted mind and provides us with new challenges every day. She has attempted to shuffle downstairs a couple of times, leaving her Zimmer frame on the landing. We're not expecting this because we encourage her to come down on the stairlift every day, but she always refuses. One day we hear her shouting and discover that she's managed to get down as far as six stairs from the top, and now she's unable to move any further up or down. With great difficulty we push, pull and coax her upstairs again and sling a rope across the top to remind her not to try it again.

'We should put a how-shall-I-say?' Sophia announces. 'I mean, what is stop the children when is fall down the stairs.'

'You mean a stairgate,' I say. 'That won't stop her, she's too big.'

'You are tamplar, *you should make one,' she instructs.*

'I am what?'

'Tamplar. Who work with the wood.'

'Carpenter,' I say. I was indeed a carpenter for thirty years or so before I re-trained as a psychotherapist. Taking this as a challenge, I build a stairgate so strong it would survive a nuclear explosion.

'Ah!' Sophia says when I instal it. 'Is not bad. Let's see if it stop the Mumia.'

Lizzie complains loudly about my stairgate, but we explain that it's only there to stop her falling down the stairs and hurting herself. 'You can come downstairs whenever you want,' we say, 'but you need to use the stairlift.'

'Yes, but there's no need for this,' *she says, pointing at the stairgate.*

'It's to keep you safe,' we explain. ' You're a bit unsteady on your legs sometimes. We don't want you to have an accident.'

'You don't care if I have an accident,' she complains. 'You want to make me a prisoner in my own house!'

'Aha,' I say, taking advantage of her confusion. 'So this IS your house, after all!'

Lizzie scowls at me, and shuffles back into her bedroom.

She's getting weaker, too. She can no longer get up off the loo; we have to add a plastic extension to make it high enough for her to stand up again once she's sat down on it. She can't stand up when she gets out of her bed, so we persuade the solicitor to fund a proper hospital bed, known as a 'profile bed', which can be configured into various different positions and heights. It also has sides that can be raised to stop her falling out.

'Is coming soon that she will need them,' says Sophia ominously.

Lizzie is very confused about the difference between night and day. She is almost always awake in the wee small hours, when she spends her time randomly re-arranging the contents of her wardrobes, or hiding things by wrapping them up in multiple layers of clothing, or shuffling out onto the landing every so often and calling 'Yoo-hoo! Yoo-hoo!'. She usually sleeps during the morning and for a while in the evening as well, if we're lucky.

She often forgets how to use the telephone so whenever she wants to call someone on an 'off' day, she has to get out of bed, shuffle across the landing and call 'Yoo-hoo!' until one of us does it for her. There are about six or seven people she still calls from time to time; if they don't answer, she'll demand to call them again and again until they give in and pick up the phone, so we get plenty of exercise running up and down stairs for her.

She often calls Amy to complain about us, because we can't (or won't) give her what she wants, but the man she calls most often, much to saintly Amy's evangelical discomfort, is Jolyon, Lizzie's long-lost gay stepson.

Sophia starts noticing that after Lizzie has had a phone conversation with him, she gets agitated about money. She wants to see the solicitor and 'sort out her affairs'. Then she wants to know how much it's costing her to have 'the girl' living in her house.

All this talk about money makes Sophia very suspicious, because it only happens after she's been talking to Jolyon, so she starts listening in to their conversations on the spare phone. Before long, she hears Jolyon asking Lizzie whether the solicitor has been to see her recently, and whether she's sure he's looking after her affairs properly. Lizzie says she hasn't seen him 'for ages', and she wishes he (Jolyon) would sort it out for her.

One day, Jolyon calls me and starts asking questions about the solicitor. Who is this man? How did he come to have power of attorney for Lizzie's finances? What do I know about him?

I give him the bare minimum and email the solicitor to warn him about what Jolyon is doing. At this stage, I'm still insisting that Jolyon is just a harmless old busybody who thinks he's helping, but Sophia is quite sure he wants to get his hands on her cash. It was his father's cash before Lizzie inherited it – of course he wants his share! Wouldn't you? I think she has a point.

The solicitor sends me a reply saying that 'this gentleman' has already called him and asked a lot of questions, but of course he wouldn't let him have any information about Lizzie's affairs because of client confidentiality.

Sophia tells me I should call Jolyon and tell him to 'fuck off'. She swears copiously in English, even though there are much more colourful expressions that she could use in her native tongue, most of which I learned from Valentina, who is younger and more carefree than Sophia. I agree, but my middle-class English background won't allow me to be quite so direct, so I call him and thank him for his concern. I advise him to address his questions about Lizzie's affairs to me rather than her because she's a vulnerable adult suffering from dementia and we are obliged to safeguard her interests. He apologises profusely, assures me that he understands and says he doesn't want to do anything that might upset 'poor Lizzie'. So that's where we leave it.

Sophia shakes her lioness head and calls me a 'taitsel ud'. She got that from Arnie Schwarzenegger; in her own language, it means 'wet noodle'; it's what Arnie called President Trump after his first meeting with Kim Jong Un. 'He will not give up,' she says. 'I tell you smack his face, but you just stroke his ass.'

I think she meant the other way round, but never mind.

🍃

We have spent the last two months in the intervals between Lizzie's mad episodes preparing for our equally mad journey to the Peruvian Amazon. Sophia has made sure that Lizzie will be cared for by her colleague, Valentina. This will be the third time Valie has looked after my mother-in-law while Sophia has been away on holiday.

Sophia wants to make Valie's stay as trouble-free as possible because she won't be able to contact us when we're in Peru. She makes sure Valie knows all the details about what's happening with Jolyon, and advises her to contact the solicitor if it gets any worse. She also calls the doctor and asks him if he can prescribe something a bit stronger than Lorazepam because it doesn't always do what it's supposed to do. Lizzie can still become very anxious, and when she's agitated she can do silly things like forgetting where she is and looking for the loo in Sophia's bedroom.

'One day she find loo in there and make kakat', she says, as if this is something they all do in the end. I start locking my bedroom door during the day.

Just before we leave for Peru, I get a call from the doctor.

289

He says he will try Lizzie on an anti-psychotic called Risperidone, and I can collect it from the chemist whenever I want. I pick up the drug and bring it home for Valie to dish out when we're gone. We hope this will calm Lizzie down while we're away, but we have no idea what the Fates are busy arranging for poor Valie.

We're due at the airport at 4am for the first leg of the journey to Amsterdam. There's no point in trying to sleep, so we all stay up (Sophia, Valentina and I) until we're due to depart in my ancient Ford Focus.

At 2.45am, I take the last small item of luggage out into the blustery, freezing darkness, stow it in the car, slam the rear door shut – and realise I've locked my keys inside. I lost the spare key a long time ago, so there's nothing for it but to smash the passenger side window, open the rear door from the inside, and retrieve my keys. We patch the shattered side window with a black polythene rubbish bag and some duct tape, and depart half an hour late.

As we depart, Lizzie leans over the banisters and starts yoo-hooing loudly. 'What's going on? Who's that in my house? I'll call the police! Yoo-hoo! Who's down there? What are you doing in my house?' and more like that.

'Bye, Valie,' I say, and give her a goodbye hug. 'Sorry it's such a mess. Good luck with Lizzie. See you later!'

❧

The journey to Peru is a nightmare. We arrive at Bristol airport in good time, despite the delayed departure and the frantic flapping of black polythene, but by now the blustery wind has become half a gale and the Amsterdam flight is delayed by two hours. Ours is the last flight into

Schiphol that morning, as the wind is gusting to 80 mph, and we're lucky not to be diverted to somewhere half a continent away. Then they keep us cooped up on the plane for another two hours because the movable stairs are being blown over by the wind – we see three of them lying on their sides on the tarmac – and they decide to stop all passenger movement until the gale subsides enough for us to be taken off the plane safely.

By the time we find ourselves traipsing up the long corridor at Schiphol, Sophia hasn't had a cigarette for nearly six hours. The only place she's allowed to smoke is in a tiny cupboard at the other end of the terminal. No doubt this is intended as a deterrent, but it makes Sophia even more enraged than she is already. It's lucky I know how to keep calm under duress because the slightest thing might set off a nuclear explosion.

The Lima flight is delayed by three hours but it's uneventful, just twelve hours of sitting still watching old movies and trying to sleep. We've been looking forward to a good long sleep in Lima and a leisurely breakfast before catching our Latam flight to Iquitos, but once again the fates are against us.

'Can we have breakfast at eight?' I ask.

'I advise you get taxi at six,' says the desk clerk.

'But it only takes twenty minutes to the airport!'

'Yes, usually it does, but tomorrow morning comes Il Papa to Lima, so many roads will be closed and journey will take two hours, maybe more.'

'Oh, fuck!' says Sophia. 'We choose the one day in twenty years when is coming to Lima the fucking Pope. Oh my God.'

Never mind. We managed to reach Iquitos, and had three days to relax and get accustomed to the climate. Mercifully, it wasn't as hot as we had expected. We were in the tourist part of town, where the Ayahuasca influence was visible everywhere in the artisan shops and the cafes. Ayahuasca menus; Ayahuasca paintings; American hippies in their sixties with their taut twenty-five-year-old Peruvian girlfriends; local craftswomen laden with beautiful, printed textiles or handmade jewellery – it was all there, and much more. We soaked it up for three days, and then we did the thirty-mile boat trip upriver to the community which hosted the Temple of Shamanic Healing, and our ordeal began.

We had chosen this particular place because we wanted to take Ayahuasca in its traditional context of plant healing, rather than just using it as an exotic way of getting high, so we couldn't really complain about the discomfort. But nothing could have prepared us for the sheer extremity of the experience. The heat and humidity of the jungle, the ferocity and persistence of the biting insects, the constant discomfort, the frequent purgatives, the awful salt-free diet and the stomach-heaving effects of the ayahuasca itself would have been enough to put anyone off, were it not for the stubborn belief that we were doing this for the sake of our souls (and, of course, the fact that we'd paid $2,500 each for the privilege).

There were ten of us on the retreat and, although most of us grumbled and got angry at one time or another, we bore the discomfort with a stoic sense that there really was a 'higher purpose' to it all, as the facilitators kept reminding us, and we were going to 'satisfy our deepest longings' through it, come what may. If I was going to get a bit closer to the Divine Feminine, she was asking a very high price. I hoped she would be worth it.

The first ordeal was the purging. They gave us some kind of foul-tasting liquid to drink (the first one was called *sangre del grado,* which means 'dragon's blood') and then we had to drink enormous quantities of water – five or ten litres of it – until we threw up. There we were, all ten of us, throwing up lustily into the undergrowth.

There were three of these purges, each one more extreme than the one before. My stomach still tightens up when I hear the words *Bija bija*, the awful liquid we had to drink for the third one. The stated aim was to get rid of the toxic stuff we'd allowed to build up in our gut over the previous twenty, thirty or (in my case) seventy-five years, so that the plant medicines could get into our system properly and do their job.

Then there were the vapour baths every day for six or seven days, where we were suspended from a wooden frame that looked like a medieval instrument of torture over a large vat of plant medicines dissolved in very hot water. There was a plastic sheet over us so that we were forced to breathe this hot vapour for fifteen minutes, after which they laid us out on a wooden bed and blew *mapacho* smoke over us for another ten minutes as a cleansing ritual.

Then there were the cold baths full of noxious stuff like onions and garlic, and the 'love baths' which smelled lovely and fragrant but were full of green slime that we weren't supposed to wash off for at least two hours. There was the special diet that contained no salt, spices or stimulants, which tasted so awful that it was a real effort to swallow anything. Porridge without any salt, or chickpeas without any spices, turn out to be gut-churningly horrible.

Then there was the constant heat at 100% humidity, and the mozzies waiting to bite any skin surface that presented itself, and the lack of anywhere comfortable to sit or lie. The beds themselves were OK, but the rooms were insufferably hot during the day and there were no fans to cool the air, let alone *punkah wallahs* or Nubian slaves with ostrich feathers.

This was no hippie hangout where we could lie around all day and just 'do some Ayahuasca' every other night. Mother Ayahuasca requires her supplicants to go through a bloody ordeal, not at all like the warm maternal fantasy suggested by the words 'Divine Feminine'. She can be fierce and uncompromising, like Kali or the ancient Egyptian Sekhmet. She wants to clean out the cupboards and get rid of the crap. She's not anyone's lovely soft mummy, and she's definitely not their nice compliant little girlfriend. If you stroke her the wrong way, you may end up with bloody claw marks all down your front.

This aspect of the experience of Mother Ayahuasca is not much mentioned in the publicity material of the various temples and foundations, which are keen to emphasise 'love and light', because this is what the average Euro-American punter, driven half-mad by the zombie culture with which we have surrounded ourselves, is literally dying to hear.

✎

The Ayahuasca ceremonies themselves were a journey into the chaotic beauty of the underworld, with occasional glimpses of heaven (if we were lucky enough). Each ceremony lasted five hours or more. We would assemble in the *maloca* at 7pm, when it was already completely dark, and do a meditation. After a while the maestro, Don Miguel, who was an experienced healer in the Shipibo tradition, would give each of us a cupful of the thick, viscous, bitter-tasting liquid, and after another half an hour or so he would start singing the *icaros*, the traditional songs that invite the various plant spirits to join the ceremony and do their work under the direction of the spirits of the Ayahuasca and Chicruna plants.

The action of the plant medicines starts slowly and builds up to a long climax. During this time, there is a great deal of exuberant vomiting because Ayahuasca is a strong emetic. This caused me great discomfort because I hate throwing up and will resist it if at all possible. At the same time, the participants may have 'visions', which may be anything from beautiful colours to dream-like events involving animals, people or strange spirit forms – or almost nothing may happen. Alternatively, as in my case, something may change deep in the subconscious mind and is only noticed afterwards.

Sophia, on the other hand, experienced hours of almost unbearable pain in her body, which the facilitators told her was the traumatic effect of her mother's violence and neglect. Mother Ayahuasca opens the door, but you never know what her partner Chicruna is going to present you with when it's open. Maybe it will be something you need to learn the hard way.

We were told that if we had a strong intention for the ceremony, something would happen that would be related to that intention. Although I had agreed to come on this crazy trip in the hope that I might get closer to this mysterious entity called the Divine Feminine, I soon realised that my search for a spiritual revelation, something that would carry me above and beyond the boundaries of everyday experience, was constantly being held back by my need to feel in control. It's an existential anxiety, an insistence that I must know what's *really* going on. Why? Probably because I was fed up with being lied to when I was a child, so I had to spend my life searching for some kind of reliable truth as a result. Whatever came to me, it didn't seem real until I'd nailed it down, possessed it like another book on my bookshelf, written my name on it and put it in a box.

Looking back on this now, I can see that it's just another expression of our collective conditioning into 'machine thinking', which demands consistency, reliability and predictability, and hates ambiguity or uncertainty. I had been doing what rebels often do: trying to use machine thinking to repudiate machine thinking.

As a strategy for rebellion, this search for the 'one consistent story' has an upside and a downside. The upside (for me) is that I'm not easily conned into a state of passive compliance by the agents of the Machine. The downside is that I have to feel like I know all the answers or, to put it another way, I can't tolerate not knowing. The reward of having a consistent story is the feeling of superiority you get because you're always right; hence the proliferation of conspiracy theories at this time of *anomie*. In its shadow is a gnawing sense of anxiety that it may still, after all, be just another delusion. How would you know?

🍃

Which way round am I? Wait a minute. Ah, there's the

throwing-up bucket. Need to turn around. Feet go this way. Where are my feet? I don't feel too good. Mustn't get too far from the bucket. What if I throw up all over the mattress? Maybe I should sit up for a while. I'm in the examination chair. Who's examining me? There are frogs all over the floor.

Ah, there's the bucket. I'm going to throw up. There are colours coming out of the bucket. Iridescent lines of blue, red and purple. A forest of red-blue trees, coming from some place deep inside the bucket. I'm wandering around in a red-blue forest, there are birds hiding in the trees, calling me. Where are my feet? Where am I now?

Ah, they are singing the plant songs. I know this one. I'm in a valley where three rivers meet. The valley is spinning slowly round me. I'll go this way. The plant song is everywhere, coming out of the river, the sky. There's a big purple moon. Am I OK? I haven't thrown up yet. Whoops, here it comes.

Woah! That's better. The colours are still coming out of the bucket, faster now. Where's the loo roll? I need to wipe my mouth. Someone else is throwing up right next door to me. Who's that? A giant turtle just came out of his mouth.

Where am I? I'm not feeling too good. This restaurant is terrible but the singer is good. I could listen to him all night. Take the food away, I'd rather listen to the singer. I fancy a drink of water right now. We're not allowed to drink any water in this fucking restaurant. I'll speak to the manager tomorrow. He's over there, hiding in the trees.

Now we have a different singer. She's good too. They are dancing on the stage over there. Something Spanish, what is it called? Famingo. Famenco. Fam... I don't know.

Jesus loves you. You're just saying it, I don't believe a word. Great dancing, though. I feel like getting up and joining them but I'm very heavy. Much too heavy to dance. I'd rather just lie here and dream. Love and Light. Well, it's lovely but it's dark. Very dark.

Which way round am I? I might need that bucket again…

🍃

Something in me wasn't going to give in to all this 'love and light' without a struggle. After four or five ceremonies, a mood of resentment began to develop. I felt as if I were expected to buy into a completely bizarre set of beliefs and practices in the hope that they would eventually work, when all the evidence was that they did me a lot of harm and left me exhausted and unable to function. We had to take it on faith that all this would have a good outcome, even though it didn't bear any kind of critical examination. There was a lot of talk about 'your highest good', which I really wanted to be true, but so far there was no evidence that it represented anything real. And we were expected to believe that a transformation as profound as this could be delivered in three weeks.

Sitting in the communal dining area one day, I told one of the facilitators, Adrian, about the ball of resentment that was gathering inside me. I told him I'd spent all my life trying to understand what 'the plot' is, and I felt this was being subtly denigrated as a mere mental exercise. I said it had been very important to me to have a grasp of what's real, but this would never feel complete without some kind of revelation, which is why I had brought myself all the way here … and it still eluded me, despite the talk of love and light. Where was the evidence? I didn't see it.

'Maybe the revelation you feel you need can only be accessed through faith and trust,' Adrian said. 'You could make this your intention for tonight's ceremony.'

'Yeah, maybe I could,' I said, unconvinced by his enthusiasm.

'Try it,' he continued earnestly. 'But don't expect any particular outcomes. They'll just get in the way.'

This was all too much for me. Part of me wanted to strangle the man, and another part wanted to give up and go home. Then I fell to pieces, overwhelmed by seventy-five years of accumulated grief, not to mention twelve days of inedible food and several nights without sleep. I couldn't stop the tears coming. This time it wasn't just about me, it was about the whole historical tragedy of our culture and its doomed attempts to bring everything in the world under its control. I thought I'd pretty much freed myself from all that, but now I realised just how deeply complicit I was with the whole pattern. There was no escape, even in the Peruvian Amazon. Fuck this crazy universe, I cried, flipping over totally into victim mode, it cares no more about any of us than it does about a fly on a turd.

After a while I found myself laughing at the absurdity of it all. What's the point? We control everything, and then what? We get to be masters of the universe – and then we die.

By this time I had acquired an audience which applauded my performance with gusto. So much for my desire to be taken seriously.

That evening was the sixth ceremony. Having fallen to pieces earlier, I was finally able to bury my cynicism enough to ask Mother Ayahuasca to show me how I could get past this impasse. Also, for the first time, I managed to stay present with all the craziness instead of becoming preoccupied with what was 'really' happening – in other words, I didn't put up any resistance.

I found myself vomiting with unusual violence but afterwards felt very relaxed and awake, in a weirdly hallucinatory way. The strange thing was that there was still a subtle 'something' there underneath all the craziness that wasn't affected by it, so I was able to meet the energy that was flowing through me with a degree of welcoming and self-care. It felt as though this was being given freely without any need for me to do anything, as if it were saying, 'It's OK, you can let go of your fear now, nothing bad will happen.' It wasn't intense or overwhelming, just subtle and deeply reassuring.

Then I realised that the *Icaros* was being sung by a mysterious woman really close to me on my right-hand side, as if she was singing to me personally. The power of her song was indescribable; it wrapped itself around me like the Ayahuasca vine wraps itself round the tree. There was a hunger for completeness in it, an eerie intensity that commanded the space like nothing I'd ever heard before. She wanted something from me, not something sexual, not an attitude, not a gift – it wasn't personal. She was telling me something, and she wanted me to really hear it.

Opened up by the plant medicine, in a receptive state where I had no desire to resist or argue, I could hear her really well, and I could *feel* what she was trying to convey. It's not something I can ever forget because it was there in her voice, in the music; I can still hear it today just as clearly as I could on that night in the Peruvian Amazon. It's very hard to put into words but, as an experience, it left a unique 'taste'.

Later, when I had returned to my normal habit of boxing up everything neatly so I could think about it more easily, for some reason I cast her as one of those legendary French *chanteuses*, like Edith Piaf, singing about love and life in that wonderful bittersweet voice that only a French *chanteuse* can produce. Perhaps my more rational side preferred to think that Mother Ayahuasca was merely reflecting my own hyperbole. The thought that I could have been so close to such a primal energy didn't sit well with my inner cynic.

Whatever I made of it later, at that moment and in that place she *was* my Divine Feminine. If I could have met a woman like that in real life, her sheer emotional power would have scared me completely shitless. She was definitely not an angel.

Looking back on it, I can see why Abrahamic man has so typically abused women as the 'evil temptress' (or else put them on a pedestal as the 'pure ideal'). It's because, deep down, we know the power of the Feminine, we (men) know what she wants from us, and we don't want the responsibility.

I was completely spaced-out after the ceremony and sat on the side of the bed, swaying gently from side to side. Sophia had some fun trying to persuade me to take off my clothes and lie down, but I had no desire to move and stayed there for hours, quite contentedly vacant. Eventually I managed to shed a few clothes and lie down. I slept very well for the few hours that remained until sunrise.

Adrian told me later that when I threw up I had vomited out a bad spirit, which had lived in me for quite a while and was responsible for a pattern of highly negative physical, emotional and spiritual energies, including my need to feel in control. He congratulated me on my determination to let go of it. I said it didn't seem like such a big deal. I just kind of gave up struggling.

'It never is a big deal,' he said, 'and that's the tragedy of it. We can so easily let go, but we don't because we're afraid. We've always been afraid, but we can't acknowledge it because we don't really notice it – until we let it go.'

🍃

Sophia went on her own journey that same evening. She had been anticipating this for a long time, several years in fact, and was finally able to do it because her body was relaxed enough. Normally, she says, she feels tense most of the time.

On her journey she searched for, and found, the spirit of her grandma, of whom she'd been very fond when she was a child. Her grandma had taught her what love feels like, unlike her mother, who had taught her how to manifest an almost unlimited level of defiance when under attack. Her grandma appeared as a Being of Light, and they recognised and held each other in a loving embrace.

Then she went on a different journey, to find the violent *mafioso* who had used and abused her when she was a young woman. Some years after she had escaped from him at great personal cost, he had died from a heart attack. She found him in a room full of dead people, looking like a partly decomposed corpse. He was very surprised to see her, and even more surprised when she said she had come to forgive him. She just said it and left; there was no need for any more.

Sophia is full of surprises.

🍃

Professionally speaking, the facilitators, Marnie and Adrian, were very good at what they were doing and took great care to protect us. They were presenting what the temple had to offer very much in the manner of a cult, with characteristic fundamentalist fervour, along with core phrases (Love & Light, Your Highest Good, etc.) and essential initiation ordeals (purging, dieting, etc.).

I was suspicious of this because I have some experience of cults and I know their tricks. The retreat was *apparently* structured in the classic manner of an initiation (the descent into the darkness, the search for the light, the journey through many perils, etc.) but the participants, like all spiritual tourists, had to be protected from the real perils, the real terrors of the dark side. It was tailored for a modern Western clientele, which is unprepared for this kind of encounter. We had all signed up for this retreat in the hope that we'd see the spiritual light, but nobody was talking about the darkness.

Adrian had been on his Ayahuasca journey for only a year or two before taking on the job, so I suspect he wasn't quite so well acquainted with the dark side. About half way through our stay, Don Miguel came under some kind of demonic attack. Knowing the dangers, he stopped officiating at the ceremonies for a while and Adrian had to take over.

That night, during the ceremony, we were aware of Adrian singing the *icaros* with desperate urgency for three hours without a break, as if his life depended on it. Later the same night, Sophia was woken up by the sound of a man screaming. Adrian told us afterwards that he too had suffered a sustained attack, both during the ceremony and afterwards, by a *brujo* (a bad spirit). He appeared very relieved to have survived.

Sophia hadn't drunk the sacred brew that night, but she was in the *maloca* with the rest of us and she told me later that she had seen his attackers. She saw three enormous, shadowy figures, almost as high as the ten-metre roof of the *maloca*, trying to envelop and overwhelm him. At one point she saw a huge snake appear through the floor and go for him, 'So I cut it' she said, meaning that she was able to imagine the cut into the other world. This, she said, is based on a trance technique used in NLP[2] to cut through obsessive thought patterns.

She wondered whether Adrian had been trying to go somewhere too deep, too fast. She could easily be right; he was prepared to take things to extremes. Judging by his account of the life he led before he became a *curandero*, he could get a bit blasé about the dark side.

❧

These experiences with Mother Ayahuasca confirmed what Conrad was trying to tell me on the night of my vigil in the Coombe about standing with one foot in each of the two worlds. Not just the ordinary world that we experience 'out there', but also the numinous world that we experience more from the inside, if we are aware of it at all. The enormous shadowy figures and the huge snake that Sophia saw that night existed in this numinous world, not in the world we usually call 'real'.

It's not easy to balance these two worlds; the kind of direct inner awareness that sees the numinous world can't easily exist side-by-side with our ordinary common-sense experience. We could say that the shadowy figures represented some kind of energy that Sophia was 'picking up', but that doesn't convey the vividness and immediacy of the actual experience.

The medicinal arts of the indigenous South American people survive from a time thousands of years ago when the separation paradigm had hardly begun to establish itself in our human world. The mindset of its practitioners is not the same as the mindset that we have grown used to over the last couple of millennia, and it's not easy for us to abandon our way of experiencing the world to make way for theirs.

In our modern world of separation, critical thinking has become a very powerful weapon. The world of oneness cannot survive a sustained attack by unbalanced critical thinking. In recent years, almost everything we can experience in our inner world, especially those experiences we call 'spiritual', has been mercilessly attacked by such thinking, whether it's Richard Dawkins' aggressive atheism or Ben Goldacre's gentle mockery of 'alternative medicine' in his Bad Science column in *The Guardian*.

The world that was opened up for me by Mother Ayahuasca was no exception. My inner critic – my Tyrant – pounced on the experience like a secret policeman in a totalitarian state, just in case some small taste of inner freedom should slip through.

The challenge for us in our era is not to abandon critical thinking entirely, but to apply it appropriately in situations where it's really necessary so that it supports our fragile inner experiencing rather than automatically destroying it. The medieval scholastics, like Thomas Aquinas, made a serious attempt to do this in the centuries before the so-called Enlightenment bowled us over with its uncompromising pursuit of reason at the expense of our innate sense of the sacred. Little remains of this innate sense in our common discourse now; it has been almost completely destroyed by our relentless drive to become masters of the universe and bend everything to our will. It's going to be very hard for us to deal with the results of tempting that particular genie out of its bottle.

*

On our way back home from Peru, when Sophia and I were in Iquitos again for three days of de-acclimatisation, I noticed a peculiar trick of perception that had the effect of removing the veil between the Two Worlds and allowing me to live for a time with one foot in each of them, like a kind of alternative reality.

We went up to the promenade on the Saturday evening, when everyone was out and about enjoying the balmy air and making music, and strolled along it for a while. Everything stood out as if it had come alive, and the air was full of energy. In this state, it's very easy to see that the world we normally inhabit is permeated with another magical one where some of our fellow beings (human or animal) can become larger than life, as if in a surrealist dream. Maybe this happens more easily in South America, the birthplace of magical realism.

At the same time, on this numinous evening nothing mattered. There was no agenda and nothing to worry about. We were in an open-focus state, not at all like the closed-down, narrow-focus state that we usually inhabit, which is always full of 'the next thing' or 'the last thing'.

I'm familiar with the practice of 'being in the moment' or

'waking up', but this usually requires a deliberate decision and a certain amount of work. To slip into it so easily and so thoroughly was new to me. I could do it to order then, and I still can to some extent, especially when I'm walking in the woods.

In this state of awareness, beings from the spirit world might very well appear, alongside our everyday reality. Sometimes they do, disguised as birds or small animals. When I'm touched by this state, I can experience a tree or a crow as if it were as sentient as I am, which it probably is in its own way. The universe is a strange and wonderful place.

Not long after we got back from Peru, a beautiful green-and-gold scarab beetle contrived to find its way into my bedroom in Lizzie's house and ended up on my pillow, like a hidden message. I was aware that I could see him in two ways. In one sense, he was a fairly common type of beetle that had somehow strayed into my bedroom. In another sense he was no ordinary beetle, he was *Ra-Kheper*, the scarab, the ancient Egyptian symbol of transformation, whose ancestor emerged from the primeval waters and started the cycles of life on Earth. There was something about his appearance in that time and that place that made me see it as a sign that everything had changed for me, although I didn't know how or in what way.

❧

Recently I read an interview with a Colombian singer called Almunis Alejandra Ortiz[3], who mentioned Ayahuasca in connection with spiritual tourism. Ayahuasca, she pointed out, is a medicine not originally intended for seeking self-knowledge in the modern Western sense. People from other cultures who go to South America in search of spiritual fulfilment find themselves in a kind of psychological no-man's land because they aren't sustained by the tradition. She regards the *Icaros* – the sacred songs used by the healers to invite the spirits of the plants into the healing ceremony – as being potent enough in themselves without any drug.

Her words reminded me of my vivid encounter with the Divine Feminine in the sixth ceremony, as well as the extraordinary inner landscapes into which the songs translated themselves when I heard them for the first time.

When I mentioned this interview to Sophia, she saw the sense of it straight away. 'Is right,' she said. 'I feel like intruder when I go in jungle.'

I asked her what she meant by that.

'Is something in us that remember we are deep connected with the Nature,' she said. 'Is like our soul want the pure water, because she have nothing but shit all her life, so we jump in it like idiot, but the water is hundred metres deep and we forget we are never learn how to swim, and is too much for us.' Sophia can be very elegant with words, even in a language that still causes her head to ache.

I have to ask myself why I needed to go all the way to Peru to discover something about the Divine Feminine when I live in a country where there is still so much natural beauty, despite our efforts to reduce it to a theme park or a chemical food factory.

🌿

The last word in this small saga needs to come from the healers of the Shipibo community themselves. It says something that needs to be heard by everyone who, like me, has indulged in what the representatives of those healers have called 'spiritual extractivism'.

Two months after we got back to the UK, a Canadian Ayahuasca tourist rode his motorbike into a small town not so far from Iquitos and shot dead eighty-one-year-old Maestra Olivia Arévalo Lomas in a dispute he was having with a relative of hers over money. The local Shipibo community, which revered Maestra Lomas as a great healer, reacted instinctively by catching and killing him in revenge. There was an immediate and severe reaction from the Peruvian police, who don't normally take much interest in the Shipibo community, because this was very bad publicity for the tourist trade.

In the fallout from this tragedy, the representative council of the Shipibo-Konibo-Xetebo peoples of the Peruvian Amazon convened a conference of traditional healers in the city of Yarinacocha in August 2018, the result of which was the Declaration of Yarinacocha[4]. In this, they are very clear about the dangers of unrestricted access by foreign spiritual tourists to the riches of the indigenous tradition. It says, in part:

The fallout from the murder of Maestra Arévalo Lomas is emblematic of a common problem, [which] we are framing as spiritual extractivism...

People come to the Amazon to heal themselves of the culturally specific ailments of industrialized, individualistic societies – from addiction to depression to sexual, military and other forms of trauma to eating disorders and diseases and illnesses that have found no real cure in the halls of Western medicine. Then they get to leave but they leave behind traces of their ailments, trails of inequality, frustration, violence, and sometimes legal cases. But their consciousness has expanded! They have experienced the Way of Light!

This is spiritual extractivism. We have to recognise that ayahuasca tourism is part of a much wider spiritual ecology and political economy, part of structures of global inequality, of predatory capitalism, of Euro American lifestyles and thirst for growth, of the rampant militarism and corporatism of states that everyday affect the health of the Amazon and its peoples.

Will the enlightened and the healed help the overwhelming fight against big companies eating up the rainforest and destroying the territorial survival of the very Shipibo communities from whom they are receiving so much benefit? Will they put their bodies and resources on the line? Or will they be part of what Franz Fanon, referring to colonialism, called 'the greater organism of violence'?

Will we, indeed? I doubt it. We'll sign petitions and agonise over the destruction of the Amazon forest, which is moving at an accelerated pace now that the fascist Jair Bolsonaro has been elected President of Brazil. But we won't do much to help the indigenous people protect their ancestral land; we'll be too busy trying to protect our own land from the fracking wells, the open-cast mines, the giant infrastructure projects and the expanded airports demanded from us by the insatiable Machine.

References

1 www.globalissues.org/news/2018/01/06/23842
2 Neuro Linguistic Programming, a therapeutic modality that makes much use of trance states. Sophia was a trained NLP practitioner.
3 Interview with Amisha Ghadiali, 30 August 2018, on www.thefutureisbeautiful.co/
4 https://amazonwatch.org/news/2018/0906-in-the-declaration-of-yarinacocha-shipibo-healers-organise-to-resist-spiritual-extractivism

- 13 -
Psychosis

2 FEBRUARY 2018

A REPORT IN *The Guardian* today gives details of 197 people who were murdered in 2017 for defending land, wildlife or natural resources, as revealed by the Global Witness network. For every defender killed, many others (in some cases, thousands of others) are displaced, their culture and way of life ruined in the name of 'progress'.

'The slaughter of people defending their land or environment continued unabated in 2017, with new research showing almost four people a week were killed worldwide in struggles against mines, plantations, poachers and infrastructure projects', says the article.

The toll of 197 in 2017 – which has risen fourfold since it was first compiled in 2002 – underscores the violence on the frontiers of a global economy driven by expansion and consumption.

Most of the killings occurred in remote forest areas of developing countries, particularly in Latin America where the abundance of resources is often in inverse proportion to the authority of the law or environmental regulation.

Extractive industries were one of the deadliest drivers of violence... Mining conflicts accounted for 36 killings, several of them linked to booming global demand for construction materials...

Agribusiness was the biggest driver of violence as supermarket demand for soy, palm oil, sugarcane and beef provided a financial incentive for plantations and ranches to push deeper into indigenous territory and other communal land.

With many of the tensions focused in the Amazon, Brazil – with 46 killings – was once again the deadliest country for defenders. Relative to size, however, smaller Amazonian neighbours were more dangerous.

We hardly ever see this kind of outrage reported in the mainstream news. I wonder why.

🍃

Valie waves good-bye to us as we set out on our journey to Peru. It's 3.30am, and she's shivering in the wet, blustery wind. When she goes back into the house, she finds my mother-in-law halfway down the stairs, quivering with rage. Somehow, in her anger, she has managed to open the impregnable stairgate.

'What's going on?' Lizzie shouts. 'Who are you? What are you doing in my house?'

Valie braces herself for a fight. 'I'm the carer,' she says. 'What are you doing on stairs? Go in bed please.'

Lizzie lets go of the banisters, raises her fist and shouts, 'Don't you tell me...' She loses her footing. For a moment she teeters on the edge of a catastrophic fall but, by the grace of God, she manages to grab the banister and steady herself in time. It frightens her and gives Valie time to race up the stairs and hold on to her.

'Careful, Lizzie,' she says. 'Hold on to me and try to relax.'

Lizzie does what she's told and stops struggling. Valie pushes, pulls and coaxes her up the stairs again and back into bed. She sits on the bed for half an hour until she's sure Lizzie is settled. She explains that Sophia will be away for a while, and she (Valentina) will look after her during this time.

'Don't you remember me, Lizzie? I was here before when Sophia was on holiday. I'm Valentina.'

Lizzie shakes her head and looks away. She mutters about how scandalous it is that no-one tells her what's going on, then gradually sinks into a kind of torpor.

Valie waits to see if it's just another coma drama. After a while, when she thinks Lizzie's probably OK for the rest of the night, she falls exhausted into her own bed and goes straight to sleep.

No more than half an hour later, she is woken up from a deep sleep by Lizzie banging on her door and shouting, 'Are you in there? I want to know what's going on! What's happening?'

Wearily, Valie falls out of bed and opens the door. 'Lizzie, nothing is happening. I am very tired. I am trying to sleep. Please go in bed, you need also to sleep. It is half past four in the morning.'

Lizzie is having none of it and continues to shout that she wants to know what's going on. Valie steers her back to her bedroom. Once again she sits on the bed and patiently explains that she is looking after her while Sophia is away, and there's no need to worry about it. Once again Lizzie sinks gradually into a kind of torpor and Valie goes back to her own bed, exhausted.

And once again, she's woken up an hour later from a deep sleep by the sound of Lizzie banging on her door and demanding attention. And so it goes on.

Valie parks the stairlift at the top of the stairs and locks it in place; even if Lizzie somehow opens the stairgate again, she can't get past it to try and kill herself. It's a damn nuisance because Valie has to struggle to get past it too, but she can't take any chances.

Over the next four days, Lizzie becomes more and more anxious. Gradually she stops eating and sleeping normally and becomes increasingly aggressive. By the fifth day, she's indulging in an extended orgy of throwing things, shouting, and calling all and sundry on the phone.

As Valie listens on the other phone, she hears Lizzie making serious allegations about what 'the girl' is doing to her – hitting her, trying to kill her, locking her in the bathroom and amputating her leg (literally!), and she begs them to come immediately and save her life. Most of them are bemused by this, but Jolyon takes at least part of it seriously and tries to interfere.

Lizzie tells him a similar story about being locked in the bathroom and having something amputated, which he doesn't quite believe, but he certainly thinks Valie is maltreating her in some way. He promises he'll come at last and see her on January 31. He instructs her not to tell the carer when he's coming or she'll have time to prepare for it, and he wants it to be a surprise. He says he'll come 'with a strong man, so we can throw her out of the house, and then we'll make sure you can move to a nice home where they will look after you, and you'll be able to watch TV whenever you want to, and they'll give you only the food that you like, and make sure the doctor sees you whenever you need him.'

Having been warned about Jolyon, Valie is listening on the other phone. She feels like butting in and telling the idiot where he can stuff his 'nice home', but she manages to hold her tongue, and tells the solicitor about it instead. He promises he'll support her and advises her to call the police if anyone tries to come into the house without her permission.

Lizzie finds the strength for some surprising feats, like throwing her Zimmer frame across the room at Valie when she suggests it's time for a shower. If Valie doesn't come when Lizzie yoo-hoos she repeatedly bangs the bedside table against the wardrobe. She bangs on Valie's door at night with the Zimmer frame and throws things at her when she comes out. Valie is getting no sleep; in fact, she even tries to sleep downstairs for two nights so she can get some rest. It's a real nightmare.

She asks for support from EuroCare, but they say they can't change anything without doing another assessment, and they can't arrange that for another two weeks. They say they can replace her 'if she isn't happy with the placement', but Valie has given Sophia her word and she refuses their offer. She can't ask Sophia for advice because we're deep in the Amazon jungle, miles away from the nearest phone signal. The only real support she gets is from Sue, who does some shopping for her on Mondays, and Amy, who lets her go out and take a break on Thursdays when she comes for her weekly visit.

Meanwhile Jolyon calls Lizzie every other day and talks to her for an hour at a time about how he's going to sort everything out, what a lovely home she'll be going to, and how Jane is waiting for her in the Kingdom of Souls. She keeps begging him to come down now, not to wait until

January 3l, but he keeps saying he can't. He's had to arrange a driver because it's too far for him to drive and he can't leave his sick and ageing partner on his own.

Finally he gets irritable with her and tells her she'll just have to be patient, but he picks the wrong time to do it because she's also feeling irritable. She shouts at him that he's useless; all he can do is chatter on about the Kingdom of Souls but he's got no real intention of helping her. Then she throws the phone across the room and shouts for Valie to come and pick it up again.

Valie calms her down, calls him back and explains that this behaviour is typical of Lizzie at the moment. The phone is not the only thing she's thrown across the room during the previous week. He listens to what she says for a change and at last the light begins to dawn on him that Lizzie is completely mad. He begins to doubt that he's doing anything useful. He has a long conversation with Valie, apologises profusely and says he'll 'try and make amends'.

Valie realises quite quickly that Lizzie's behaviour isn't just a reaction to the events on the night we departed, which she would normally have forgotten about after a day or two. She thinks it might be the result of a UTI (a urinary tract infection that often unhinges very old people), and sends some urine for a test. God knows how she gets the old relic to provide it, but she does.

Valie finds out that there's no infection. The only other significant change in Lizzie's routine has been the so-called anti-psychotic drug Risperidone, which she started to take on the day we left, so it seems possible that the drug is the culprit. Valie tries to talk to the doctor about it, and after a while she manages to persuade him to come and visit, but he still insists that the reason for Lizzie's bad behaviour is that

I've gone away and the carer has changed, so he won't alter the prescription.

After ten days of hell, Valie simply stops giving it to her and waits to see the result.

Lo and behold! The bad behaviour stops almost at once, and the Mumia relapses into her usual torpor. She is suddenly very hungry as well. Valie keeps this up for three days, then calls the doctor and tells him that Lizzie has been refusing to take the Risperidone, but for some strange reason the disturbances have magically stopped. The doctor reluctantly agrees that the drug may have been responsible for the disturbances. Valie should stop trying to give it to her for a while and see what happens.

Now Lizzie needs to go back on Lorazepam, which is the only drug that has actually helped with her relentless agitation. Valie has a struggle with the pharmacy to get the prescription renewed, but eventually she succeeds. Fortunately, Lizzie is so exhausted by her ten-day psychotic spree that she is torpid for the next four or five days and doesn't need medicating. This gives Valie a chance to recover from the continual stress and lack of sleep.

Jolyon duly comes for his visit, minus the threatened 'strong man'. He turns out to be a rotund, jolly man, to match his jolly name. He brings two enormous bouquets of flowers, one for Valie and one for Lizzie. By great good fortune he has decided to come on a Thursday, so saintly Amy, the scourge of the Antichrist, is there already. She's sitting with Lizzie upstairs in her bedroom, massaging her hand and talking about Jesus.

Valie offers Jolyon a cup of coffee, which he accepts gratefully and manoeuvres himself into a chair in the kitchen. He talks non-stop while Valie arranges the flowers.

He's full of praise for her wonderful qualities and apologises over and over again for not recognising them before. After a while Valie gets bored with this and asks him if he'd like to go up and see Lizzie.

'Maybe I should wait until her friend has gone?' he suggests anxiously.

Valie can't wait to see how saintly Amy will react to the presence of the Antichrist, so she says, 'Oh I think it's OK. She comes here every week and sometimes she stays for hours. Anyway,' she adds mischievously, 'I think she would like to meet you.'

'OK,' says Big Jolyon, and heaves himself out of the chair. He pauses at the bottom of the stairs and puts his hand on the stairlift, which is parked at the bottom again since Lizzie has calmed down. 'Could I use this thing?' he asks, giggling like a naughty child. 'I've never used one of them before.'

For a brief moment Valie wonders whether it's built to take that much weight, but she quickly dismisses the thought. Sending him up in the stairlift will be much more fun. 'OK,' she says. 'Sit on the seat and I will do the safety belt.'

The belt is only just long enough to reach round his ample girth, but she straps him in and up he goes, singing, 'Funiculi, funiculi, funiculi, funicula-a-a' under his breath, winking at Valie and swinging his vase of flowers from side to side in time with his singing.

He makes a grand entry into Lizzie's bedroom and bows extravagantly. 'Hello, my dear, how lovely to see you! And you're looking so well, too!' He reaches down, takes her hand, kisses it, and looks round for somewhere to put his vase.

'What lovely flowers!' says Lizzie. 'And who are you?'

'I'm your long-lost stepson Jolyon,' he intones.

Amy jumps out of her chair and backs away. Jolyon sees

the small black Bible lying on the bedside table, moves it to one side and carefully sets down the vase. He extends his hand to introduce himself, but Amy ignores it, darts forward and retrieves her precious Bible.

'Jolyon Pickton,' he says. 'Pleased to meet you.' But Amy is already marching out of the room, stony-faced, and starting down the stairs. Jolyon shrugs, sits down heavily on Amy's chair and picks up Lizzie's hand again. 'Well, my dear,' he says. 'Long time no see!'

Now she's really getting some attention! Lizzie laps it up. 'How lovely of you to come, dear,' she says dreamily. 'Will you stay for a while?'

In the kitchen, Valie manages to suppress her laughter as Amy comes stiffly down the stairs with her Bible in her hand. 'I think I'll go now,' she says. 'Don't worry, I'll see myself out.'

Jolyon stays for two hours, chattering away about the good old days and whatever else comes into his head. Lizzie has no idea what he's talking about, but she's blissfully happy that he's there and he's not talking about Jesus. When he goes, he leaves behind a 'special' letter full of pompous utterances about her life and the wonderful people she has around her. Even I get a fulsome mention, despite being AWOL.

When Amy comes back the following Thursday, she's all smiles, and doesn't even mention the Antichrist. It's as if nothing ever happened. She still brings her little black Bible, and she still talks to Lizzie about Jesus.

A few weeks later, when she is very confused, Lizzie is in the habit of wiping herself not just with toilet paper but with whatever she can find lying around – clothes, towels, plastic bags, newspaper. One day we find the bemerded remains of Jolyon's tattered 'special letter' floating in the loo.

Perhaps that's the most appropriate end to this story that the universe could devise. She literally wipes her arse with him. He would have laughed till he cried. It's a shame she isn't able to appreciate the perfection of her own gesture.

❦

It can be very shocking when someone like my mother-in-law, who's often 'difficult' but not usually aggressive, starts behaving like that. There are plenty of examples of people turning nasty in the story book of dementia, but it's still a shock when it happens to someone you know, especially if it's your mother or your husband.

Psychoactive drugs have unpredictable effects. My dear old mum could be quite embarrassing after the doctor started her on one of the newer antidepressants in the 1980s, having been on Valium for half a lifetime. Valium turned her into a zombie, whereas the new drug simply disinhibited her so she could no longer stop herself from expressing the angry feelings that she had been trying to suppress for the previous seventy years.

I was with her one day when she went to the local grocer to buy some bananas. 'I'm awfully sorry, Mrs Wilson,' said kindly old Mr Skidmore, 'but I won't have any until tomorrow.'

'Oh, *fuck*,' muttered my mother, turning on her heel and heading for the door.

One or two of Mr Skidmore's customers who knew her swiftly adjusted their TV sets (this phrase won't mean anything to you, unless you had one of those ancient analogue receivers, which went out forty years ago). Until that morning, none of us had ever heard my mother say

321

anything more hardcore than 'damn'.

'I'm terribly sorry, Mr Skidmore,' I said, as she stomped out of the shop. 'It's the antidepressants. She's not normally like that.'

It can be even more shocking when someone becomes violent or aggressive because they have fallen under the influence of an ideology. It's not unusual when someone has gone off and joined ISIS, or planted a bomb, that their friends and family express astonishment that they could have done such a thing. 'He was such a nice, friendly boy,' they say. 'I can't believe he would have done that.'

The famous 1971 Prison Experiment, carried out by Professor Philip Zimbardo at Stanford University[1], showed how easily ordinary people can slip into roles that expect or require them to behave in cruel ways. According to Zimbardo, four out of the twelve participants who were playing the role of 'guards' exhibited genuinely sadistic behaviour when they were given the opportunity, even though they knew they were only playing a role.

This study has received a lot of criticism that it was unscientific, which is no doubt justified from the point of view of orthodox science, but anyone who reads the accounts given by Zimbardo and some of the participants cannot doubt that it says something very significant about how people behave when the social pressure to be nice to other people is replaced by the suggestion that it's OK to be nasty. If you've witnessed the behaviour of any hostile crowd, you will probably have seen many examples of this. Donald Trump's MAGA crowds were rife with it.

At times of extreme social disruption when law and order breaks down, it can get very much worse. All kinds of violent and horrific entities come out of hiding disguised

322

as ordinary people, and roam around looking for victims. Francisco Goya's brilliant and disturbing etchings in the series known as *The Disasters of War*, created during and after the Peninsular War of the early 1800s, bear witness to these horror stories in graphic detail.

We can't predict how often this kind of thing will happen as our society starts to fall apart, but similar things have been happening for a while in the USA where mass shootings and brutally racist police behaviour are now commonplace[2]. It also happened on a large scale in Bosnia and in Rwanda in the mid-1990s, and in Iraq after the Bush-Blair invasion. In these countries, neighbour turned against neighbour, mixed families were torn apart, and ordinary people turned into gratuitous sadists and torturers. It has often happened before and it will probably happen again when tensions are running high enough.

✒

When I think about the tendency of our Western culture to breed so much violence, the word 'evil' keeps cropping up. So I find myself asking questions like, when does bad behaviour become evil? And what exactly *is* evil? Is it merely 'the privation of Good', as St Augustine wrote? Or is it substantial and embodied, which is what we imply when we call somebody a 'bad person'? Are there evil entities out there, sabotaging everything we do? And how is it that some people behave like quiet heroes when things descend into chaos, while others behave as if possessed by the devil? What's the difference? Are all the baddies really evil, or is that just a word we throw at them?

These are not just academic questions, they are

necessary questions if we're interested in how to orient ourselves towards the current situation out there in the 'real world'.

The traditional view is that people who do bad things are acting out some kind of disembodied evil that's working through them because they rebelled against God's law. This is 'the work of the devil' in Christian mythology. He tempts us and we fall for it. Most of us don't believe in this 'devil' any longer, but if he *does* exist this won't bother him very much, because we continue to fall for the temptations which are opened up by our own negative states. It's not hard to see how these negative states (greed, anger, hatred, the lust for power) can lead directly to actions that we tend to describe as 'evil'.

There are different ways of understanding this. One of the most interesting has been described by Paul Levy, and it starts from the Native American notion of *Wetiko*[3]. According to this notion, whatever evil is in a metaphysical sense, it *behaves* like a non-localised psychological virus. Rather like a physical virus, but without a physical form, it lurks unseen until it is presented with an opportunity. It infects the person whose inner disposition (or state of being) gives it the opportunity, and works through them to cause whatever damage it can. *Wetiko* is a symbol for the quality of 'evil-ness' that is being manifested in someone's bad behaviour. We might say, 'Something got into him.'

For the Native Americans, bad behaviour included anything that upsets the harmony between humans and the world of Nature, which they experienced as 'all one world' with the Spirits and the Ancestors. Robin Wall Kimmerer has some memorable descriptions of *Wetiko* behaviour (her Anishinaabe people call it *Windigo*), which

324

are associated with excessive consumption, with taking too much for oneself: *Windigo*, she writes, *is the name for that within us which cares more for its own survival than for anything else.*[4]

In their culture, before it was almost destroyed by the European invaders, it would have been quite easy to identify the actions of *Wetiko* (or *Windigo*). In ours, it's not quite so straightforward. In most situations, especially when it applies to the natural world, for us it would be a matter of opinion.

Take, for example, the protest that was mounted at Solsbury Hill in 1994 against the destruction of the woods to make way for the A46 Batheaston bypass. People were laughing at the antics of the tree-huggers living in their squalid camp, but these social outcasts saw much more clearly than their 'straight' critics just how *Wetiko*-laden the whole project was. Having less to lose, on the whole, they were courageous enough to mount a serious challenge.

I worked with one of them when I was a therapist. She was a gentle soul, but she had the courage of her convictions. She was still suffering from PTSD five years after she'd been manhandled out of a tree forty feet up by men on a hydraulic platform with their bolt-cutters, their chain saws and their determination to get her out of there before the lunch break.

Levy writes that the *Wetiko* virus gets most of its opportunities when human beings 'fall asleep' and stop paying attention to what is motivating their attitudes and their actions. According to the formidable cosmologer and sage G. I. Gurdjieff, most of us are 'asleep' most of the time; it's our default position[5]. This is easy to verify, if we want to. We walk around dreaming about what we should have said to the guy who just annoyed us, or what a wonderful life we're going to have when we move in with the girlfriend, or what an asshole the new office manager is. We're up in our heads, either in the past or the future; we're rarely present here and now.

The radical psychiatrist R. D. Laing made the same point more forcefully when he wrote: *The condition of alienation, of being asleep, of being unconscious, of being out of one's mind, is the condition of normal man... Normal men have killed perhaps 100 million of their fellow normal men in the last fifty years*[6].

This condition is, of course, mediated by social pressure. We are social animals, constantly looking for validation from the social groups with which we identify. We take with us to the bar (or the pub in the UK) the things that we're daydreaming about, and sit there for hours gossiping with our friends, who daydream in the same way about the same things. When times are hard and our mutual daydreams take on a resentful character, it just takes one charismatic leader (or one issue like Brexit) to articulate and focus the resentment, and before long all these conversations spawn a mass movement. It's very easy for a charismatic leader to manipulate people when a large number of them are literally begging to be manipulated. This is where we stand right now as far-right movements across Europe and America start flexing their muscles for a fight.

A mass movement is just like a cult, only on a much larger scale. The veteran journalist Chris Hedges wrote recently about Donald Trump[7]: *[He] has transformed the decayed carcass of the Republican Party into a cult. All cults are personality cults. They are extensions of the cult leaders.*

The cult reflects the leader's prejudices, worldview, personal style and ideas. Trump did not create the yearning for a cult leader. Huge segments of the population, betrayed by the established elites, were conditioned for a cult leader. They were desperately looking for someone to rescue them and solve their problems.

Cult leaders are narcissists. They demand obsequious fawning and total obedience. They prize loyalty above competence. They wield absolute control. They do not tolerate criticism. They are deeply insecure, a trait they attempt to cover up with bombastic grandiosity. They are amoral and emotionally and physically abusive. They see those around them as objects to be manipulated for their own empowerment, enjoyment and often sadistic entertainment. All those outside the cult are branded as forces of evil, prompting an epic battle whose natural expression is violence.

Here in the UK we're apt to say, 'Oh well, that's how it is in the USA, but it couldn't happen here. We're much too polite and well-behaved for that kind of thing.' Looking at our recent history, and the new style of political leadership it has thrown up, I'm not so sure we have any grounds at all for this kind of complacency.

🍃

Most of us, most of the time (myself included) don't really want to wake up from our customary sleepiness. It feels too much like hard work. I think one of the reasons for this is that we get confused between 'waking up' and 'trying hard to be a good person'. The whole Woke culture is predicated on this; if we don't learn the 'right' way to behave, we're a very bad person. This evidently comes from the action of the inner Tyrant and has little to do with waking up, because Wokesters often compete with each other to appear the most Woke, and to hurl the most venom at those who are not Woke, which people who are genuinely awake (in the sense I'm using the word) probably wouldn't feel the need to do.

Our cultural indoctrination seems to tell us that waking up should be rewarded with a large number of brownie points, because you have to be such a 'good person' to do it. I remember my first impression of the Gurdjieff Centre in London way back in the 1960s, when I first went there as a neophyte seeker. Although I quickly suppressed it, the image that came to me was of people walking round with a cucumber up their ass[8] because they were trying so hard to be 'awake'. Perhaps I was being a little unfair, but that was the image.

Nevertheless, I'm prone to making the same mistake myself, imagining that because I've made some efforts in the direction of waking up, I'm somehow a better person than those who (I tell myself) clearly haven't. This, too, is an action of the *Wetiko* virus, which can find its way just as easily into people who are addicted to 'self-development' as anyone else. It's a kind of narcissistic self-absorption, not very different from that which consumes the *jihadi*, or the white supremacist shooter when he is engaged in his ideologically-driven crusade.

The pursuit of spiritual growth in the Western world is such a specialist activity that people who engage in it are almost bound to think of themselves as 'different'. People like me, who come to it through a massive sense of disillusionment with the society that raised them, can end up feeling that we are the special ones who managed to escape from the conformist prison.

The terrorist, the neo-Nazi, the conspiracy theorist and the religious fanatic all feel that they are the special ones in exactly the same way.

It's not possible to 'wake up' by ingesting an ideology, however spiritual it looks, or by beating oneself over the head repeatedly with a book of rules. If we're really interested in waking up, the first step (according to a wide variety of spiritual teachers) is to notice what's really going on inside us, *not to try and change it*. This kind of attention needs courage and impartiality rather than cleverness or will-power. It's because we lack the courage to face up to our own negativity, and because we're so easily affected by the norms of the social groups to which we belong, that we project our bad feelings onto those others – and projecting our shadow is one of the main foundations of *Wetiko*.

The trouble is, this kind of work seems to need a lot of time, commitment and support. This is because everything in our culture pushes us in precisely the opposite direction. We are comprehensively indoctrinated into a social world where lying about oneself is endemic, vulnerability is despised, and psychological predators are lionised.

Our best hope is that, as our society starts to disintegrate and throws up movements like Extinction Rebellion, this orientation will change in a way that makes it easier for people to imagine living a different kind of life. This may happen on a large scale or in small pockets, but wherever it does happen it will provide nourishment and validation for those people who are courageous enough to try to deal with their own negative states instead of projecting them onto others.

Another way of looking at evil is through the developmental lens used in most Western psychotherapy, which understands bad behaviour as a result of psychological distress that, in turn, comes from not getting enough love and support as a child. There are two main weaknesses with this model. One is that it often seems to end up blaming parents for everything, ignoring the fact that the parents' behaviour is itself the product of a sick social system – they don't behave like that because they are 'bad people'. The other is that it's almost exclusively about human relationships with other humans, so it doesn't include crimes against Nature, such as cutting down a 200-year-old oak tree so that you can build a bypass. Native Americans would certainly have regarded this kind of behaviour as *Wetiko*-inspired, because they were careful not to upset the harmonious balance that exists throughout the natural world.

Our Western understanding of the roots of evil doesn't go far enough, but it does have merit on its own terms as an explanatory framework. As an example, consider the work of the courageous Muslim activist and award-winning film maker Deeya Khan. She interviewed a number of Muslim jihadists for her 2015 movie *Jihad: A Story of The Other*, and a number of white racists in the USA for her complementary 2017 movie *White Right: Meeting the Enemy*. Both of these movies demonstrate that the emotional driver that most often underlies extremism is the experience of being rejected, of not belonging, not having any meaning in one's life.

In a January 2019 interview for Vox online mag[9], she

330

said: '...*these movements are deeply rooted in a sense of victimhood.*' She was also very aware of the part played by group validation. She pointed out that when people join an extremist group: '...*suddenly they have a sense of meaning in life, a belief that they matter, that their voice matters. It's as though they were once invisible, and now they're seen.*'

Speaking of jihadist groups, she said that many of their members: '...*are not particularly religious, are not particularly well-versed in their faith at all. For them, it's about feeling righteous and believing that they are doing something important and meaningful in life... They also do it because they know it scares you.*' That is, it gives them a sense of power, whereas before they felt powerless as well as victimised.

It's not hard to see how our individualistic, competitive society forces people to adopt attitudes that divide other people into worthy and unworthy, good and bad, winners and losers. These attitudes are instilled into children as they grow up. If they aren't examined, they become entrenched and socially normal, and are passed on from generation to generation.

It's well known that people who have been bullied often turn into bullies, and men who have been abused turn into abusers. This is a similar dynamic, and it works at all levels from the personal to the global. But even if those Muslims who resort to violence and become *jihadis* do so because they have psychological issues, it's worth remembering that we have made it very easy for them to justify their behaviour by endlessly disrupting their lives and attempting to bomb them into submission in the Middle East. This started with the British 'punishment bombings' of Iraq in the 1920s, and has continued in one

331

way or another right up to today's American drone strikes. No wonder they feel a certain resentment towards us.

⟡

We can also look at evil through the lens of addiction. Habitual negative feelings take up residence in us in the form of patterns of tension in the body, tensions we can feel in the neck and shoulders, the belly, the thighs, or wherever else we store them. It's as if we become addicted to these patterns, just as we become addicted to the psycho-physical effects of alcohol or narcotics. One of Gurdjieff's acerbic sayings was that the hardest thing for man to let go of is his suffering. People become addicted not only to anger and resentment, but to loneliness, self-harm, victimhood and self-denigration.

It's easy for anger to become an addictive behaviour pattern because of the tension that is built up and then released in one very satisfying splurge. I have my own cautionary tale about this. I have a notoriously bad temper, as those who know me well enough will probably agree. When I was a builder, I often used to lose it when something went wrong with the job.

Seeing how much I appeared to enjoy getting angry, one of the guys I worked with started wondering if he was repressing his anger too much and decided to try letting it out when anything went wrong for him, just like I did. Once he'd got over the initial difficulty, he started to enjoy his new-found freedom, until he realised that he too was becoming addicted. At that point he tried to stop and was dismayed to find that it wasn't so easy to let go of his new habit. He was right: he was becoming addicted to getting angry. The demon had got into him and now it wouldn't let go.

Addictive behaviour is grist to the mill for the *Wetiko* virus. The more addicted we get to a set of negative feelings associated with a pattern of bad behaviour, the more opportunities it gets to use us to do some damage in the world. And there's a great deal of addictive behaviour around these days, in all areas of life. Addictions to sex, food, power, comfort, being a martyr, being universally admired, winning...

These addictions are the direct result of the alienation we feel from ourselves, from each other and from the natural world as a result of living in this culture. It is, as Levy says, 'a *Wetiko* culture', and this characteristic has been getting stronger for a very long time.

In her book *Psychological Roots of the Climate Crisis*[10], psychoanalyst Sally Weintrobe goes deeply into this aspect of our culture, highlighting the addictive influence of the economic and social belief system known as Neoliberalism, which has fostered what she calls 'a culture of uncare'.

This is one of the underlying reasons why it's going to be so hard for our Western societies (and others that are busily imitating us) to change direction and stop inflicting all kinds of violence on other people and on this sacred Earth. As all substance abusers are aware, it can be really difficult to kick the habit.

*

Another writer who has gone into the addictive and entity-like nature of our negative emotional states is the spiritual teacher Eckhart Tolle, with his notion of the Pain Body[11].

The Pain Body is his image for the bodily residue of all the emotional pain we have suffered in our lives.

If you look on it as an invisible entity in its own right, you are getting quite close to the truth. It's the emotional pain body... Anything can trigger it, particularly if it resonates with a pain pattern from your past... Some pain bodies are obnoxious but relatively harmless, like a child who won't stop whining. Others are vicious and destructive monsters, true demons...' (p.29).

Tolle is very clear about how we can recognise this entity in ourselves. '*Watch out for any sign of unhappiness in yourself, in whatever form – it may be the awakening pain body. This may take the form of irritation, impatience, a sombre mood, a desire to hurt, anger, rage, depression, a need to have some drama in your relationship, and so on. Catch it the moment it awakes from its dormant state.*

'*The pain body wants to survive, just like every other entity in existence, and it can only survive if it gets you to unconsciously identify with it. It can then rise up, take you over, "become you", and live through you. It needs to get its food through you. It will feed on any experience that resonates with its own kind of energy, anything that creates further pain in whatever form: anger, destructiveness, hatred, grief, emotional drama, violence and even illness. So the pain body, when it has taken you over, will create a situation in your life that reflects back its own energy ... for it to feed on.*' (pp.30–31).

This description of the Pain Body is almost identical to Paul Levy's description of the *Wetiko* virus. In effect, Eckhart Tolle succeeds in reconciling all three of the 'stories' we have looked at so far: the *Wetiko* story, the psychotherapeutic story and the addiction story.

He says that the way to deal with the pain body is not to fight it, which only creates yet more negative energy on which it feeds voraciously, but to simply be aware of it and watch what it does. Watch how it twists and turns, how it shape-shifts, how it tries to keep you identified with it: '*Sustained conscious attention severs the link between the pain body and your thought processes and brings about the process of transmutation. It is as if the pain becomes fuel for the flame of your consciousness, which burns more brightly as a result.*' (p.33).

Paul Levy also has this in mind when he writes that the most extraordinary thing about *Wetiko* is its dual nature. It's not just a psychological virus that exploits our tendency to live our lives in a kind of sleep, it is also the principal means through which we find opportunities to wake up and inhabit ourselves more consciously. Unless we're willing and able to look into our own inner darkness, it never occurs to us to yearn for the light.

Gurdjieff referred to this process of waking up as 'self-remembering', and linked it with the action of our 'real conscience'. What is normally called 'conscience' may not be the same thing at all; it's more likely to be an aspect of the inner figure that Philip Shepherd calls the Tyrant, the entity inside us that reinforces whatever psycho-social identity we have come to regard as being our own. Real conscience is more like a witness, a moment of clear insight, that gives us the opportunity to see how these suppressed emotions are allowing the *Wetiko* virus (or the Pain Body) to take us over. Such a moment of truth gives us the opportunity to let go of the need to act them out, not to suppress the urge all over again as the Tyrant demands, but simply to see it as the pettiness it really is. We catch sight of our enemy's humanity and in that moment we find he's just like us, so we cannot hate him. We catch sight of our own urge to tighten into an aggressive posture and it just looks ridiculous, so we let go and relax instead.

We don't have to overcome anything; we don't have to force ourselves to be heroically 'good'. Maybe this is what Jesus Christ meant when he said 'resist not evil'. We simply see it for what it is, and that gives us the choice to let it go because it's banal and unnecessary, and because it violates our essential humanity.

Sometimes it's funny to catch a glimpse of what we're really up to. When I notice the red-faced two-year-old boy inside me, who's having a tantrum because he can't get the printer to work, I have to laugh. Sometimes it's not funny at all, it's excruciating, because I feel how strong the urge is to go back to my default position, to fall asleep again, to avoid having to bear the fact that *this is what I'm really like*. That, I guess, is the action of 'real conscience'.

On the rare occasions when I manage to stay with it and keep it in awareness, the urge to get angry or to feel like a victim fades away quite naturally. But then, if I breathe a sigh of relief and fall asleep again, the urge can sneak back easily and take over once more, just when I'm least expecting it. Maybe this is what Jesus Christ was talking about when he told us to 'watch and pray', or why Tolle recommends 'sustained conscious attention'. It's a basic theme for all genuine spiritual teachings and it's also implied by what we suggest in our clinical psychotherapy.

🍃

One of the hardest things to see, and one of the most fruitful for the *Wetiko* virus, is our tendency to project our own shadow. Whenever we do this, we feel a strong sense that what we're doing is absolutely justified by the other person (or people). Indeed, it often provokes the very attitude or behaviour that we're projecting, which confirms our estimation of the other person and escalates the situation. If we believe that the people who voted for Donald Trump are 'deplorable', they will behave like that and revel in it.

This is how projection becomes a *pas de deux* instead of a one-way street. For example, the bully projects his own deeply held fear, which he violently disowned many years ago when he was a child, onto his victim and the victim really feels it. Maybe she, in turn, projects her own rage that she was also forced to repress when she was a child onto the bully, then they act out their own unique tragedy as if it were a play written specially for them.

The bully 'smells out' victims with unerring accuracy. An abusive man (often one who has been abused himself) knows exactly which women he can successfully terrify. He is addicted to feelings of power and domination, which is a strong attractor of *Wetiko*, and he's always on the lookout for victims. He may not be aware that's what he's doing, but he's doing it, nonetheless.

That's one of the reasons why non-violent protest is much more effective than violence. If you're not projecting violence and badness onto the police, there is nothing to which they can attach their aggression. This doesn't mean they won't be aggressive, but it's much harder for them if you're smiling and not showing any sign of anger or fear.

I learned about this more or less by accident, although

not during a protest. Years ago, I was confronted by a very angry neighbour who was squaring up to wallop me. For some reason (not because I was trying to be good, I have to say) I just stood there, completely relaxed, and waited. I could sense how badly he wanted to hit me but he couldn't bring himself to do it because there was nothing his anger could grab on to and use as a justification.

In the end he relaxed as well, we both started laughing and I invited him in for a cup of tea. Non-violence doesn't always work but, when it does, it's sure as hell better than starting a fight.

Working with the shadow can be painful and difficult because we try so hard to keep it hidden. It doesn't have to be difficult, but it often is because we're so attached to our negative attitudes. Maybe this is the essence of 'spiritual work': it's mundane, it's practical, and it gets its hands dirty. *Wetiko* is defeated not in one mighty confrontation but in a thousand small and intimate encounters with oneself. From this point of view, it's not such a big deal after all. Or is it?

❦

If we don't take these opportunities to 'remember ourselves' (as Gurdjieff put it), our sleepiness can end up as a very big deal, especially in a society which is so obsessed with personal freedom.

Levy describes what *Wetiko* looks like when a person has allowed it to grow in them until they are taken over completely. He translates it as 'malignant egophrenia', meaning something like 'the self-perpetuating tendency to put one's desire for personal satisfaction ahead of the need for harmony within a larger whole'. The larger whole can mean a relationship, or one's community, or the Earth as a community of life-forms, or presumably even one's own body if personal satisfaction includes such self-destructive habits as using strong drugs or over-eating.

In its extreme form, it can also mean the same as 'cannibalism' in the sense of feeding off the life force of other human beings, whether through violence, abusive behaviour, slavery or other forms of exploitation[12]. In this respect, it shows up most clearly in behaviour we would normally categorise as psychopathic. The psychopath (as normally understood) is a person so heavily afflicted by *Wetiko* that he's no longer in touch with his own humanity, therefore he cannot connect with the humanity in others. He can be very charming but he uses this charm to serve the purposes of the *Wetiko* virus. He can even appear banal, lacking in imagination and hardly a fit vessel for the perpetration of any kind of violence.

The banality of evil is a theme usually associated with Hannah Arendt's words about Adolf Eichmann, the Nazi mass murderer[13]. This has been a puzzle to many because Arendt certainly acknowledged the scale and awfulness of what Eichmann did to Jewish prisoners in Nazi Germany. In effect, she was confirming the *Wetiko* story, that evil is like a non-local psychological virus that can take control of us when we're not alert to what's really going on in our own shadow. She found Eichmann to be thoughtless, disengaged, a bland bureaucrat unable to think from the standpoint of another person. He was not inherently evil, but had made himself available for the *Wetiko* virus to use because he lacked the spiritual awareness – or perhaps the feeling intelligence – to understand how he was betraying his own essential humanity.

Alternatively, you could say that he was a good but unconscious servant of the ubiquitous Machine, like most of what we now call 'the 1%', the elite group of the wealthy and the 'successful' who feel entitled to their status because they believe they're 'worth it'. They are certainly not all psychopaths but their privileged position is backed up by a legal system whose ultimate guarantee is the threat of state violence. If you're on a low income, with few privileges and little hope of escaping your situation, this system looks as if it were designed to be unfair, uncaring and oppressive. As the film-maker Ken Loach once said in a memorable TV interview about benefit sanctions, '*It's conscious cruelty.*'

🌿

Psychopaths are often construed as 'missing something', but my own experience – both personal and professional – suggests that these men are deeply frightened of showing any kind of vulnerability. (It tends to be more visible in men as it fits better with the prevailing patterns of domination set up by the patriarchy.) At the same time, they are in denial about this; they have cut off their own capacity for self-reflection because it might show them something they don't want to see. They are, in that sense, incapable of behaving differently. Levy writes, *They can seem confident and self-assured, but in reality they are covering deep insecurities and fears through an inflated self-image. Intense feelings of revenge, fury and out-of-control rage manifest when their fear is exposed and their narcissism threatened*[14].

An obvious example of this is Donald Trump, judging by

340

the accounts of those who have found themselves on the wrong side of him.

Several studies have shown that a large proportion of successful businessmen exhibit character traits that are usually classified as psychopathic[15]. The same could be said of the behaviour of corporations like those that populate the fossil fuel industry, or of predatory agribusinesses like Monsanto.

Robin Wall Kimmerer sums this up succinctly in *Braiding Sweetgrass*: *...multinational corporations have spawned a new breed of* Windigo *that insatiably devours the earth's resources 'not for need but for greed'. Their footprints are all around us, once you know what to look for.*

They stomp in the industrial sludge of Onondaga Lake. And over a savagely clear-cut slope in the Oregon Coast Range where the earth is slumping into the river. You can see them where coal mines rip off mountaintops in West Virginia and in oil-slick footprints in the Gulf of Mexico. A square mile of industrial soybeans. A diamond mine in Rwanda. A closet stuffed with clothes. Windigo *footprints all, they are the tracks of insatiable consumption....*

Every item in this depressing list – which we could easily extend until it covered the whole Earth – is a product of the Machine. The *Windigo* or *Wetiko* virus is closely related to the entity known as Ahriman, the presiding deity of the Machine, who lives inside us and feeds off our psychic energy. Each of them is an aspect of the other.

The fear for me, she continues, *is far greater than just acknowledging the* Windigo *within. The fear for me is that the world has been turned inside out, the dark side made to seem light. Indulgent self-interest that our people once held to be monstrous is now celebrated as success. We are asked to admire what our people once viewed as unforgivable. The consumption-driven mindset masquerades as 'quality of life' but eats us from within. It is as if we've been invited to a feast, but the table is laid with food that nourishes only emptiness, the black hole of the stomach that never fills. We have unleashed a monster.*

In a way it's illogical to blame the corporations because that's what they're supposed to do. Legally, they must maximise their profits whatever the 'external' cost. In this way, they are behaving like good servants of the Machine, or the *Wetiko* virus, depending on which way you look at it. Not always unconsciously, either. Evidently the fossil fuel giants have been well aware for decades of the harm they have been doing to our planet, as the recent (2019) Congressional hearings have revealed[16]. And it can't have escaped the attention of the Bayer executives that their neonicotinoid insecticides are a significant cause of colony collapse disorder in bees.

In this way, we have set up a society that literally cannot help itself but must press on at full speed towards the oncoming disaster, unless something changes at a fundamental level.

The existing institutional structures can't facilitate this change because all they know how to do is to foster consumption and growth. The consequences of this, from climate breakdown to mental illness, are regarded as side issues that have to be addressed, like everything else, from within the growth paradigm – as if that were possible.

It seems to me that the changes will have to come from a completely different place at the level of our own personal experience, not the level of governments or globalised businesses. At the moment this is not easy but perhaps when people really start to see how destructive and dangerous our civilisation has become, enough of them may want to look for an alternative way of living and will want to support each other in this journey.

It's been said many times before, but I hope you will forgive me if I say it again: the changes we all need must start within ourselves.

References

1 See https://www.simplypsychology.org/zimbardo.html

2 Author, activist, teacher and dissident Chris Hedges gave an extraordinary talk about the rise of what he called 'American Sadism' at The Sanctuary for Independent Media in Troy, NY, on June 27, 2021. Well worth watching. See Chris Hedges "American Sadism" - YouTube.

3 Paul Levy, *Dispelling Wetiko* (North Atlantic Books, 2013).

4 Robin Wall Kimmerer, in 'Windigo Footprints' from her classic memoir, *Braiding Sweetgrass*.

5 See G.I. Gurdjieff, *All and Everything* (Routledge & Kegan Paul, 1950) and numerous commentaries on his work by P.D. Ouspensky, J.G. Bennett and others who worked with him.

6 R.D. Laing, *The Politics of Experience* (Ballantine Books, 1971), p.28. Quoted in Levy, op cit. p.xvii.

7 Truthdig, 29 October 2018. https://www.truthdig.com/articles/the-cult-of-trump-2/

8 I have to confess that this image wasn't mine. It was supplied by Lawrence Durrell's aphorism from *Justine*, the first book of the celebrated Alexandrian Quartet: *Life is like a cucumber. One minute it's in your hand, the next minute it's up your ass.*

9 See https://www.vox.com/world/2019/1/14/18151799/extremism-white-supremacy-jihadism-deeya-khan

10 Sally Weintrobe, *Psychological Roots of the Climate Crisis* (Bloomsbury Academic, 2021).

11 See Eckhart Tolle, *The Power of Now: A Guide to Spiritual Enlightenment* (Hodder & Stoughton, 1999).

12 In his discussion of the effects of Wetiko, Levy acknowledges his debt to Jack Forbes, who wrote *Columbus and Other Cannibals* (Seven Stories Press,

N.Y., 2008).

13 Hannah Arendt, *Eichmann in Jerusalem: A Report on the Banality of Evil* (Viking Press, 1963).

14 *Dispelling Wetiko*, p.128.

15 See, for example, https://www.telegraph.co.uk/news/2016/09/13/1-in-5-ceos-are-psychopaths-australian-study-finds/

16 See also Chris McGreal's article in *The Guardian's* Climate Crimes series, 30 June 2021.

- 14 -
Coming Home

7 JULY 2018

A PAPER PUBLISHED today by the Institute for Leadership and Sustainability (IFLAS) entitled *Deep Adaptation: A Map for Navigating Climate Tragedy*[1] is causing a minor sensation in the world of climate scientists. One of their number has finally broken ranks and publicly declared that what he's looking at is so out of control that some kind of civilisational collapse is now inevitable. Scientists are not supposed to say that kind of thing in case they frighten the horses and cause a scandal. His words cannot be dismissed easily, because twenty years of work has already earned him a great deal of respect in the scientific community.

Within a year, *Deep Adaptation* will have been downloaded more than half a million times. Activists all over the world are breathing a small sigh of relief. At last there's someone in the know who's telling the whole truth, not just a sanitised version of it. It has been a hard road trying to convince people, but it's suddenly become a little bit easier.

🍃

It's a weird experience to arrive back in the middle of the English winter after a month in the Peruvian Amazon jungle. I'm relieved to regain a modest degree of physical comfort after living for three weeks on the awful Ayahuasca diet, but I'm also thinking, 'Oh my God, here we are back in the madhouse again.' For all the craziness of the Ayahuasca experience, it felt much saner than our desolate, screaming world of jet aircraft, smartphones and endless shopping.

It's only February, so the phrase 'deep adaptation' hasn't been coined yet, nor has much else changed. We're still riding a turbo-charged handcart to hell and still no-one – except a few activists, and a bunch of hysterical Doomsters – is talking about it.

🌿

Valie is very pleased to see us. On our first evening back she tells us all about the frolics she enjoyed with a deranged and uncontrollable Mumia. She keeps breaking into rapid-fire Romanian because her English, although good, is too slow for the story line. We are up till 3am, hiding in the back room downstairs.

'She did what?,' we keep saying. 'Oh my God!'

Next day, my sister calls. 'Have you heard?' she asks.

I automatically assume she wants to tell me something about bloody Brexit, which I know she's very concerned about, so I'm a bit acerbic. 'What is it now, Sis? I've only just got back from the other side of the world.'

'Mike just died,' she says.

'What? When? How?' Mike is my younger brother; he can't possibly be dead. My sister tells me he died of a heart attack, just like that, while standing in a post office queue. I

know post office queues can be a pain, but he's a very calm person; I am quite sure it wouldn't have killed him to wait for twenty minutes just to send a parcel.

I find it hard to concentrate on what she's saying. Mike was in much better shape than I am; he was hardly ever ill physically, despite his tendency to adopt a melancholic attitude to life. He never smoked, he didn't drink very much, ate the right food and kept himself fit by going out for long walks in the country.

I'm quite sure he'd never even thought about taking ayahuasca, although he was one of the few people I know who would have had something constructive to say about our adventures in Peru. He would have wondered why on earth I had to go so far away and endure such stomach-churning ordeals to feed my obsession with the Divine Feminine. He would probably have communed with her quite effortlessly whenever he felt the need, down by the weir on the tree-lined banks of the River Severn a couple of miles from his home. 'Typical of you,' he would have said, 'doing such a simple thing in such a complicated way.'

R.I.P., dear Bro.

❦

Winter gives way to spring and Lizzie's garden, unlike its unfortunate owner, is coming back to life again. The hellebores are still in flower, snowdrops are peeping through, daffodils are springing to life among the weeds. Sophia and I distract ourselves from the ongoing drama in the back bedroom by digging them out (the weeds, not the daffodils) and sowing a few seeds – hollyhocks, nasturtiums, cosmos – in case we're still here when summer comes. Who knows how

348

long Lizzie might last?

I'm trying to write, but since we've been back I've found it increasingly difficult to work. Sophia is concerned. 'Are you OK?' she says.

'I don't know. Now that I'm back writing about all the shit that's happening in the world, I think about it a lot and it's making me wretched. I wake up every morning and wonder why I bother. What's the point? It's all going to get much worse whatever I write. And there's Lizzie yoo-hooing every ten minutes, and it drives me mad.'

'What you wanna do then?' she says, practical as ever.

'If I still had it, I'd go back to living in my camper van. Somewhere far away from my wretched mother-in-law. At least then I could work in peace.'

Sophia thinks for a minute or two. 'What about the Mumia shed?'

There's a shed at the bottom of the garden. It was probably built as a workshop because it's quite substantial, has an electric light, and there's a power socket on the wall. It's full of broken furniture, old paint cans, dusty spiders' webs, a couple of ancient bicycles and other assorted rubbish. I doubt whether Lizzie has ever even gone inside to take a look. We keep the garden tools there, but there's not much room for anything else.

'What – that rat-infested shithole?' I say ungraciously.

'You could work in there, or you could read a book,' she says. 'I can make very good place for the meditation.'

'Really? You think so?'

'Why not? Is only full of kakat', she says. 'Is quite a lot of space, if we take all to the dump. We will start tomorrow, OK?'

Bless you, I think. I would have spent hours weighing up

349

the pros and cons. Sophia just goes for it.

It takes us a week, and five visits to the municipal dump, to clear the place and remove all traces of its four, six and eight-legged inhabitants. I spend another two weeks repairing the door, fixing the guttering and drying out the wall beneath it where the rain has been coming in for the previous ten years. We go to B&Q and buy some paint. Sophia slaps it on the breeze-block walls and is pleased with the result. She finds some old pieces of carpet and covers the cement floor.

We name it 'The Hidey-Hole'. Over the next week, Sophia raids the house and finds a few homely items with which to furnish it – a table, chairs, a clock. Lizzie won't notice, because she never comes downstairs these days. I knock up some shelves and hang my framed sketches of Swaledale, which have been stowed away in a box for the last few years.

When it's all done, I take some books down there and instal a fan heater. I spend a few hours working then declare the place habitable, although draughty.

I discover that it's a great place for meditation, as Sophia had predicted. The window is quite large and, now that she has cleaned it, all you can see outside is the verdant greenery of Lizzie's wonderfully unkempt garden. The house itself is hidden behind an enormous hypericum bush, which will soon be covered in bright-yellow flowers. It reminds me of the one that Jane had in her garden when we met.

I decide to try sleeping down there on my big green folding recliner, which I've slept in many times before when there was no bed to sleep in. It's a blissful experience, wrapped up in a duvet.

At 3am, I get up and sally forth into the moonlit garden for a pee. It's chilly out there but very quiet, just a gentle rustling in the April breeze.

'Yooo-hoo!' comes the call from somewhere beyond the hypericum bush. 'Yooo-hoo!' It's surprisingly loud. The poor bloody neighbours have been living with this for a while now but no-one has complained. I wonder what they make of it.

🍃

Spring morphs gradually into summer. I sleep down there a lot on my big green chair to escape the nocturnal clamour.

During the months after we returned from Peru, I've relied more and more on my meditation practice to lift the brooding fog of heaviness that goes with the work I'm doing. Although I still pay regular visits to the Coombe, and Sophia is a cheerful companion at home, there are few distractions in my life and I'm still getting a shedload of mostly dire political and environmental news through the Internet every day.

I hear about a group in Bristol where they do something called a 'Gaia meditation', which celebrates our inner connection with the Earth in a very imaginative way. I join them for their weekly group meeting, and it makes a big difference to my life. Although none of the members of this group are activists, those who stay behind to talk after the meditation say that they too are concerned about the ongoing war against Nature. They feel that their practice helps them make a better connection with the 'soul of the Earth', the inherent presence of the divine in the natural world. They don't use those words but they're moved by the same spirit.

Carla, who runs the group, refers to this as 'coming home'.

🍃

During these months, since the demise of Lightning Tree, my friend Max has been very busy. He's working on something new, but he's not saying very much about it. Every now and then he shows up at a protest somewhere and posts his adventures on Facebook.

He asks me if I want to join him in Preston for a week to do a bit of work with the anti-fracking protesters at the Cuadrilla site, but I'm weary of the whole thing so I turn him down. He spends a lot of his time with a mysterious group of people in Stroud, a trendy little town in the Cotswolds where (as far as I know) nothing much happens. I ask him what he's up to but all he'll say is that working with these guys is a bit like Lightning Tree, only ten times harder. I find it difficult to imagine something that hard, but I admire his persistence. Max doesn't give up easily.

I tell him I'm working with a new meditation on the Divine Feminine. He says he'd love to hear more about it sometime. I worry that he's thinking I've lost my activist spark or that the Ayahuasca has left me permanently blissed out.

Max asks me if I'd like to look at something and give an opinion. I say yes, and he sends me a 'manifesto', which has been worked up by this Stroud group. It's a scream of rage and defiance about the ecocide that our civilisation is perpetrating all over the world. They announce their intention to start a campaign of mass civil disobedience, this being the only way to compel the government to take any notice of the science.

I agree with everything they're saying, although I don't believe the political system is capable of doing anything that's so completely at odds with the current paradigm. They might make declarations, set targets and produce lots of window-dressing, but they dare not do anything that threatens the Holy Grail of economic growth.

In typically Churchillian fashion, it starts with the bald statement: 'This Is Our Darkest Hour'. I agree with that, too, but I would never have the cojones to put it into a manifesto.

I tell him what they're doing is great, but I fear they might not make much of an impact. It reminds me of the Committee of 100, the radical wing of the Campaign for Nuclear Disarmament, set up by the philosopher Bertrand Russell in 1960. This also advocated mass civil disobedience but was fatally weakened by internal disagreements and by the determination of the authorities to suppress it. When people saw that their colleagues were actually being arrested and imprisoned, they weren't so keen on it. People may understand that climate change is a potential menace, I say to Max, but on the whole they don't yet see how it affects them personally. They're unlikely to risk being thrown in prison for civil disobedience when it's about something that's happening somewhere else, like the Amazon rainforest or the Arctic icefield.

I like the name, though. They've called themselves 'Extinction Rebellion'.

I was wrong about XR, of course. Something was changing, and Max and his colleagues chose their moment with impeccable timing; so did the icon of this change, the teenager Greta Thunberg.

Greta's celebrity status is no accident. I have no idea what she's like personally but it's what she *represents* that I find interesting. She stands for the archetype of the Virgin Warrior[2], a figure dreamed up from deep within the collective unconscious, once symbolised by goddesses like the Greek Artemis or the Roman Diana. She's an archetypal figure in the same tradition as the fifteenth-century saint known to us as Joan of Arc, whose strength of spirit was manifested in qualities like simplicity, purity and single-mindedness – the same qualities that people see in Greta today. The denialists who troll her on social media even use some of the same tropes as those who railed against St Joan: a political puppet manipulated by sinister forces, a mentally ill child. (In Joan of Arc's case it was 'innocent child possessed by the Devil', which is why they eventually burned her alive.)

Apparently Greta isn't ambitious or self-seeking[3]; she simply responds to what's in front of her, whether it's an august body like the UN or a tricky situation like the tiny sailing boat in which she was transported across the Atlantic. She's undoubtedly intelligent and very good with words (she apparently writes her own speeches), but she's not some kind of populist leader with a desperate hunger for personal power. Nevertheless, like any archetypal figure, she evokes strong responses wherever she goes.

In a way, her recent prominence is a product of the powerful forces that are being generated in the human collective unconscious, waiting to find some outer expression. Who knows what else may emerge from the same deep source before this saga is over?

❧

Max, one of the founders of XR, is another true warrior. I wouldn't like to speculate about what archetype he embodies, but he leads by a kind of heroic example. He has had many personal difficulties in his life, but he is absolutely steadfast in his values; he knows what he's living for and he's not afraid to put himself into some very uncomfortable – and even dangerous – situations to stand up for his principles.

He's moved by a very strong spirit, you might say. The spirit that moves him comes from essentially the same inner source as the spirit that moves my fellow meditators in the Gaia group, although Max's is a warrior spirit so it manifests much more actively. What he does wouldn't normally be described as spiritual, but at its root it's just as 'spiritual' as any meditation. This is also true of Greta, although her visions derive their authority from science rather than God, as you'd expect in this secular century.

Like most activists, Max is a complex character who won't allow himself to rest while all he sees around him is denial, complacency and a tendency to bargain with the truth. ('*Tell The Truth!*' says XR's pink sailing boat.)

We do what we can with the promptings of the spirit. Usually we're moved to convert them directly into action, whether it's helping the blind lady to cross the road or stopping the traffic altogether by sitting in the middle of the same road for several hours with our XR colleagues, singing protest songs.

Sometimes it's good to balance all this outward activity by taking a more inward, contemplative route.

My friend Conrad used to say that the promptings of the spirit are a bit like a river. Usually, those of us who respond will simply jump in and go with the flow but sometimes it's good to turn the other way and swim upstream, maybe even as far back as the source to find out where it's coming from. The source is our true spiritual home, and the inner journey back there is what reconnects us with the oneness from which we have become so estranged in this culture of separation. It's this essential inner journey that mystics have been making throughout recorded history.

The man (or woman) of action often has a certain disdain for this kind of 'upstream' effort. 'But the house is on fire!' they say. 'It's no use just meditating about it, we need to put the fire out!' Fair enough; without this sense of urgency, people might not even be aware that there is a fire at all, or they might prefer to run away, or bury their heads in the sand. But then what often happens is that the man of action tries to put out the fire with another fire, because fire is what they have been given to work with. As the Greek philosopher Heraclitus said, when taken to an extreme, everything turns into its own opposite.

Many (perhaps most) political revolutions turn into their own opposite. They start with the promptings of the spirit towards harmony and one-ness, a healthy response to injustice and oppression, but they end up substituting one kind of despotism with another. It's a very difficult dilemma. XR have done their homework; they recognise that non-violence almost always works better in the long run than trying to overthrow something by using force, but it may be a difficult line to hold in the current divisive atmosphere. Phrases like 'climate change fascists' are already being used in social media, and it won't be long before anti-terrorist legislation will be used against protesters when their actions really start to bite.

🍃

Many environmental activists, my friend Max included, understand very well that what they do is primarily a spiritual activity because it comes from their deep love for Nature. This is a very powerful force, which, if uncontained, can make extraordinary demands on them because they become so driven. The inner tyrant needs them to 'stay strong', so he won't ever let them rest. If they pause for reflection, it's so they can devise better strategies for more action, not to go inside themselves or indulge in anything contemplative, especially if it involves being open about their feelings.

In this sense, poor suffering Nature may be a surrogate for their own injuries, especially the times when they were under attack as children and could not defend themselves. I would guess that this is a common theme for campaigners against any injustice; they really feel it, because it reminds them on some level of what was done to them.

This is not to denigrate the valuable work they do, which is essentially a creative response to our collective historical trauma, but that same trauma is often their Achilles heel because they drive themselves so relentlessly that they eventually burn out. Many of them simply dismiss any shared spiritual activity as 'woo-woo' because it makes them feel awkward and embarrassed. Their inner tyrant is scared it might weaken them rather than strengthen their resolve.

This is a great shame because any activism needs a source of strength and legitimacy that's greater and more widely shared than its own crusading zeal.

Andrew Harvey and Carolyn Baker, in their book *Savage Grace*, say it like this[4]: *Unfortunately, many activists have an understandable but profoundly limiting rejection of religion and any form of spirituality. This is extremely dangerous because only an activism grounded in a spiritual perspective and rooted in simple but galvanizing spiritual practices can be both effective and sufficiently persistent in this exploding crisis... Gandhi could never have been effective in overturning the British Empire without the spiritual depth of his enterprise. Martin Luther King could never have prevented a racist bloodbath without appealing to the nobility of Christ consciousness... More recently, the extraordinary manifestation of courage and truth-telling that blazed from the Standing Rock resistance would not have been possible without the grounding of that resistance in constant ritual, prayer and meditation.*

It's not only spirituality that some activists are cynical about, it's psychology as well. This is more than just unfortunate, it's perverse. They must surely be aware of how many of their colleagues have ended up suffering from depression, disillusionment and burnout. Some activist organisations have recognised this and are doing good work that's intended to address it. For example, XR devotes a lot of time and energy to the wellbeing of the people who take part in its actions. It's not a soft option to sit in the road and stop the traffic when people are yelling obscenities at you and the police are hauling away your friends and throwing them into police vans.

The doyenne of this kind of work is that wonderful old spiritual activist, Joanna Macy. Her activism is driven by a love of Nature, but it's channelled and informed by her Buddhist practice and her involvement with the 'deep ecology' of Arne Naess. Many of her books, for example *World as Lover, World as Self*[5], explore the question of how we can find and nurture the courage we need if we really want to make a difference. Anger and defiance on their own are not enough, and can even be counter-productive.

There's a story in that book that I can never forget, having seen a video of her telling it at a time when I was full of confusion and despair. This is the ancient prophecy of the Shambhala Warriors. There are various YouTube versions of her telling this story[6], which I thoroughly recommend. About forty years ago I had a very vivid dream which had a similar theme and I've never forgotten that either – although I understood it differently at the time.

She and her co-workers have developed a set of practices known as 'The Work That Reconnects', which is designed to provide a safe space where people can express their feelings of fear, sorrow, rage and despair about the ecological devastation that's proceeding all around us. The aim of this work is to 'open the heart' and refresh the spirit in a place that can often feel very dark. There is little understanding or support elsewhere in our society for people who feel they must work against the flow of our destructive, materialistic culture.

I have done Work that Reconnects workshops three times now, and it's definitely not an easy option for someone conditioned into the notorious English stiff upper lip culture that all septuagenarians like myself were born into – not to mention the boarding school ethos that rammed it down my throat. Despite my years of training as a psychotherapist, I still find it quite scary to be part of a group where people are encouraged to express their feelings freely, so I really understand the difficulty that many activists have with this kind of activity. It evokes an old, deep-rooted feeling of embarrassment about my own vulnerability that I learned as a child from my father, and even more so from my school, which continues to get in the way no matter how much I've worked on it. Apart from occasional outbursts of anger or explosions of grief (which always happen when I'm least expecting them), I'm usually quite restrained in my expressions of feeling. That doesn't mean I don't feel anything, just that I'm not always very good at showing it.

I find it easier to connect with those feelings of rage, despair and confusion through the medium of my Focusing practice, which is a much quieter, less cathartic process. The aim here is to establish a relationship with the part of myself that is angry or despairing so that I can actually learn to understand what it needs, instead of either unconsciously acting it out or suppressing it.

These feelings still come back and haunt me at 3am as I lie there unable to sleep, wondering if anything I'm doing will make the slightest difference. But later, when I have the energy for it, I can take some time, invite them back and sit with them for a while, so that they can unfold into consciousness and help me to orientate myself in this toxic trauma field we call 'life in the twenty-first century'.

🍃

There's some hope that psychospiritual practices will gradually become more mainstream in the activist world. One of the reasons for this is Jem Bendell's courageous decision to publish *Deep Adaptation*, the IFLAS paper mentioned earlier, in which he not only discusses the likelihood that climate change will lead to near-term societal collapse, but is also quite open about what this means for him and the feelings that it evokes.

He chose to do this because, having worked in the field for twenty years, he knew what his fellow scientists, as well as the bureaucrats at the UN, for example, with whom he has often discussed the ramifications of climate breakdown, had already been secretly thinking and feeling for quite a while. They were reluctant to say anything about it because of the widespread belief that it's dangerous and unprofessional to do so. It is considered 'dangerous' because it might lead to a kind of climate despair, which discourages people from doing anything, and 'unprofessional' because neither scientists nor bureaucrats are supposed to express their personal feelings. If they cross that line, they can expect to be condemned by everyone, not least their own colleagues.

There was some negative reaction to Bendell's paper but not nearly as much as might have been feared. It was published on 7 July 2018, and in the following year it was downloaded on average about 1500 times *every day*. That's a measure of how badly it was needed. Of course, there have been criticisms because there is still this belief in scientific objectivity, but many people feel that it has done a power of good. Even in academic circles, it's now beginning to be acceptable to express one's feelings of fear and doubt, to seek emotional support, and to respond to the situation as if it really is an emergency rather than a vague threat that we can trust (or hope) the authorities will do something about.

Professor Bendell is a supporter of XR, and was invited to give the opening speech at Oxford Circus on 15 April 2019, when they started their week-long occupation. He told the assembled crowd: '*We gather and rebel not with a vision of a fairy-tale future where we have fixed the climate, but because it is right to do what we can. To slow the change.*

To reduce the harm. To save what we can. To invite us back to sanity and love. The truth is we are scared and we are brave enough to say so. The truth is we are grieving and we are proud enough to say so. The truth is we are traumatised and we are open enough to say so. We are angry and we are calm enough to say so, and invite others to join us.[7]'.

❧

XR has provided a focus for many people who have been feeling uneasy or just plain scared about the damage that the Machine is doing to our Earth. Jennifer C., a remarkable young woman I worked with at Fire Valley, is one of them; like Max, she is a warrior for Gaia and was born with a fiery spirit. I asked her if she could tell me something about her experience with Extinction Rebellion, and this is what she wrote:

Extinction Rebellion seemed to thrust itself into my consciousness in a way that nothing has ever done before. I felt like the words of its message were coming directly from my heart. Attending meetings with people who were determined to carve a more just future for all species of life was a humbling, uplifting and inspiring experience. Watching the women elders of my local community taking turns to mind my baby, enabling me to speak my heart's truth, were gifts of freedom that meant so much to me. Walking into a room full of people from mixed backgrounds, people I would probably have never spoken to before, knowing that if I shared my grief for Earth ... I would be seen and heard and held and would never again be told 'there's nothing you can do, it's just the way the world is'. What a relief and a blessing that was!

*My journey has been re-enlivened by Extinction Rebellion...
I have been mobilised to help build resourced, resilient,
more self-sufficient and sustainable communities that may
become the fabric of our future. My work is grounded in
the needs of my children, who will learn practical skills to
empower them to live gently, build an inner capacity to cope
with the difficulties of the world and develop meaningful and
honest relationships with other people.*

🌿

To live in service to the Earth, and to learn how to repair
the damage, is quite a challenge. There are many places
where people have taken up this challenge but few have
done it so thoroughly, or had such a direct impact, as the
Findhorn Community in north-east Scotland.

The community started very small, and almost by
accident, in the early sixties when Eileen and Peter Caddy,
and their friend Dorothy Maclean who managed the Cluny
Hill Hotel in the town of Forres, were made redundant by
the hotel's owner and ended up (together with the Caddy's
three children) living on a caravan park in the nearby
village of Findhorn. Feeding six people on state benefits
wasn't easy, so they decided to have a go at growing their
own veg.

Dorothy, through her meditation practice of 'inner
listening', discovered that she could communicate in some
way with the plant spirits. She was able to use the intuitive
knowledge she gained to coax the most amazing plant life
out of the rather unpromising sandy soil around the park.
The extraordinary success of their 'garden in the sand' (and
the highly unusual way in which they achieved it) soon

became famous in the burgeoning New Age atmosphere of the sixties, and led to a rapidly growing community of people attracted by the apparently miraculous nature of what was happening up there on the wild Scottish coast.

All three of the community founders had had years of meditative practice, with Eileen Caddy receiving very clear inner guidance from 'the still small voice within'. This voice started to give specific guidance on the development of the community, which Peter had complete faith in and followed. This guidance also included fundamental spiritual principles and teachings that formed the basis of the growing community.

Eileen started to publish her guidance and attracted even more people, including a Canadian spiritual teacher, David Spangler. His influence led to the community's first education programmes, which focused on putting spiritual principles into daily practice.

During the 1970s the community expanded massively, buying (mostly through donations) ten properties in the locality including the Cluny Hill Hotel that the Caddys had been forced to leave a decade earlier. The Findhorn Foundation (now a charitable trust) adopted this as their educational guest centre and offered a range of programmes that continue to this day.

Having leased part of the Findhorn Bay Caravan Park, and lived in temporary accommodation for almost twenty years, in the 1980s the foundation was finally able to purchase the whole park, plus adjacent farmland and dune land, and start to build an 'eco-village' of environmentally sustainable housing.

I've never been to Findhorn, but my friend Hilary M. was very active there between 1980 and 1989 when she was a young woman. I asked her what was so special about her experience there. This is what she told me.

'*They had it the right way round. The community started by growing vegetables and working in harmony with Nature, and this led into growing people. The personal work that we did while we were there wasn't done just for our own benefit, it was done so that we could learn how to be what we called 'Stewards of the Earth'. Service was our big thing, not 'spiritual growth' for its own sake. Planetary service.*

'*There was a tangible sense of love and care that developed between the people who were there, but it didn't result from a self-conscious attempt to love and care for each other. It was more about believing there was a higher purpose, and then co-operating to achieve it. The love and care just came naturally from the work because unless people feel respected, valued and understood, they are not able to put the needs of the group/community/planet at the forefront.*

'*We had a saying, that I've never forgotten, and I've always gone back to it when I've needed a kind of compass bearing in my life: "Work is Love in Action".*

'*It's very simple but not easy to do – to bring love into whatever we are doing. In the community everyone at some point had to spend time working in a service department such as house-care, kitchen or garden to learn how to do that. It is a rather Buddhist approach and akin to what we now refer to as mindfulness.*'

I asked her if they had a spiritual practice at Findhorn, like a meditation that they all did or some kind of ceremony which they all attended. She told me there was no compulsory meditation practice, although most people attended regular scheduled meditations that they referred to as 'going to sanctuary'. Only the group 'attunement process' was a community ritual, which they went through before starting any group task from having a management meeting to cleaning the loos. What was that, I asked?

'It was to acknowledge that everything we did was an act of service, and as such it was an opportunity to be present and focus on the task at hand, and to do it with love for the task and each other. It was a way to acknowledge that by connecting spiritually we could create something that was greater than the sum of the parts, that we could tune into something greater than us and channel that through our activity. We used the process too for group and community decision-making – a chance to let go of ego, opinion, and search for the best and highest answer for the whole. I suppose most people would think this was ridiculously idealistic, but all I can say is that it worked, without feeling at all heavy or artificial, and I wish there were more opportunities like that in the "real world".'

❦

Places like Findhorn are like beacons of hope in the darkness – places which can have a life-changing effect on the people who live there for a while and get some experience of what psychological transformation is about. The important principle at the centre of this is service: it's about giving rather than taking. The culture of service to the Earth is naturally friendly towards psycho-spiritual work, unlike the alienating, competitive, hyper-individualistic culture which has come to dominate the world we now live in.

The ideal of service doesn't feel like a burden in a place like Findhorn, or indeed Fire Valley (where I worked), because we live our lives there completely immersed in the sheer beauty of our planetary home, and with love and respect for the creatures that live here with us, including our fellow-humans, and realise just how lucky we are to be alive.

Findhorn was a product of the spiritual renewal that flared up and illuminated our lives for a few years in the l960s. My guess is that we're due for another, perhaps more intense renewal, during the next few years as our complex societies start to unravel and people really start to think about who we are and what we're here for. In some ways, for example, in recent social movements like #MeToo, Black Lives Matter and Extinction Rebellion, this has started already. It will be a natural progression from the activities of XR, which will generate some serious self-examination in its supporters as it proliferates and runs into a lot of really determined opposition.

A number of writers, including Charles Eisenstein and Paul Levy, have interpreted the current situation in a similar way. They point out that 'something new' is already emerging. It's taking many different external forms, but at their heart is a completely different perception of what human life on this planet is all about, a perspective that values caring for each other and for the natural world rather than limitless competition and casual ecocide. It's as if a whole section of humanity is becoming aware of itself as a tribe and beginning to tear itself away from the mindset of Progressivism in an effort to find a healthier direction.

From the perspective of something new being born, Charles Eisenstein has said that the conditions we're living in right now look like the third stage in the four-stage gestation and birth process described by the visionary psychiatrist Stanislav Grof. He has written about this in an essay[8] with a very evocative title that many mothers will recognise: 'Time to Push'. Here, the individual birth process is seen as a metaphor for a collective birth process that we are all witnessing together:

As the cervix opens, the contractions do not subside; they intensify. We are on the brink of social convulsions beyond anything we have seen in America for 160 years, and in Europe for 70. (In other places this process is telescoped into a shorter time span and mashed all together in an accelerated nonlinear jumble.) The contractions may take the form of economic collapse, natural disasters, political turmoil, or social conflict. Old certainties, generations or even centuries standing, will dissolve with astonishing speed.

The 'new breeze' stirring has blown in a storm... We hear the rumble of thunder before the deluge: supply chain disruptions, forest fires, floods, and droughts, civil disturbances, transportation system breakdown, internet and power outages, political extremism, accelerating inflation, and so on.

As the saying goes, this is when 'the shit gets real'. For many people it already has: the underclass, the sick, the persecuted, the hungry...

Also, we might add, the migrants forced to move away from impossible conditions in their homelands and rejected everywhere as unwanted invaders. Eisenstein continues:

In other words, we are entering a period of struggle where it is obvious that something important is at stake and our actions matter. We are moving down the birth canal. Immense pressures will bear down on us, pause for a while, then bear down again.

For most of my life, in the national and global arena

each passing year seemed much the same as the last, a predictable deterioration. That is changing. The year 2020 was no aberration. Normal is not going to return...The stasis that rendered us hopeless and cynical is over.

Eisenstein has been watching the situation closely for a number of years so his words carry some weight. The birth analogy isn't something he just dreamed up on a Saturday night; it's a thoughtful synthesis of a number of trends that are now coming together to facilitate a deep transformation.

🍃

Paul Levy has also written an interesting essay[9] about the process we're going through from a slightly different perspective, this time using a medical analogy:

In my lifetime I've never seen the extreme polarization that is playing out in the world today. We are at a severe "crisis" point ... which, medically speaking, always tells us that our process has reached a dangerous climax. We truly live in dark times. Jung reminds us, "there are times when the spirit is completely darkened because it needs to be reborn".

We may recognise times like these in our personal lives – times, for example, when we become disillusioned with the life we're living but we don't know what kind of change to make. These times can be very uncomfortable, especially in a culture like ours where we're taught to make decisions by thinking them through in a logical way. This never works at a time like that because our discontent comes from the soul, and we can't adequately respond to it by some rational process of goal-setting.

Levy continues:

Commenting on this polarization, Jung points out that if it doesn't kill us, what he calls our 'sickness of dissociation' is a harbinger of rebirth. This is an expression of the timeless archetypal process that one of the opposites is born out of the other; in our case, that the light (of consciousness)... is – potentially – emerging out of the darkness.

The widening of consciousness is always presaged by conflict, upheaval and darkness. Not only is darkness known through light, but conversely, light is known through darkness. It is an archetypal idea (found, for example, in the Kabbalah), that some form of conflict, destruction or disintegration is a prerequisite for individuation and is necessary for the birth of the Self (the God within)...

The conflict and polarization in our world can be recognised to be the footprints, so to speak, of this higher-dimensional birth projected into ... our third-dimensional world. Becoming conscious of this deeper process of birth that is revealing itself through the state of extreme polarization ... creates the womb for the Self to be born within us, and by extension, in the world at large. Once we have this realization, there's then plenty of work to do in the world, but recognising this deeper archetypal creative process that we are all participating in changes everything, including ourselves. Recognizing what is being revealed to us helps us to find ourselves, remember what we are here to do – assisting us in discovering our true mission in life – and helps us remember who we are. We are reborn in the process.'

Claire's story (in Chapter 2) is a good example of what Levy is writing about here.

❧

There's an analogous story of transformation that comes to us from the insect world, the story of the chrysalis in which the caterpillar undergoes its metamorphosis into the butterfly. Actually all insects undergo a similar process, but the butterfly in particular has always been a powerful symbol of transformation because of its astonishing beauty and delicacy. The caterpillar literally disintegrates into a kind of soup inside the chrysalis; for a long time people wondered how on earth this soup could reconstitute itself into something as complicated and beautiful as an adult butterfly.

It has since been shown that there are microscopic structures in the insect larva, sometimes called imaginal discs, that don't have any apparent function in the larval stage. When the organism reaches the pupal (chrysalid) stage and turns itself into a soup, however, they come alive and grow into the characteristic jointed legs, wings and other body parts of the adult insect. They were always there but they were hidden from view until the biologists became curious and started looking for them.

Bruce Lipton[10] has written (and spoken) about this as an analogy for the transformations that are under way in human society. There have always been people who are aware of the limitations of the current industrial paradigm, including groups who have been disadvantaged or dispossessed by it. Some of them have been inspired to experiment with different ways of doing things, including regenerative agriculture, co-operative enterprises, re-localisation, restoration of 'the commons'[11], etc. These more sustainable, and usually more locally-based, initiatives are practically invisible from the point of view of the mighty Machine, but they are linked into a loose network that enables them to inspire and learn from each other. They play little part in the global economy, but they will be available as exemplars when the industrial systems start to fail, just when we urgently need to find viable replacements.

Lipton points out that the world-wide network that links these different initiatives has a direct analogy in the developing chrysalis; it is a neural net that enables the imaginal structures to co-ordinate with each other, as if intelligence was distributed throughout the organism, not concentrated in any one place. This *distributed intelligence* is found throughout the natural world, in contrast to the conventional view that intelligence is a command-and-control function and must therefore be concentrated in one place.

🍂

Writer and environmentalist Paul Hawken has been interested in the transformations that are under way in human society for a while now. In his book, *Blessed Unrest*, he takes a good look at what he calls 'the largest social movement in history' – the myriad groups that have arisen in the last century, and especially the last half-century, to redress the balance between suffering Nature and the common people of this Earth on the one hand, and the oppressive power of the Machine which exploits them on the other.

When asked ... if I am pessimistic or optimistic about the future,' he writes, my answer is always the same: If you look at the science that describes what's happening on the earth today and aren't pessimistic, you don't have the correct data. If you meet the people in this unnamed movement and aren't optimistic, you don't have a heart. What I see are ordinary and some not-so-ordinary individuals willing to confront despair, power and incalculable odds in an attempt to restore some semblance of grace, justice and beauty to this world[12]. Having met members of many thousands of such groups over the years and organised a unique database on which many of them were listed[13], he writes that he believes there are between one and two *million* such groups world-wide, all working to make a difference.

There's a sense in which the entire human community can be viewed as one organism, a view normally associated with the French Jesuit priest and philosopher Teilhard de Chardin (1881–1955). From that point of view, Hawken suggests, this global movement – this enormously diverse collection of groups, these imaginal cells in our societies, all focused on restoring and regenerating what is most characteristically human in all of us – could be regarded as the immune system of the single human organism:

Just as the immune system recognises self and not-self, the movement identifies what is humane and not-humane... The word immunity *comes from the Latin* im munis, *meaning 'ready to serve'.*

The immune system is the most diverse system in the body, consisting of an array of proteins, immunoglobins, monocytes, macrophages and more, a microbestiary of cells working in sync with one another, without which we would perish in a matter of days, like a rotten piece of fruit, devoured by billions of viruses, bacilli, fungi and parasites, to whom we are a juicy lunch wrapped in jeans and a T-shirt...[14]

The immune system is a good example of distributed intelligence. There is no director to co-ordinate its action or to tell it what to do. Nature abounds with examples of this; think, for example, of a murmuration of starlings, where huge flocks of birds behave like a single organism, or of colonies of ants or bees, which behave like a highly differentiated organism but without any elite that gives orders or makes plans. Recent research has shown that even the trees in a wood communicate with each other and co-ordinate the way they respond to various disturbances, mainly through mycelial networks that are in intimate contact with their root systems[15]. Indeed, the entire natural world is organised like this on every scale from a single cell to a whole ecosystem. No-one is in charge of it – not even God – and yet it has maintained itself impeccably over several hundred million years, responding to every disturbance (including some really massive ones, like the asteroid impact sixty-six million years ago which killed off 75% of all life on the planet), gradually evolving and becoming ever more complex and differentiated without needing a plan or a specialised command-and-control structure of any kind.

Bruce Lipton applies the same notion to the individual cells that make up the bodies of all creatures in the natural world. We tend to think of the intelligence of the cell as if it were concentrated in the nucleus where the DNA is found. However, Lipton has shown that it manifests more as a property of the membrane that surrounds the cell – the cell wall – than the nucleus[16]. The study of epigenetics has shown that the body as a whole is much more openly responsive and less pre-programmed than the traditional DNA-centred view would suggest.

We tend to think of intelligence as concentrated in one place because we identify intelligence with left-brain thinking which glorifies hierarchies, hates complexity (which it sees as 'disorder') and imposes a top-down approach to everything. But the non-human world, the world of Nature, is alive with innumerable different forms of intelligence – or rather, one could say, different aspects of the One Great Intelligence that permeates everything. We tend not to recognise these different forms as 'intelligent' because, once again, we don't see a mechanism that resembles the highly specialised structures through which we humans manipulate the physical world around us. We think of intelligence as if it were language-based, a kind of clever mechanism whose principal functions are classification, organisation, command and control.

Nature doesn't work like that. It's an emergent, open-ended system that doesn't have any specific goal in mind except to be *more itself* in all its beautiful, delicately balanced diversity, and, in doing so, to manifest its own creative intelligence in response. Unlike the Machine, product of our hubristic cleverness, that seeks to control, dominate and standardise everything it touches, without limit.

*

We can bring the Findhorn ideal of service to the Earth into our own personal work if we dedicate our spiritual practice to Gaia rather than to our own private enlightenment.

I spent some time with Carla, who leads the Gaia meditation group in Bristol, talking about the contribution that our inner work can make as a response to the war on Nature. I started by telling her all about our adventures in Peru. When she'd stopped laughing, she asked the obvious question: had it made a difference?

'Yes,' I said, 'it's left me with the persistent feeling that it would do us all good to just *let go.*'

' Of what?' she asked.

'Well, in my case,' I said, 'of the elaborate mental frameworks I've erected around myself to protect my own version of reality. The mental frameworks that give me the feeling that I've got it all sussed.'

'Got what all sussed?' she asked.

'The story about spiritual growth, and beyond it the whole story around climate breakdown and the collapse of our civilisation. All the stuff I've been reading and writing about for the last few years.'

Carla suggested that one way of letting go is to stop using meditation as a way of gaining something exclusively for oneself – enlightenment or inner peace or whatever, and think of it as a way of participating in something greater than oneself. This is what they put into practice very successfully at Findhorn.

It has been pointed out many times before that we have a tendency in our culture to regard spiritual practice as a personal achievement that deserves some kind of spiritual 'brownie points'. 'Look at me, how spiritual I am, how enlightened, how worthy!' The Tibetan Buddhist teacher Chogyam Trungpa called this 'Spiritual Materialism':

The problem is that ego can convert anything to its own use, even spirituality. Ego is constantly attempting to acquire and apply the teachings of spirituality for its own benefit. The teachings are treated as an external thing, external to 'me', a philosophy which we try to imitate. We do not actually want to identify with or become the teachings[17].

Perhaps that was why I was finding Carla's Gaia meditation such a satisfying and useful practice. My attitude to inner work had been strongly influenced by Conrad's brand of spiritual individualism, with its Nietzschean values of 'rising above the common herd' and aspiring to be some kind of Superman, which has a very obvious dark side. My experience in the Peruvian Amazon showed me that there comes a time when this no longer serves us and we have to let go of it. Recognizing this, Carla's suggestion made a lot of sense to me.

Recently I found an article about spiritual practice in service to the Earth written by the Sufi teacher Llewellyn Vaughan Lee[18]:

We are living in a time of fundamental change, a period of increasing divisiveness, tribalism, isolationism, even as a global consciousness of one-ness struggles to be born. Surrounded by accelerating ecological devastation, climate change, loss of species, many of us—and especially young people—are awakening to the need to respond, to care for climate justice and the living Earth—to embrace life's interdependent unity, the web of life that supports us all...

Our materialistic culture with our dependence upon fossil fuels has created this crisis, and any shift in consciousness is also dependent upon us. And our spiritual practice is an essential, if little understood, catalyst for this change. Spiritual energy has the potential to change our individual consciousness, the patterns that define our existence, our day-to-day life. We know this from our own journey: how meditation, prayer, mindfulness can bring a deeper awareness into our life, and free us from the patterns that constrict us, the ego identity that isolates us, the wounds and defenses that define us. What we have yet to fully realise is that what is true for the individual is also true for the whole...

...if we are to live the real potential of our spiritual practice, we need to break free from the focus on our own individual journey. We need to reclaim the simple truth that spiritual life is not solely about ourselves, and open to a larger, all-embracing vision. If spiritual life is not about the whole, it has lost its true nature; it has instead been subverted by the ego and its patterns of self-concern. Everything that has been created is in service to life, to the real purpose of creation. This belongs to the 'Original Instructions' that were given to the earliest wisdom keepers. We are not separate from each other or from the Earth, and we need to recognise how our individual spiritual journey, our praise and thanksgiving, are part of life's sacred purpose and can nourish life in different ways...

I am not suggesting that spiritual activism is the sole form of activism needed to help humanity and the Earth in Her time of distress. There are many ways to bring our hands and hearts into the arena of service, to respond to the 'cry of the poor and the cry of the earth.' What I am suggesting is that spiritual practice is a little understood catalyst of global change, accessing a power that can help real transformation, a foundational shift that combines the power of the land with the light of our spiritual self. Those who are drawn towards spiritual practice can make a vital contribution to the well-being of the whole. And the first step is the simple but often revolutionary awareness that 'it is not about me.'

...Awakened consciousness is a powerful agent of transformation, of real change. And the light of our spiritual self is our most precious offering, our greatest contribution.

☙

How can a meditation practice help to bring about the transformation that's needed on a global scale? From a common-sense point of view, it can't have any real effect at all because meditation is an entirely inward process that can't bring any external force to bear on anything. But transformation has nothing to do with external force. The oneness that fosters transformation doesn't issue commands, it issues invitations.

From the common sense point of view, the action that Vaughan Lee describes is a mystery, but from another perspective it's no more mysterious than the phenomena of quantum physics, which are well-known and have been exhaustively described even though no-one has yet been able to give us an explanation of how they work. There are ways of thinking about the actions of subtle energies that can help us to imagine what might be going on[19], but they're not amenable to what we call 'common sense'.

For me, it helps to remember that *everything* is a mystery. From a common sense point of view, we're not happy with mysteries; we like to think that we know how everything happens or, if we don't, we soon will as science expands its boundaries to take in the whole of creation. We need to feel safe in our alien, disconnected world of things interacting with other, separate things. Anything obviously mysterious, like the extraordinary productivity of the veg gardens in the thin, sandy soils at Findhorn, tends to get rejected as nonsense because we can't identify a causal mechanism. That means, for those of us who are immersed in this point of view, *it couldn't possibly happen*.

But mysterious things happen all the time, right in front of our faces. The way that Gaia has maintained herself over hundreds of millions of years is a mystery. Our ordinary human capacity to call up memories and 'see' them in our consciousness is a mystery. The action of the immune system is a mystery. We think that as soon as we've uncovered a mechanism, we've solved the mystery, but we haven't solved the mystery at all, we've just uncovered the mechanism that makes it possible for a process to manifest itself in the material world. As we uncover more and more of the almost unbelievable complexity of life processes, which keep themselves going in a remarkably adaptive way, apparently without a recognisable hierarchy of command and control, we never ask ourselves how the overall system maintains its integrity. What's behind it all? We don't know.

I remember when I was a teenager, my father (who clearly thought I was in danger of growing up a little too different for comfort) gave me an expensively produced book called *Explaining the Unexplained*. He was only trying to help, but I'm afraid it was, without exception, the most pompous, boring, inane book I have ever read. It saddens me to think how thoroughly the education machine likes to trample all over our children's sense of the mysterious and the sacred. It's a tragedy without end, a wilful abuse of a very precious part of our innate humanity, and it has helped to turn our civilisation into one of the most crass, insensitive machines that has ever existed.

It's not easy to let go of our deeply embedded sense that the universe is a giant machine, whether or not God has his hands on the levers. We've spent the last three or four hundred years dreaming it up, and it's now the firmly established basis for what we like to call common sense. But when we start to question it, we find that common sense is, in essence, just another collective set of beliefs. If we manage to loosen the hold these beliefs have over us, we can see that there are other possibilities, and if we open ourselves to these possibilities – if we can make that small but crucial leap of faith – we can make them real.

References

1 https://iflas.blogspot.com/2018/07/new-paper-on-deep-adaptation-to-climate.html

2 For a concise description of the Virgin Warrior archetype, see Savitri Bess on the Ask Astrology website, at https://askastrology.com/archetype-of-the-virgin-warrior/

3 Simon Hattenstone did a very good interview with Greta Thunberg in *The Guardian* newspaper, September 21, 2021, which highlighted the contrast between her straightforward, fearless pursuit of climate ethics and her perfectly normal development as a young woman who has a deep appreciation of the value of friendship and mutual support and apparently no desire to capitalise on her celebrity status.

4 Andrew Harvey and Carolyn Baker, *Savage Grace* (iuniverse, 2017), p.49.

5 Joanna Macy, *World as Lover, World as Self* (Parallax Press, 2007).

6 For example, this one from the Spirit Rock Meditation Centre. https://www.youtube.com/watch?v=Y2Y10cdOE3M

7 See Jem Bendell's article in *Resilience* magazine, 17 July 2019.

8 Available at https://charleseisenstein.substack.com/p/time-to-push

9 See https://www.awakeninthedream.com/articles/rebirth-in-an-age-of-polarization

10 Dr Bruce Lipton is a developmental biologist, one of the pioneers of the science of epigenetics, who has unconventional views on how we can shift deep-seated unconscious patterns of self-sabotage. His website is www.brucelipton.com. Many of his videos are available on YouTube, and he has a considerable worldwide following.

11 'The Commons' refers to anything held in common on behalf of a group, usually a local group. This includes common land, water supplies, wood for fuel, etc. Much of the traditional commons have been stolen from the people during the last few centuries, until there is now very little left to steal.

12 Paul Hawken, *Blessed Unrest* (Penguin, 2007), p.4.

13 This is (or was) on the Wiser Earth website. The project had to be abandoned because things were changing so rapidly that it proved impossible to keep up, and the database was archived.

14 Paul Hawken, *op. cit.* p.142.

15 See, for example, Peter Wohlleben, *The Hidden Life of Trees: What they Feel, How they Communicate* (Greystone Books, 2015). This is mainly based on original research by the Canadian ecologist Suzanne Simard, whose interesting TED talk on the subject is available on YouTube. She was recently interviewed for *Emergence* magazine (see Finding the Mother Tree – Emergence Magazine).

16 See Dr Bruce Lipton, *The Biology of Belief* (Hay House, 2015).

17 Chogyam Trungpa, *Cutting Through Spiritual Materialism* (Shambhala, 1987), p.13.

18 From the Working with Oneness website at https://workingwithone-ness.org/articles/including-the-earth-in-our-prayers-spiritual-practice-as-a-catalyst-for-change/

19 My own teacher, J.G. Bennett, was very good at this. See Bennett, *Energies: Material, Vital, Cosmic* (Collected Works, Vol.12. Create Space Independent Publishing Platform, 2016).

– 15 –

Village Building at the End of the World

JULY 2018

THE WORLD'S FIRST regenerative hubs on a bioregional scale were launched in July when a gathering of experts from more than twenty organisations met at the eco-tourism retreat centre of Rancho Margot in the high mountain rainforests of Costa Rica. At this meeting, they set up an organising platform for regional development that can be replicated in other areas for regenerating the natural life-support functions of the Earth.

Joe Brewer writes in *Resilience* magazine[1]: *I had the great honor and privilege to be at this meeting. It felt like the spirit of Gaia had stirred in the hearts of these men and women, awakening us to the profound truth that we are of the Earth and the only way we continue to exist is by earning the right to serve as the consciousness of our dynamic home planet by transforming all human communities into superorganisms that serve the homeostatic needs of the Living Earth...*

We are all of us living in a globalized world of parasitic

384

extraction and excessive consumption. Measure humanity's footprint and you will see that it exceeds what the Earth is able to regenerate on its own... [Bioregional regeneration] offers a glimmer of hope for something truly worth aspiring for.

They have an ambitious programme based on a peasant economy rooted in the existing communities that already live on the land. Costa Rica has a good conservation record based on decades of experience, including nature tourism and excluding as far as possible the disruptions caused by large-scale mining and agribusiness. Let's hope they succeed with this vital enterprise.

All good things come to an end, and our collapsing techno-civilisation has already pushed itself a long way past the point of no return. Fortunately, a surprisingly large number of people have realised this and are trying to live in a way that puts them in a radically different relationship with the Earth.

For my mother-in-law, however, there was only one way her story was going to end, which is the same for all beings that enjoy the gift of life on this extraordinary planet. After we returned from Peru, she soldiered on for another six months before she succumbed to the Grim Reaper. He was never very far away during this time, and we often caught a brief glimpse of him in and around her bedroom.

There were times when she'd be suddenly frightened, for no particular reason that she could name, but I think she was catching a glimpse of the man with the scythe too, and she knew who he was despite her befuddled state. She'd look at me desperately and say things like, 'What's going to happen to me?'

I'd be thinking 'Well, I guess you're gonna die at some stage, probably quite soon,' but out of my mouth would come some cheerful comment like, 'Don't worry, dear, you'll be fine! And we've got some nice fresh chicken for supper.'

She wasn't able to use the phone any more, and there were many days when she couldn't be bothered even to ask if we could phone someone for her. Then there were days when she'd obsessively want to phone a particular person – usually Saintly Amy or the alleged Antichrist, Jolyon, and she'd ask us to call them over and over again.

She pretty much stopped talking about Jane. Jolyon congratulated himself, thinking that she'd finally understood that her dead daughter was hanging out somewhere in the Kingdom of Souls, but actually she just didn't have the energy for it any longer. Her obsession with 'going home' and finding 'the houses' went the same way.

This was the beginning of the end of Lizzie's long struggle. You could feel the death energy in the air, alongside all the craziness. It was a strange time.

🌿

Sophia goes away on her six-week summer break, and Valentina takes over. Poor Valie always seems to draw the short straw. A few days after she takes over, Lizzie develops the habit of slowly tearing her padded pants to bits piece by piece. This requires considerable force and commitment, but she still manages to shred them regularly, going through six or seven pairs a day.

Valie sits with her for long periods, calming her down

and making sure she's OK. I go in from time to time and sit for a while. Lizzie thinks I'm some kind of special doctor and greets me with intense relief, as though I can somehow rescue her from this nightmare. I wish I could, but in reality there isn't much I can do to help her.

After two or three weeks of this, the inevitable happens: she gets out of bed at 3am, falls over and breaks the other hip.

Once again she's carted off to the hospital. They call us in the morning and say that it will be very risky to operate, but even more risky not to. I find it hard to imagine just how awful it would be for her to live for any length of time with a broken hip, so I say OK, I guess you'd better operate. I'm beginning to realise that I've put myself in a position where I'm being asked to make some serious decisions on Lizzie's behalf, even though I don't have power of attorney for her health. That's a sobering thought.

The operation takes a few hours, but she survives it. They also find out that one of her kidneys is no longer functioning.

Valie goes in for three or four hours every day to calm Lizzie down and bring the kind of food and drink that she likes, because she won't touch the hospital food and she doesn't trust the nurses. We have a long argument with EuroCare about this, because their rules say that their carers are not supposed to have anything to do with the client while they are in hospital. But the solicitor with power of attorney has confirmed that he agrees with this arrangement and is prepared to pay for it with Lizzie's money, so they grudgingly allow it.

Lizzie has been catheterised, but she soon pulls it out again. Whatever they put inside her, she pulls out. When they try to reinsert the catheter, it takes four of them to hold her down and stop her from struggling. Valie witnesses this, and says she never again wants to see something like that being done to a ninety-six year old, however bad the alternatives might be.

I am summoned to a meeting with the doctor, Tania, a lovely woman from who knows where in Eastern Europe. She asks me how I feel about keeping Lizzie alive using 'aggressive interventions'. I ask what would be the point. Tania agrees that it would be futile. They may be able to extend her life by a few days or weeks, but only with great difficulty. They could do it, but what would be the human cost?

After my interview with Tania, I join Valie on the ward. Lizzie is pleased to see me but she doesn't have any idea who I am. She has been trying to get out of bed and escape from the hospital. This has aggravated the wound from her operation. To cope with this behaviour, they have lowered the bed almost to floor level and placed it next to the wall with mattresses all round. I watch her as she sits up in bed, pulls one of the mattresses towards her, leans over it, stares into the tiny void and, in a feeble voice, utters the immortal cry: 'Yoo-oo-oo-hoo! Yoo-oo-oo-hoo!'

She thinks she's leaning over the banister in her house. Do you laugh, or do you cry? If it were my mum I'd probably cry, but it's Lizzie so there's only one way to go.

There are four women on the ward, all of whom have some degree of dementia. Maisie used to be some kind of public figure, so she calls the room to order.

'Quiet, please!' she cries. 'Would anybody like to make a comment?'

Ellen shouts 'No! No!' That's her normal response to any suggestion at all, but Maisie thinks it means something.

'Speak up, please,' she commands.

'No!' cries Ellen. 'I can't do it!'

Meanwhile Jean, in the opposite corner, gets fed up with this ongoing argument and shouts out her characteristic phrase: 'Get out of my house! All of you!'

This meaningless jousting unsettles poor old Lizzie, so she sits up and does another feeble 'Yoo-hoo!', whereupon Maisie pipes up again.

'What was that?' she says. 'Speak up, please!'

My impression is that Lizzie is shutting down and hoping that the world will go away, but she still has moments of lucidity. In these moments, when she's not anxious, she's often unguarded and a different human being rises to the surface. She confides to Valie that she's had a difficult life and she's glad she won't be around much longer.

We're told she will be moved out of the hospital soon and the next step will be hospice care. But Lizzie keeps surprising them by reviving – or rather, almost reviving.

'We'll try some physiotherapy tomorrow if she keeps on like this,' they say. But when tomorrow comes, Lizzie reverts to her coma. She stops responding to anything, has great difficulty breathing and hardly even opens her eyes.

The man with the scythe is playing with his victim now. He pulls her down until she's almost done in, then he lets her go at the last moment and leaves her alone for a day or two. We all wonder whether she'll make a miraculous recovery after all, then two days later she's back on death row. They move her into a side room where she can get some peace from the continual noise of Maisie and Ellen slugging it out in the Mad Ward.

Saintly Amy also visits every day now, sometimes for two or three hours at a stretch. Valie is beginning to get fed up *with her because she's always trying to take charge. Why isn't Lizzie getting more pain relief? Has she had enough to drink? Why don't they make her more comfortable? The nurses try to ignore her and speak to Valie, but Amy is always butting in and demanding to be heard.*

❧

Lizzie learns how to use a bedpan, which is amazing in view of her fear of looking undignified. She doesn't wear incontinence pants any more because she still can't stop herself shredding them, but she has remarkably few 'accidents', given her situation.

After a week in the side room, they move her to a posh nursing home paid for by the NHS under an end-of-life scheme. Valie thinks she probably won't be needed there as they are not as short-staffed as the hospital, but once again she has to spend many hours educating them about how to handle Lizzie's quirky behaviour. For example, one of the nurses tells her, with great surprise, that they heard Lizzie singing during the night. 'Ah,' says Valie. 'Did it sound like this: Yoo-oo-oo-hoo! Yoo-oo-hoo!'

'Why yes,' says the nurse. 'Does she often sing like that?'

'That's not singing,' says Valie. 'That's calling for help. When she makes that noise, she's probably in pain or she's thirsty or she needs the bedpan.'

'Oh,' says the nurse. 'Has no-one taught her how to use the call button?'

Valie sighs. 'You try,' she says. 'If you can do it, you can have my job.'

Lizzie repeats the same pattern in the nursing home: one day she'll respond to people, have something to eat, drink a *little water or some fruit juice; the next day she'll lie on her back, breathing heavily, eyes closed, dead to the world.*

Saintly Amy still comes in nearly every day for two or three hours. Valie tries to avoid her but sometimes they overlap. One day she comes in just as Amy is trying to get Lizzie to pray with her.

'Now Lizzie, repeat after me: "Jesus Christ, have mercy upon us".'

Lizzie makes a valiant attempt to respond. 'Jesus Christ,' she says, and then there's a pause. 'I'm desperate for the bedpan,' she continues.

Valie, who's waiting respectfully just outside the door, can't stop herself from laughing.

Amy looks round and pretends nothing is happening. 'I think she needs the bedpan,' she announces.

'I think so too', says Valie. 'Shall we ask Jesus if he will bring it with him when he comes?'

Valie doesn't object to praying as such; in fact she's quite religious in her own way. There's just something about Amy's religion that doesn't feel right, especially after her outburst about homosexuals and the Antichrist. There's something weirdly unpleasant about the way she has fastened herself onto Lizzie's death process. Anxious, earnest Tony gives the same impression. They are like a pair of vultures circling the not-quite-dead prey, waiting for the moment. Valie says there's a word for this in Romanian; they call them ceocli, meaning something like 'vultures of the death process' – a sort of specialised vampirism.

At Sophia's suggestion, because she and Valie talk on the phone nearly every day, we ask the nursing home if their chaplain can spend some time with Lizzie. We all agree she might benefit from something cleaner and less vampiric.

One day he comes to see her, fortunately when Amy isn't around. They say the Lord's Prayer together. When they finish, Lizzie looks at Valie and asks in typical Lizzie fashion but with a rare smile on her face, 'So who's idea was this?'

Fortunately the vicar has a sense of humour, so he just laughs.

Two days later, she's dead.

Valie is holding her hand when she dies. It's one of those afternoons when both Saintly Amy and anxious, earnest Tony are there together. As always, they are concerned about Lizzie's pain relief and are discussing whether or not they should call one of the nurses and complain.

'What do you think?' Tony asks Valie.

She just says, 'I don't know, but I've had enough of this complaining, I'm going outside to smoke a cigarette.' And with that, she leaves.

She's only half way through her cigarette when she feels the need to go back. The champion worriers are out in the corridor harassing one of the nurses. Valie sees that Lizzie is waving her right arm, which means she wants her hand held, so she sits by the bed and holds it. 'I'm here, Lizzie,' she says.

Lizzie swallows hard, which is unusual for her, and it reminds Valie of something her grandma did just before she died. 'There's nothing to be afraid of,' Valie whispers to her. 'Just let go, and follow the Light.'

Lizzie grips Valie's hand tightly, swallows again, and lets out a gasp – 'Aah!' Then she swallows a third time, lets go of Valie's hand and dies.

When I arrive a short time later, Valie tells me, 'Is when she made "Aah!" that her soul come out from her body. I feel it go. It doesn't stay here very long, then is gone.'

I'm surprised to see that there are tears in her eyes. I give her a big hug.

'It's rushed off to look for the bus to the Kingdom of Souls,'
I say.

🍂

Everything that's alive and growing eventually gets tired, stops growing, dies and becomes food for something else. Even our remarkable techno-industrial civilisation will become food for something else, like all civilisations in recorded history however 'special' they believed themselves to be. We don't know how long this will take or what will replace it, because this is a time of truly transformational change. At a time like this, while everything is up in the air (so to speak), it's very difficult to make that kind of prediction.

There are many possible futures but it seems to me that they tend to resolve themselves into one of two directions. The first, which we have so far tended to follow by default, is the direction of 'progress'. Analysts like to call this 'business as usual', but the label conceals as much as it reveals. Its more enthusiastic devotees (like Ray Kurtzweil and his colleagues at Google's Singularity University) are actively dreaming up a hi-tech future, where all our problems are solved by techno-fixes and we acquire absolute mastery over nature.

This dream implies that we will become more or less completely dependent on the Machine in the sense that technology, in the service of our overriding need for power and control, becomes the sole driver. This has the advantage (for some) that it's left-brain-friendly, so it doesn't require any inner work on our part. However, it does imply a high degree of emotional shutdown and the acceptance of severe limitations on the scope and intensity of our inner lives, as Aldous Huxley foresaw ninety years ago in his novel, *Brave New World*. It also implies an indefinite extension of the culture of extreme individualism and 'uncare', so that human power continues to grow without limit, but human relationships become increasingly shallow and transactional.

We don't hear the enthusiasts talking about this aspect of their dream, probably because they are not even aware of it. But it's hard to see how it could be avoided, given the route we would have to take in order to arrive at this future. The Machine can't tolerate much human anarchy and it doesn't care at all about the Second Law of Thermodynamics[2]. No matter how thickly its devotees cover it with greenwash, it will continue to exploit and destroy the natural world until there's nothing left to destroy.

The other direction, which we've been exploring in this book, is towards restoring the Life of the Soul, including the spiritual relationship between our human world and the natural world that supports us. This means renewing our appreciation of organic (natural) wholeness, a much more right-brain process, and implies (over a long period of time) a resurgence of the Feminine and the complete transformation of the role that humanity plays in the ecology of the Earth. It involves living humbler lives, taking our inner experience more seriously, letting go of our need to control everything, and putting much more energy into caring for each other and for the health of our communities. It also implies that we accept a very different, rather less comfortable lifestyle.

This doesn't mean we have to go back to the Stone Age,

as critics of this dream sometimes say. We will still need a high degree of technical and social organisation, partly because there are several billion more of us on Earth now than there were five thousand years ago, partly because we will have to adapt to extreme conditions caused by climate breakdown, and partly because we will need to clean up the mess that the industrial growth economy will leave behind as it falls apart. But this won't work unless the technical and social effort serves our human soul-life, rather than serving the Machine. This is an arrangement which the Machine is not used to; as an entity, it doesn't understand it, or may even see it as a threat, so it might have to be fought for. Or, if we're lucky, it may be supported by some version of a Green New Deal. At this stage, we can't predict what might be possible.

Anyway, the unquestioned dominance of the 'progress' (or 'business as usual') agenda may not last very much longer. The economy suffers from too many internal contradictions for it to survive undamaged in its present form. But the Machine will do everything in its power to survive and a collapsing economy will give it many opportunities, as Covid-19 has shown. Vaccine passports, restrictions on where we can go and what we can do, widespread monitoring of our behaviour – in the context of a pandemic these might be sensible precautions, but they can also be read as warnings. The conspiracy theorists do us a valuable service in reminding us about this, whatever we think of Bill Gates and his alleged nanobots or the sinister architects of the New World Order.

We need to be very clear about this: *the Machine will do whatever it takes.* It is not interested in democracy or human rights unless they can be used as an excuse for imposing more technology on us. It gets its strength from its ability to turn everything into a business opportunity. Worse, it is gearing itself up to cause even more catastrophic damage to the Earth than it has already in the race to mass produce renewable energy systems and electric vehicles. Those of us who want to limit this damage will have to resist it in whatever way we can.

We can be inspired in this resistance by people like Joanna Macy, who has been doing it for so long now that she has it in her bones. It's worth watching some of the talks she has given which are available on YouTube like The *Hidden Promise of our Dark Age*[3], the address she gave at the 2009 Bioneers conference.

We can't know how this trial for the soul of humanity will turn out in the end, but we can be pretty sure that the longer the industrial growth economy manages to keep going, the more unpleasant life will become for many (perhaps most) human beings now living on this Earth, whether it's through 'austerity', inequality, resource wars or the direct effects of climate change. The circle of victimhood is gradually expanding; it will continue to expand until it affects even those of us who currently enjoy an affluent lifestyle with good prospects for a bright future. Many young people have already stopped believing in these bright futures, and by the year 2030 it's likely that most of us will have joined them as we head towards a new low-energy life on earth.

It's hard to contemplate the suffering that's likely to be visited on vulnerable populations by this relentless contraction. Borders are already closing all over the developed world; those who try to cross them in a desperate search for some kind of safety are treated with hostility wherever they turn. The current migration pressure is mild compared to what we'll get in the coming years as crops fail and weather patterns become more extreme. Where will they all go?

Equally terrible to contemplate is the devastation that will be suffered by our one and only home, this beautiful planet Earth. According to the 2018 report of the World Wildlife Fund, we've already lost at least 60% of our terrestrial wildlife and an even larger percentage of our aquatic wildlife *since 1970*. If we keep on throwing up populist leaders like Trump, Modi or Bolsonaro, this destruction can only get much worse. There's no easy way to stop these disastrous *Wetiko*-infected vandals now that it has become OK to vote for them in national elections.

If we're very unlucky, the world could even unleash its nuclear arsenals as an accidental result of the unrestrained scramble for survival. Accidental – but by no means unpredictable. That doesn't even bear thinking about.

🌿

There's a profound anxiety out there. The obvious effects of climate breakdown (drought, forest fires, floods, the melting of the Arctic) have made people aware that something has gone badly wrong, and that politically nothing much is being done about it. At the same time, most of them have jobs, family responsibilities, debts. We are caught in a system which has extended without limit the power of money, but for ordinary people there's less and less of it about, so there is little time to do anything but earn it and then crash out in front of the TV.

It becomes harder to slow down and reconnect with

ourselves, with other people or with the natural world that sustains us. There's no way out for most of us, beyond making minor changes in our personal habits. Recycle more, fly less, buy local produce if possible, that kind of thing. But people aren't stupid; they realise this won't be enough to really change anything.

What will happen to us? We don't know, but at the moment most of us still prefer to live in a state of suspended denial, rather like Lizzie did until she began to recognise that this was it, her time was up.

This pervasive anxiety, and the combination of emotional numbing, disconnection and increased reactivity that go with it, are very reminiscent of PTSD (Post Traumatic Stress Disorder). I've worked with traumatised people so I've seen these symptoms before, and it seems to me that our entire culture is now immersed in a kind of trauma field[4], a deep sense of unease that isn't acute enough for us to attach it to any specific thing until something happens in our lives that makes it explode in our face. Covid-19 has been a striking example of this kind of pattern externalised in the form of a catastrophic event. We have been living in a semi-conscious trauma field for a long time and we've become so used to it that we think it's normal.

The word 'trauma' means wound, and this wounding is very common in our society. It's mainly caused by repeated violations of our human need for safety and protection, especially in childhood. These come in the form of emotional abuse and other more subtle rejections, including the refusal to listen or to acknowledge our hurt[5]. They have a cumulative effect that is normalised by our alienated, competitive lifestyle until we can hardly imagine anything different.

This background anxiety is not new. Existential angst was identified I50 years ago by the philosopher Soren Kierkegaard, when it was still an obscure condition that was only of interest to a few intellectuals. It was described very vividly by writers such as Jean-Paul Sartre and Albert Camus in the I940s, since when it has become more commonly recognised as a feature of life in the modern age with its abandonment of the sacred and its deep uncertainties about who we are and where we're going.

As Richard Tarnas pointed out in his epic study, *The Passion of the Western Mind*[6], the development of science has presented us with a difficult dilemma: how can we reconcile our felt need for some sort of meaning in our lives, for deep connection, for participation in cooperative communities, with our intellectual preference for materialistic reductionism? We've been told for a long time that we're alone in the universe, which is like a huge machine devoid of meaning or purpose. To put it another way, how can we reconcile the two 'stories' we tell ourselves that represent the two major modes in which we perceive reality: the story of separation, and the story of interbeing?

I believe one thing is certain: the more we depend on the Machine, the more our lives will come to resemble a hideous nightmare where human warmth and intimacy are replaced by ubiquitous control and a pervasive sense of inner emptiness.

In the short term, I think it's highly likely that the idea of a hi-tech lifestyle will persist and be developed still further, but the supposed benefits of such a lifestyle (insofar as they exist in reality) will be enjoyed by a smaller and smaller proportion of the population as the existential crisis gets deeper. The current inequality will probably persist and will make life steadily worse for a large proportion of the population, which will find itself in a kind of never-ending emergency where the struggle to survive will become more and more relentless[7]. We have been told so many times that technology will save us but, as we've seen, the price we pay for this 'security' is that it enables the Machine to dominate our lives until we can't live or work without it.

The human population of the Earth can only be maintained at its present level and in its present form (i.e. living in big cities remote from the land) by the availability of a large energy surplus. When the surplus starts to disappear, so will the population that depends on it. It sounds heartless and cruel to say that, but no-one has yet thought of a way in which we can escape this awful dilemma.

Meanwhile we are beginning to develop more and more of our own street-level ways of looking after each other (for example, urban community farming, which is becoming quite well-developed in the USA), and the elites in their hi-tech wonderland will no doubt become less and less relevant as the unravelling continues and intensifies.

One of the tasks we could be addressing right now is to build up our community life so that it's there for us when we really need it. Every serious writer who has looked at our possible futures agrees that extreme survivalism isn't viable; it really isn't wise to spend your money on guns, ammo, tinned food and a cabin in the mountains. In any case, there's no wilderness left to retreat to in the UK; every square foot of land is either privately owned or heavily regulated by some public body that won't allow you to camp on it unless you're on a designated site. If you're a billionaire you might be able to buy yourself an island somewhere – in which case, good riddance – but most of us are not billionaires so we couldn't do that even if we wanted to.

It's quite likely that central governments will struggle to cope as the unravelling gains momentum and spreads. For the growing number of poor people in our communities, they're already making a bad situation worse with their punitive approach to public service provision and their tolerance of extreme inequality. Thus, for example, in the UK a lot more money is spent on the relatively small problem of benefit fraud than is spent on the huge problems of tax evasion and tax avoidance[8].

&

What might a global collapse actually look like in the long term? One of the most comprehensive studies that I'm aware of is John Michael Greer's *The Ecotechnic Future*[9], which examines the changes we're likely to go through between now and the kind of society we may be heading towards in the far future, when the current unravelling completes itself and humanity starts to recover. This study is based on the concept of succession, which is used by ecologists to describe what happens when a piece of land is colonised by Nature.

If you take an ordinary plot of land in the temperate zones of Europe and North America - one that hasn't already been ruined by industrial chemicals - and clear it down to the bare earth, it will soon be covered in tiny plants. These are opportunistic weeds, the fast-growing annuals that can convert energy into growth at the highest possible rate but lack durability, relying on a yearly cycle of birth, death and re-seeding. They create the ideal conditions for the next 'sere', as the ecologists call it, where a few more hardy plants have started growing. These gradually displace the annuals and settle down into a yearly cycle of birth, partial death and rebirth from the same durable rootstock. Bushes and small trees start appearing, and within a few years there's a pioneer forest of young trees growing where once was bare earth. After many more years – centuries, even – we get to the stage of the mature forest, where the trees grow much more slowly and can last for hundreds of years if undisturbed. Each sere adapts to make optimal use of the conditions set up by the preceding one, reaching more and more stable conditions as they follow each other.

If we apply this model to civilisations, Greer writes, we can see our industrial civilisation, with its extravagant use of energy and its colossal wastage, as equivalent to the first sere. This is the stage of the fast-growing annuals, with their ability to make maximum use of the resources available. That may sound paradoxical, as our civilisation has arisen at the end of a long period of evolution, so how can it be the first sere?

I think the answer lies in the thoroughness with which it has tried to obliterate all previous ways of life, including indigenous ways that have survived almost undisturbed for thousands of years, so as to bring all of us humans into its sphere of operation. In effect, we abandoned centuries of history and started again with a clean slate. We are tearing up the rainforest, burning it to a cinder, and replacing it with palm oil plantations and soya farms.

As the resources on which our civilisation depends

start to run out, Greer writes, we will have to learn how to conserve them so that we lean more towards durability than growth. As we go further down this road, we will learn how to salvage the resources that are at present locked up in those huge industrial fortresses – the factories, office blocks and other structures we have built around our extravagant way of life – and use them more wisely. One he singles out in particular is steel, of which we have used literally billions of tons in our structures and other artefacts. Steel can be re-purposed relatively easily for common items of hardware such as tools, nails, etc.

After industrial society starts to collapse, he imagines three broad categories of successor cultures. The first of these he calls 'scarcity industrialism', where the remaining energy resources are used a good deal more carefully by the relatively few people who can still afford to use them. This is followed by the 'salvage economy', which finally gives way to the 'ecotechnic society', which has learnt to apply selected technologies in a truly sustainable way so that a much-reduced and very diverse human population can live in harmony with its environment instead of trying to live way beyond the earth's carrying capacity. This is a very generalised picture and, as Greer says, it won't be the same everywhere.

It's possible that many of the local organisations that are springing up in response to the suffocating grip of the industrial economy will be able to withstand the worst of this collapse because they are deliberately avoiding the need to depend on globalised systems of consumption, including seed distribution, marketing, transport, etc., and artificial inputs like fertilisers, insecticides or GMOs.

The regenerative hub that was started recently in Costa

Rica is an example, having been set up with great care in such a way that it can survive a global collapse. As Paul Hawken found, there are more and more organisations like this, some of them with equally ambitious aims, like the Zapatistas in southern Mexico[10] and the world-wide peasant farmers' organisation known as the Via Campesina[11]. The Transition Network[12], which started in the small town of Totnes in Devon in 2006, is another example that has spawned a world-wide movement.

These are some of the more visible organisations, but there are many others where Greer's ecotechnics will be developed and tested over the years. Most of them will be small, localised, and volunteer-run.

This kind of work requires persistence and dedication. Ecotechnics are being developed already in projects based on organic and regenerative agriculture (such as permaculture), which can maintain themselves alongside industrial agriculture by developing niche markets. These methods also lend themselves to the kinds of urban agriculture that are being developed in decaying inner cities like Detroit, where the farms are worked by and for local people so they are not subject to the same commercial pressures as the big industrial farms.

My guess is that in some of them, as in Findhorn, a shared psycho-spiritual understanding of what it means for humanity to serve a higher aim will also develop. This would include caring for the planet instead of exploiting it to the point of ecocide. This twenty-first century equivalent of a religion might draw on the legacy of indigenous Earth wisdom, integrating it with the work of the many diverse psycho-spiritual pioneers who are developing ways we can reconnect with our spiritual heritage, with each other and with our Mother Earth. Communities like these, including virtual communities that meet online, might well carry the torch of civilised life down through the years in much the same way that the Christian monasteries, with their powerful mix of practical work, healing, prayer and theological scholarship, carried it for our Western culture during medieval times.

$$\pmb{\swarrow}$$

I think it's highly unlikely that those of us who see the need for radical change will be able to persuade our 'democratic' governments to do very much beyond making declarations, vague promises and tokenistic gestures of the kind they made at the recent COP26 talks in Glasgow. They derive their legitimacy from their ability to oil the wheels of the existing system (also known as 'business as usual') and make it run as smoothly as possible for those who voted them in or, more importantly, for those who support them with political donations. These are the only people to whom they feel they really owe something, in the same way that the corporations prioritise their shareholders (especially when these include their own senior execs). This may sound cynical, but I'm afraid that when the chips are down, it does tend to reflect their behaviour, as was amply demonstrated at COP26.

Although there is widespread anxiety about the future, I don't think enough people have yet realised that the system itself is the problem. Consequently, there's little understanding of how radical these changes need to be. Even if we know this on a technical level, there are limits to our collective ability to embrace a radically different set of values, to imagine and welcome a lifestyle based on cooperation rather than competition, sharing rather than exclusivity, community-building rather than naked individualism, caring for our world rather than just acquiring more stuff.

Those who have been successful within the current system won't easily allow their rewards to be taken away from them. As they have the entire resources of the state – police, armed forces, security apparatus – behind them, it's difficult to see how they can be shifted from this position.

This doesn't mean that there's nothing we can do. There are several avenues open to us as activists or change-makers that are oriented towards the new world we want to see, or as Charles Eisenstein calls it: 'The more beautiful world our hearts know is possible.'

One avenue is resistance. We can slow down the destruction of the natural world in the name of 'progress', for example by making it more difficult for the UK government to build its enormously expensive and ruinous HS2 line. The courage shown by people who occupy woodlands that are about to be destroyed is exemplary and it makes our resistance visible, even if it is only effective for a short time.

Even when there's no way we can stop these acts of destruction, as the Tree Protectors are aware, we can still bear witness. The phrase 'bear witness' means a lot more than just passively watching while something happens. It means exposing the feelings, bearing the pain of witnessing.

I will never forget an example of this that I encountered in 1983, at the big anti-Trident demo in Barrow-in-Furness where they build those giant nuclear submarines. In the midst of this huge parade of angry, chanting demonstrators,

I saw a small group of Quakers standing quietly by one of the shipyard gates. They had some candles burning and a simple declaration of their intention to bear witness to the horror on the other side of the gate, where we were building a fleet of killing machines designed to deliver a fiery death to several million innocent human beings.

I could hear the voice of my inner cynic, 'Yeah, so you're gonna stop them by standing outside the gate with a candle in your hand,' but I was curious and left the march briefly to take a closer look.

As I stood there with them and read the declaration, I felt myself suddenly overwhelmed with a feeling of profound sadness and I couldn't stop the tears. I didn't really appreciate why this was happening to me at the time, except that there was nothing fake about it.

Looking back, I can see that when the action of bearing witness is done with deliberate intention, despite one's natural inclination to avoid the pain and look the other way, it has an effect that extends over both of the Two Worlds. Those Quakers were in touch with something much deeper than a collective sense of rage and defiance. They were bearing witness to something about our human condition that drives us to the kind of madness that was manifested in the killing machines being manufactured on the other side of the gate. I could only sense it inside as an unbearable feeling of grief.

*

Art can be a powerful avenue of resistance and it's another, more expressive, way of bearing witness.

Performance art has played a big role in the XR protests.

One manifestation of this that I've found particularly powerful is the Red Rebel Brigade, with their blood-red costumes and ghostly white faces, who came originally from an immersive theatre group in Bristol led by Doug Francisco. As he says, they represent archetypal figures. I see them as spirits of the dead, sent to warn us about what we're doing to the Earth. Since they first appeared in the big XR street protests in 2019, they have begun to pop up all over the world because they are recognisable everywhere as potent symbols of the Death Machine.

The Nigerian writer Ben Okri referred to the artist's role in a recent article in *The Guardian*[13]: *We must write as if these are the last days. [...] What is called for here is a special kind of love for the world, the love of those who discover the sublime value of life because they are about to lose it. For we are on the verge of losing this most precious and beautiful of worlds, a miracle in all the universe, a home for the evolution of souls, a little paradise here in the richness of space, where we are meant to live and grow and be happy, but which we are day by day turning into a barren stone in space.*

You don't have to be a professional writer to respond to his suggestion. Recently I came across a blog post written by an Australian artist, Jessie Ngaio[14], which she posted on the Deep Adaptation Facebook page together with a beautiful piece of her own artwork. She's not a writer by trade (neither am I, for that matter), but this is the kind of writing Ben Okri was talking about. I am quoting her here because she expresses her feelings much more honestly than most of us would dare to.

In our immediate future, there is suffering beyond measure and we need to let ourselves feel the depths of our horror, rage, despair and grief. We need to feel these feelings so that we can let other feelings in – gratitude for the flowers we see blooming around us, awe at the sight of a bird flying overhead, hope for a better tomorrow and deep love for ourselves, the precious, fragile, endangered species that we are.

How do I combat the climate despair which plagues me on a daily basis? I focus on the beauty that exists now, I focus on the actions myself and others are taking but most of all, I dream. In my dreams, I see a world that has changed beyond recognition... So many of the countries that exist are underwater, massive cities have been swallowed by the rising oceans and are gone, populated now only by ghosts and sea creatures. And the land ... is covered in strange new forests that are thrumming with the hum of insects and echoing with the songs of birds. The land has been rewilded, healed through the efforts and dreams and love of a new type of human.

These new people have learned from the mistakes of their ancestors and so they are not conquerors or narcissists because the only people who survive an apocalypse are people who are able to work together, work communally. And the only people who are able to heal the world after an apocalypse are the people who are able to work with the laws of nature in a mutually beneficial symbiosis ... and so these people have become connected to the land they are on, like Indigenous people always have been.

These people are gardeners.

Humanity has a way forward but it requires a shift in the way we perceive ourselves. No longer can we be conquerors, dominators, destroyers. Instead we must be healers and caregivers of the earth. Our world is ending but life doesn't have to and we can be part of the most beautiful process of transformation, rejuvenation and change.

I'm scared to say all this, afraid that I will be judged as a naïve, ridiculous dreamer. But perhaps we all need to dream more, perhaps we all need to dream so much that we see a path forward that isn't just a living nightmare. And so I allow myself to dream and I allow myself to believe that we can all be part of discovering a beautiful destiny for humankind where we are warriors for light and love, where we are gardeners who nurture, nourish and protect the incredible miracle that is life on this planet.

And if you are like me, which I suspect many people are, your heart aches with the desire for this world to exist. And if your heart aches as mine does, perhaps this indicates something about a beautiful truth of our human nature: we don't want to destroy life on this planet. We don't. We've lost our way, we're confused and far from home but our heart knows what we want most: we want to live, we want to love and we want to thrive.

So let's awaken to the truth in our hearts and start doing what we need to do to prepare for the hard road ahead. We are an incredible species, we have music, poetry, medicine, philosophy, psychology, ecology... we have so much. Let's put it all to use and together, we are powerful.

❦

We don't all aspire to be artists, but there are many ways in which we can express the human values that we wish we could all live by: tolerance, compassion, kindness, cooperation. There's no need to spell them out because they are there in front of us, from simple everyday acts of kindness to the really difficult tasks that volunteers undertake on behalf of homeless people, refugees and other vulnerable groups for whom the state provides little or no real help.

We may think that things like this don't really matter, they just come and go like waves that disappear into the great indifferent sea of life, but they have real significance when seen against the background of a culture of 'uncare' that relentlessly devalues and marginalises such people, as if they don't really matter because they don't make much of a contribution to GDP.

We can't return to the Garden of Eden and the ancient indigenous ways of life, to live again within the *participation mystique*. We have evolved into, and become attuned to, a much more individualistic mode of living. We have released the genie of Separation from his bottle, and there's no point in trying to force him back in again. In doing so, we developed the habit of critical thought, which is no small achievement, but critical thought on its own won't take us very far; indeed, when not in service to a higher aim, on its own it leads to the kind of nihilism and despair we see all around us. We need to rebalance our thinking in a more holistic direction.

This doesn't mean we need to take a course in the history of philosophy. We can just withdraw a little from our busy lives, stop distracting ourselves and be present for a while, and ask ourselves a few awkward personal questions like, 'Do I really need such a complicated life?'

In the immortal words of Bayo Akomalafe: 'The times are urgent. *Let us slow down*.[15]'

At some point when we're called to do it, we may find ourselves compelled to go further and make a decision. Am I going to go on living like this, feeding the Machine

411

with the best part of my life energy, or has the time come to say no, and make a break? I'm reminded of the story of Claire's life-changing decision, in Chapter 2. It wasn't easy for her because it went against the whole weight of what she'd been taught was 'right' for nearly thirty years. It was only when she'd done it and faced the consequences that she could see how cramped, artificial and literally soul-destroying her former life had been. Many of us are in a similar situation, making endless compromises and hoping it will all turn out right in the end. We may find, as things get more difficult, that we can't go on doing this for ever.

As we head into the 2020s, Paul Kingsnorth makes these predictions[16]: *My own personal projections ... are a short-term future of both Breakdown and Clampdown, as those who are tasked with keeping the Machine running resort to ever more draconian measures to keep it on the rails. I expect a deepening of the current demonisation of dissent, and an acceleration of surveillance and control by the authorities, even as the shelves empty and the oceans warm. At the same time I expect an acceleration of the rhetoric of progress [and] growth, and a noisy focus on the promised transhuman/ intergalactic/hyperreal future as a way out of the mess. As we hit limits on all sides, we can expect to see, at least for a while, an even more furious denial that they exist.*

Our civilisation is breaking down, but it won't go quietly.

*

I'm reminded of the simple advice that Valie gave my mother-in-law when she came to the end of her life. 'Just let go,' she said, 'and follow the Light'.

I was with my friend Conrad when he died. Before he

drifted away into a morphine dream, I remember saying something quite similar to him about letting go. His response was heartfelt, and immediate. 'I can't let go', he cried, in great distress. '*I have to have it all taken away from me!*'

When you see someone trying desperately to hold on to their life, or rather to their story, the mental construction they have made of their life, even though they are obviously at death's door, it can feel as if they're being obstinate and perverse. But it's not that easy to let go. Conrad had spent his entire life building an interior castle strong enough to withstand anything that was thrown at it; he wasn't going to let it just fall down as if all that effort had been for nothing, especially when it was his own death that was being thrown at it.

Fortunately he was helped in his final hour by a good spiritual healer. When he finally did let go, a moment I'll never forget, the room was filled with a profound sense of stillness and peace as his soul left his body and 'followed the Light'. Something similar happened when my wife Jane died. She had less to lose than Conrad so, when the time came, she didn't need to fight so hard. She just waited a while for me to sit with her and then slipped away quietly.

Now there's a sense in which all of us who inhabit this dying civilisation will have to let go of that, too. We'll have to let go of our desperation to keep it going at all costs, our need to hold on to it inwardly, as if our lives will suddenly become meaningless without it and all the good things it has brought us will disappear for ever. Some of those things probably will disappear, tragically, but this can't be avoided in any really profound transformation.

Transformation always involves sacrifice, not just a

token sacrifice but the loss of much that's really valuable. For example, we can resist the destruction of the living world but when that fails (as it often does), all we can do is to grieve for our loss, invite others to grieve with us, and try to make the loss more bearable for each . As Conrad used to say, that is 'not nothing'. In fact I think it's probably the best expression of our humanity that we can offer the world as it changes. We can refrain from adding to the panic, the scapegoating, the damage and the negativity, and use our gifts to help in whatever way we can, just as many people do quite naturally without even thinking about it when their country becomes a war zone, or when it has been hit by a natural disaster.

Perhaps not surprisingly, a few insightful people born into cultures that we once colonised (like Bayo Akomalafe who is Nigerian), seem to have a better understanding of what we will have to relinquish than we do. (I'm using words like 'we' and 'our' here to refer to people like me, i.e. privileged white European males.) They are well aware of our addiction to power and control, our unconscious arrogance and our inborn feelings of entitlement. As we attempt to fix the crises in front of us, these addictions will get in the way and make everything worse. We need to wean ourselves off them; if we can't do that, the crisis itself will be our nemesis.

Some might say that this sounds like self-hatred or defeatism, but it's worth reminding ourselves that judgements like that originate in an arrogant culture where 'losing' is almost a dirty word, and which lionises 'success' even when it means we don't care who gets hurt; a culture saturated with its own kind of 'war' mentality (the War on Terror, the War on Drugs, the War on Woke, the War on

Poverty, etc.) and one that is rapidly polarising itself into tribal camps on every issue that matters to us, from culture wars to climate breakdown.

Not the kind of culture that can produce wise, balanced judgements.

❦

This way of responding to the situation doesn't require any heroics; as the Sufi teacher Idries Shah once said[17], the time for heroes is over. It does, however, require a certain inner steadfastness. How do we nurture that?

I think there's only one real answer to that question, and it's what Valie said to Lizzie when she was on the point of death: 'Follow the Light'. This means the inner light, the light of the Soul. People who have been through a near-death experience often describe this as an actual light, but for most of us in our ordinary lives it comes as a symbolic light, an intuition, a restlessness of the soul, that leads us to turn away from the kind of life that no longer serves us and look for a better way.

This isn't an easy call. We can't just reject the whole thing and stop going to the supermarket or buying clothes or paying our taxes. As Paul Kingsnorth points out in his essay series, quoted above, we are compelled to live under conditions that are largely set by the Machine. A few people (including Kingsnorth himself) have managed to establish a way of life that involves only minimal contact with it, but most of us don't have the skills for that, or the capacity to take big risks, or we're prevented by family responsibilities, debts, or a multiplicity of other difficulties.

Those who aspire to make a complete break may find

themselves agonising over it because of what they will lose – security, status, money, the approval of family and friends – in fact, all the inner and outer constraints that keep our society going in the way that it has done since the dawn of history. It's a considerable leap in the dark, as I know myself from bitter experience having tried (and failed) with our Heart of Devon community.

But we don't have to make such a drastic once-and-for-all commitment. As Kingsnorth says, the essential first step is to make the break inwardly, to see the Machine for what it is, and to stop insisting that our present high-energy way of life must somehow be rescued. *To liberate ourselves, steadily, one human soul at a time*, he writes[18], *we simply have to walk away from the Machine in our hearts and minds.*'

Whatever our circumstances, we can gain the necessary inner strength by cultivating practices that bring us closer to ourselves, to each other and to Mother Nature. I'm not a teacher and this book is not a spiritual self-help guide but, just for the record, here are some of the things I have found to be helpful. Bear in mind that I'm quite old and therefore probably under a lot less pressure than most of my readers.

No.1 is to do as Bayo Akomalafe suggests, and slow down. Do the things we have to do but with real attention, not dashing them off or trying to do several things at once. 'Do them with love' as they say at Findhorn. Love isn't just a feeling, it's a *way of paying attention*.

No.2 is to really listen to what other people are saying, not just hear it and immediately react. As I'm an ex-therapist you might expect me to say something like this, but we don't necessarily have to go through a long training to learn this skill. It can come quite naturally if we let go of our need to be competitive when we're in conversation and allow ourselves to be interested in another person's reality. This, too, is a way of paying attention. In our culture, we are encouraged to put most of our energy into showing ourselves off to maximum advantage and it tends to become a deeply ingrained habit.

No.3 is to spend as much time as we can in Nature, preferably wild Nature, while being present to the sensations and feelings in our own bodies. Walking in the woods is one of my personal favourites, because I love the way the trees talk to each other when they think we're not looking, but each to their own. Finding a 'sit spot' and going there as often and as unobtrusively as possible is another of my favourites.

Time spent in Nature is especially valuable at a time when the natural world is under such sustained assault, just as time spent with a loved one is especially valuable when they're ill or in need of support. Again, it's only by paying attention to what the natural world is saying to us that we can get a sense of it as one whole instead of a random collection of separate living (and dead) 'things'.

No.4 is practising tolerance in this time of polarisation. This can be really difficult because there's so much out there to get angry about. I find it helps to limit my exposure to social media, or at least to notice my reactions and not let them take me over.

All of these are ways of paying attention, and all of them start with paying attention to one's own inner life. A well-developed capacity for paying attention is the foundation for everything we do that's truly human, from engineering to competitive sport to establishing a meditation practice.

We have become very good at paying attention externally, but this has mostly been done at the expense of our own inner lives. The time has come to re-balance the way we use our attention otherwise we'll just go on using it to find more effective ways of attacking each other and destroying the Earth.

There's some good material online that can help us with this, like Eckhart Tolle's YouTube channel. Alternatively, we could use a simple, basic guide like Sufi teacher Llewellyn Vaughan Lee's book, *Spiritual Ecology: 10 Practices to Reawaken the Sacred in Everyday Life*[19]. Practices like those he describes in his book provide us with anchor points that can stabilise our lives and give us a few gentle reminders about what we're here for. Without such anchors, we can easily drift from one thing to another without paying much attention to anything at all.

I could go on for a long time airily dispensing advice like this but the main thing for anyone who's interested is that we all have to find our own best way. If you're an aspiring artist, art is probably your best way; if you're a keen gardener, it's probably gardening. We need to discover what's important to us by listening to ourselves rather than following someone else's advice.

But be reassured: if you've read as far as this already without blowing a fuse, there are plenty of people who feel the same as you do, even if they haven't all articulated it into a coherent philosophy. We are beginning to find each other at this time of chaos and renewal. This brings me to:

No.5, that it helps a lot if we can find friends with whom we can talk about the situation, and the effect it's having on us. I mean friends who can actually listen, instead of trying to deflect, criticise or dismiss what we're saying, or tell us how we should be feeling. As Chris Hedges wrote in Chapter 7 of his book, *America: The Farewell Tour*[20]:

Those who resist effectively in the years ahead may not be able to stem the economic decline, the mounting political dysfunction, the collapse of empire, and the ecological disasters. But they will draw from acts of kindness, and the kindness of others, the strength and courage to endure. It will be from these relationships – ones formed the way all genuine relationships form: face-to-face rather than electronically – that radical organisations will rise from the ashes to resist.

References

1 https://www.resilience.org/stories/2018-12-11/
   regenerative-hubs-in-costa-rica/

2 Also known as the Law of Entropy, which we looked
   at in Chapter 2. However fabulous the hi-tech
   world becomes, it will still depend on the same dirty
   industries and will still need to dump its rubbish
   'somewhere else'.

3 Available at https://bioneers.org/joanna-macy-the-
   hidden-promise-of-our-dark-age/

4 This has been explored in some depth by
   psychotherapist Steffi Bednarek in her essay, 'This is an
   Emergency' – Proposals for a Collective Response to
   the Climate Crisis, in the *British Gestalt Journal* 2019,
   Vol 28 no2, pp 4-13.

5 This characterisation of trauma owes much
   to an interview with Charles Eisenstein,
   available on https://www.youtube.com/
   watch?app=desktop&v=d36xQuvlDG4&feature=youtu.
   be&fbclid=IwAR1tfnowKeOIQLxtgVKnxBcH33ar_rtbjP-
   KmU_6RDcGF8CMZQ3lCEjo7KA

6 Richard Tarnas, *The Passion of the Western Mind*
   (Pimlico, 1996).

7 This is well described in Jim Kunstler's book, *The Long
   Emergency* (Atlantic Books, 2005).

8 There are many estimates of this. See, for example,
   https://www.economicshelp.org/blog/6348/
   economics/cost-of-benefit-fraud-v-tax-evasion-in-uk/

9 John Michael Greer, *The Ecotechnic Future* (New Society
   Publishers, 2009).

10 See https://www.theguardian.com/global-
   development/2018/feb/17/mexico-zapatistas-rebels-
   24-years-mountain-strongholds

11 https://viacampesina.org/en/

12 https://transitionnetwork.org/

13 Ben Okri, 'Artists Must Confront the Climate Crisis', *The Guardian*, 12 Nov 2021.

14 Quoted here with Jessie's kind permission.

15 See, for example, https://www.youtube.com/watch?v=9qWaWGHNvy0

16 In 'Intermission: The Machine Stops', the tenth part of an excellent essay series, *Divining The Machine*, on his Substack site, The Abbey of Misrule.

17 Paul Levy (and others in the tradition of Carl Jung) have suggested that the archetype of the Wounded Healer is replacing that of the Hero as a symbol of the 'new world' that we see being born out of the current darkness. See https://www.awakeninthedream.com/articles/we-are-all-wounded-healers

18 From 'Blanched Sun, Blinded Man', part 1 of the essay series quoted above.

19 Llewellyn Vaughan Lee, *Spiritual Ecology: 10 Practices to Reawaken the Sacred in Everyday Life* (Golden Sufi Centre, 2017).

20 Chris Hedges, *America: The Farewell Tour* (Simon & Schuster, 2018).

ABOUT THE AUTHOR

Chris Wilson started his working life as a Scientific Assistant at the UK Atomic Energy Authority research station at Winfrith Heath in Dorset. He went on to study Archaeology and Anthropology at Cambridge, and worked for ten years as part of an educational research team with scientist and writer J. G. Bennett, who was well known in the Sixties as a spiritual teacher in the Gurdjieff tradition.

By the early 70s Bennett's team had become involved in the new field of Management Communications. During an extended visit to the USA in 1972, on a joint project with the Westinghouse Learning Corporation, Chris was living in Washington DC at a time when young Americans were demonstrating on a massive scale against the Vietnam War. He became involved with the anti-war movement, and by 1974 he had tired of the corporate world and decided to simplify his life by earning his living as a carpenter.

He soon found himself working with a small team of like-minded individuals, and in 1978 they made themselves into a co-op, which in those days was a highly unusual format for a firm of small builders. But it worked well for a few years, and Chris stayed with it until 1984 when he moved to the Yorkshire Dales to live 'off-grid' with his partner Jane.

In the mid-90s they moved to the Bristol area, where he re-trained as a psychotherapist and worked for 15 years in private practice. Jane died in 2003 and after a few years Chris sold up and helped to establish a permaculture co-op in Devon. In 2021 he moved to Romania, where he lives with his wife Gina in the village of Limanu, on the Black Sea coast.

Lightning Source UK Ltd.
Milton Keynes UK
UKHW050147170522
402929UK00014B/205